A Gift of Hospitality

to

_____

from

_____

Amish-Country COOKBOOK

Favorite Recipes Gathered by
Das Dutchman Essenhaus

Volume 4

Edited by Anita Yoder
    with Bob & Sue Miller

Evangel Publishing House
Nappanee, Indiana 46550

Amish-Country Cookbook: Volume 4

Copyright © 2003 by Evangel Publishing House.
All rights reserved.

No part of this book may be reproduced or transmitted in any form or by any means, electronic or mechanical, including photocopying, recording, or by any information storage and retrieval system, without prior permission in writing from the Publisher. Direct all inquiries to:

Evangel Publishing House
P.O. Box 189
2000 Evangel Way
Nappanee, IN 46550-0189
Telephone (800) 253-9315
www.evangelpublishing.com

Scripture quotations are from The Holy Bible, New King James Version. Copyright © 1982 by Thomas Nelson, Inc.

Lay-Flat Edition:
Cover photo © Eyewire. All rights reserved.
Cover design by Jim Ferm
Text illustrations by Harriet Miller

LCCN 200194021
ISBN 1-928915-36-1

Spiralbound Edition:
Cover design and text illustrations by Harriet Miller

LCCN 200194021
ISBN 1-928915-38-8

Printed in the United States of America
10 9 8 7 6 5 4 3 2 1

Table of Contents

Publisher's Preface vii

Who Are the Amish? ix

Breads, Pastries, Pancakes & Other Breakfasts 19

Soups, Salads & Dressings 43

Meats, Poultry & Main Dishes 81

Cakes & Frostings 149

Cookies, Bars & Cupcakes 171

Pies & Candies 205

Desserts & Ice Cream 235

Snacks, Dips, Appetizers & Beverages 271

Canning & Miscellaneous 299

Index 305

Publisher's Preface

BOB AND SUE MILLER grew up in a small Amish community in Sugarcreek, Ohio. Christian teaching and good home cooking were part of their upbringing, a heritage that continued when they established their own home.

In 1968 the Millers purchased property on U.S. 20 in Middlebury, Indiana. Back then it was a 24-hour truck stop named Everrett's Highway Inn. But the Millers saw other possibilities. After renovation, the restaurant reopened on January 1, 1971 as Das Dutchman Essenhaus, a six-day-a-week Amish restaurant complete with Amish and Mennonite cooks and wait-staff.

The history of Das Dutchman Essenhaus is a story of growth — growth of a family as well as a business. When the Millers moved to Indiana, they had two small children. Today, their family includes five adult children with their spouses and 15 grandchildren. The Essenhaus has grown from a staff of 24 to nearly 500 during the tourist season. What began as a small restaurant has expanded into one of Indiana's largest and finest restaurants with a baker, a country inn, numerous shops, and a wholesale food business.

Guests to the Essenhaus restaurant, flagship of the corporation, enjoy the barnlike structure supported by heavy oak beams, each hewn and hand-fitted by Amish craftsmen. The decor is replete with old wood stoves, horse collars, rustic farm tools, quilts, and antique furniture.

On a busy day, nearly six thousand people enjoy a family-style meal here. Many stop by the bakery before leaving to purchase homemade favorites like apple cinnamon bread, chocolate chip cookies, noodles, dressings, and red raspberry cream pie.

Over the years, the Essenhaus grounds and services have expanded to include charming village shops, Amish country tours, and buggy rides along the well-kept lawns and gardens. The facilities include a windmill, a children's playground, a miniature golf course, and a covered bridge with scenic trails. Many more acres of the lake-dotted Essenhaus property have yet to be developed, except in the minds of the Millers.

Bob and Sue are dedicated to Jesus Christ and seek to operate the Essenhaus by Christian values. They believe that providing excellent service, good measure, and quality food to their guests reflects their conviction that God desires all of His creation to live in harmony.

After enjoying a memorable dining experience, many guests ask about the unique recipes prepared in the Essenhaus kitchens. The Millers have responded by compiling four cookbooks containing their own original recipes and others gathered from their employees, many never published before. *Amish-Country Cookbook: Volumes 1–4* will help you create the good taste of Das Dutchman Essenhaus right in your home.

Key to Symbols

Throughout the text, you will find these symbols denoting special recipes:

   =   "Quick and Easy" Recipes

   =   Recipes on the menu at Das Dutchman Essenhaus in Middlebury, Indiana. (NOTE: Registered trademark of the Dutch Corporation.)

Who Are The Amish?

THE AMISH are one of the most colorful and distinctive religious groups in North America. Who are these people that wear plain clothing and ride in buggies? What are they really like? Why do they embrace such distinctive practices?

It is difficult to describe THE Amish because there are more than a dozen different Amish groups—each with its own customs—across North America. The buggy tops of some groups are white, others are yellow, but most are black or grey. Some groups only permit open buggies. Farmers in some groups milk their cows by hand, but most do not. Some women bake their own bread, but many buy it in stores. Even within the same Amish affiliation, some local congregations may permit the use of power lawn mowers while others do not. Some adults till the soil while others work in factories, and still others operate their own businesses.

It is tempting to assume that the Amish are all alike, as if all 180,000 of them were pressed from the same cultural cookie cutter. However, social customs vary from one settlement to another, though most Amish communities do share some basic values and practices regardless of their affiliation.

Growth and Expansion

The Amish are growing. Many of their communities double about every twenty years. Today approximately 180,000 children and adults live in twenty-three different states. About two-thirds of them reside in Ohio (49,000), Pennsylvania (41,000), and Indiana (33,000). Smaller settlements can be found in twenty other states, mostly east of the Mississippi River. Following the big three, the next five most populous states are Wisconsin (10,000), Michigan (8,000), Missouri (6,000), New York (5,000), and Kentucky (5,000).

Amish growth is fueled by sizeable families and strong retention. Typical families have six to nine children and, in some of the groups, ten or more. The average Amish person has at least seventy-five first cousins, many of whom live within several miles. Large families, however, are not enough to make the Amish population grow. Young people must be persuaded to join the church as adults, and indeed most of them do. On average, 85 percent request baptism and join the church between the ages of sixteen and twenty-two.

Deciding about church membership is a crucial step for Amish youth. Those who join are expected to follow the rules of the church for the rest of their life. If they are baptized and later violate church standards (e.g., by driving a car or buying a television), they will be asked to confess their transgression publicly before the church. If they refuse, they will face excommunication and likely some form of shunning. Some youth join the church because it is the natural thing to do; others weigh the consequences carefully because joining entails a lifelong commitment.

On the local level, the Amish are organized into more than thirteen hundred local church districts in 250 geographical settlements. Large settlements such as those in Holmes County, Ohio; Lagrange, Indiana; or Lancaster, Pennsylvania, have 100 or more church districts. New settlements, on the other hand, may have only one or two church districts.

About twenty-five to thirty-five families live in a church district. This basic social unit of Amish society serves as parish, precinct, shop, and club. The families meet every other Sunday for a three-hour worship service in their homes. Services rotate among the homes of a district throughout the course of a year. A bishop, deacon, and two ministers typically serve as unpaid leaders in addition to their regular occupations. They receive no theological training and serve for life. Religious, social, and family life revolve around face-to-face interaction in the local district, which forms the heart of Amish life.

Religious Roots

Amish roots reach back to the Anabaptist movement that emerged in Switzerland, Germany, and the Netherlands during the Protestant Reformation of the sixteenth century. They were nicknamed "rebaptizers" or "Anabaptists" by their opponents because they baptized adults who already had been baptized as infants in the Catholic Church. The Anabaptists believed that baptism should be reserved for adults who confessed Jesus Christ as Lord and fully understood the consequences of their decision.

Early Anabaptists emphasized the authority of the Bible for daily living, the separation of church and state, and the importance of following the teachings of Jesus in everyday life. Heeding Jesus' call to love our enemies, many of them espoused pacifism and refused to wield the sword or even retaliate against their persecutors. Indeed, thousands of Anabaptists were killed for their religious beliefs. Government officials as well as Catholic and Protestant leaders hunted the despised Anabaptist "heretics," who were considered a threat to civic order. Those who were caught received the capital punishment of their day—burning at the stake. The bloody stories of Anabaptist martyrs who died for their faith are told in the *Martyrs Mirror*. This 1,100-page book is found in many Amish homes today. The severe persecution shaped strong convictions among many Anabaptists that the church should be separate from the evils of the world around it.

The *Amish* name comes from Jakob Ammann, a Swiss Anabaptist leader who converted to the Anabaptist faith more than one hundred and fifty years after its beginning. He introduced several practices, including shunning, that led to a division among the Swiss Anabaptists in 1693. Ammann's followers became known as Amish. Many other Anabaptists were eventually called Mennonites after Menno Simons, a prominent Dutch Anabaptist leader.

In addition to the Amish and Mennonites, Hutterite and Brethren groups also trace their roots to the early Anabaptists. With a few exceptions, most of the Amish came to the Americas in two waves, in 1730-70 and in 1817-60. The first migration settled in Pennsylvania and eventually moved to Ohio, Indiana, and other states. Many in the second wave went directly to Ohio, Illinois, Indiana, and Iowa.

Current Beliefs and Values

As members of the larger Christian faith, the Amish endorse basic Christian beliefs—the authority of the Bible, salvation through Jesus Christ, the church as the body of Christ, a belief in heaven and hell, and so forth. The Amish also subscribe to an Anabaptist confession written in 1632 in the Netherlands. The language of Amish spirituality emphasizes the importance of living in community, in contrast to the individualistic language of American Evangelicalism.

Beyond their basic Christian beliefs, the Amish accent some distinctive values that shape their identity. Here are a few:

Separation from the world is a key belief that undergirds many unusual Amish customs. Based on biblical admonitions such as "love not the world" (1 John 2:15) and "be ye not conformed to this world" (Rom. 12:2), the Amish teach that Christians should live apart from the larger society. Followers of Jesus, the Amish believe, should walk on the straight and narrow way of moral purity, not the broad way that glorifies violence, sex, entertainment, and pleasure.

Speaking a dialect known as Pennsylvania German or Pennsylvania Dutch helps to clarify the line of distinction between the Amish and the larger world. Separation from the world, however, does not mean a wall of social separation. Many Amish interact freely with their non-Amish neighbors.

Church authority is another important Amish emphasis. For the Amish, the church is a redemptive community whose authority spans their total way of life. Each member participates in a local congregation (called a "church district") with specific geographical boundaries formed by a road, a stream, or a township line. The regulations of the local church district govern many aspects of daily life including dress, the use of technology, entertainment, and education. Their entire way of life reflects their religious commitments. Religion is not practiced only in special segments of the week, as is often the case in modern society; religious values permeate the entire fabric of their life.

Obedience is a cardinal Amish virtue. Children are expected to obey their parents without question. Talking back or challenging a parent or teacher is not tolerated. Younger people are expected to respect and honor their elders. Married women follow the lead of their husbands in major decisions related to family and church.

Younger ministers accept the guidance and wisdom of older ministers and bishops. Obedience to traditional customs and authority undergirds the harmony of Amish communities.

Unlike most of American culture, which celebrates individual rights and freedom, the Amish emphasize *humility*. Members are expected to deny personal and selfish interests for the sake of their community. They believe the welfare of the community supersedes the rights of the individual. The church discourages activities that highlight individual achievement or call undue attention to oneself because self glory may lead to pride, arrogance, and spiritual downfall. Unbridled individualism will surely lead to pride (the most dreaded Amish fear) and disturb the harmony and equality of community.

The rejection of individualism undergirds a number of Amish practices. Posing for photographs is forbidden. Using make-up and wearing jewelry, wedding rings, and wrist watches is strictly taboo. The plain clothing worn by the Amish underscores their separation from the world and also nurtures humility. Plain dress is a collective badge of group identity, but it also discourages individuals from buying fancy clothing and designer fashions, which would be extravagant.

Amish communities hold *traditional wisdom* in high regard. Elders are reluctant to change practices that have successfully served their community in the past. Amish folk are likely to try one of their grandmother's herbal remedies before running off to visit a doctor. They are reluctant to have their members study science or take up professional occupations, but they are willing to pick some of the fruits of modern progress. For example, they use the services of outside experts—veterinarians, dentists, doctors, lawyers, and accountants. At the same time, they are more likely to tap the wisdom of seasoned elders than to seek the advice of a consultant, therapist, or financial planner. Many customs are entrenched in longstanding traditions that are resistant to change.

A Basic Education

The Amish emphasize learning practical skills that will directly help them to make a living. Until the middle of the twentieth century, most Amish youth attended rural one-room public schools.

The rise of large consolidated schools worried many Amish parents because they feared that big schools would expose Amish youth to alien ideas and friends that could lead them away from the church.

In some communities, harsh confrontations erupted between Amish parents and government officials when parents refused to send their offspring to consolidated schools. Indeed, some parents were jailed in the 1950s and 1960s for keeping their children at home. In 1972, the United States Supreme Court favored the Amish with a ruling that permits their youth to end formal schooling after eighth grade.

Today, most Amish youth attend private, one-room schools where they are taught by Amish teachers and surrounded by Amish peers. In a few communities, Amish children attend small, rural public schools operated for the Amish. The vast majority, however, attend approximately twelve hundred private schools operated by Amish parents. One teacher is responsible to teach all eight grades. Classes are conducted in English. Science, sex education, and religion are not taught in Amish schools. Practical subjects like reading, writing, spelling, and basic math are emphasized.

School regulations and practices vary somewhat from state to state. Amish parents support their own schools as well as pay public school taxes. After completing eighth grade, young people learn technical and vocational skills by working in apprenticeships in the homes, shops, or farms of their parents or relatives. The practical skills gained through Amish education prepare young people for successful lives in Amish society.

The Puzzles of Amish Technology

Some Amish practices are puzzling at first glance. Why may they hire and ride in cars but not drive them? Why is electricity from a battery preferable to energy from a public utility line? And why would God smile on a tractor at the barn but not in the field?

The Amish use of technology varies greatly from settlement to settlement. Despite public misconceptions, the Amish do use modern technology. They are not antiques in a nineteenth-century museum. Some new forms of technology, such as gas barbeque grills and chain saws, are used without reservation. Other types of technology, which they fear will hurt their community, are rejected outright. Examples include television, radio, video players, cell phones, personal computers, and use of the Internet. Outsiders are often perplexed by how the Amish adapt technology in specials ways to serve their community.

For example, they believe that owning cars would pull their community apart. Horse and buggy transportation limits mobility and keeps the community close together. A symbol of individualism and independence, private automobiles would encourage mobility and eventually fragment the community. Nevertheless, as families spread to new settlements and as more Amish became involved in business, the use of motor vehicles became more attractive. So, many groups struck a compromise. They permitted members to hire vehicles (with a driver) for special needs, but not to own and drive them. This practice of hiring "taxis" flourishes in settlements that are involved in business. More conservative groups frown on this compromise.

As public utility lines spread across the country in the first half of the twentieth century, the Amish feared that tapping electricity from the lines would tie them too directly to the outside world, make them dependent on it, and provide too easy access to unnecessary conveniences. Since they already had been using batteries, they decided simply to use 12-volt electricity from batteries for small tools and appliances. This compromise continues in many communities today. Many farms and businesses also have diesel engines to produce air and hydraulic pressure. This so-called "Amish Electricity" operates heavy equipment, pumps water, operates fans, and powers washing machines. Without 110-volt electrical current, Amish homes are remarkably quiet. They have no noisy microwaves, air conditioners, televisions, videos, or CD players.

Tractors are not used in fields because they would encourage large-scale farming, steal work from Amish youth, and possibly lead to the use of cars. However, tractors are often used at barns for high power needs—such as to blow silage, chop fodder, and pump liquid manure.

Telephones in homes are discouraged because they provide another direct connection to the outside world. Strangers could enter a home via a telephone call at any moment. Moreover, face-to-face visiting is the social glue that holds an Amish community togther. If one can talk on the phone, why visit? In many settlements, members may use public phones or one in the home of a neighbor, but not install one in their own home. In more progressive settlements, a "community telephone" for several families is permitted. In some cases, individual phones for business outside the home are permissible.

Thus, the Amish do use technology. They try to control it so that it supports rather than tears down their community. Some Amish practices that look silly from the outside are actually ingenious compromises that allow them to use technology, but with restraints, so that it serves the welfare of the community. They often make a distinction between using and owning technology. For example, it may be acceptable to use a public pay phone but not to install a phone in the home. These many compromises create the riddles that enable the Amish to tap the power of technology without sacrificing their community life and identity.

Amish Food and Cooking Practices

The Amish are known for their beautiful gardens and hearty tables. Some of their food traditions such as pie-baking trace back to their roots in Switzerland. Other food habits can be tracked to Germany as well as colonial America. Food practices vary considerably from settlement to settlement, but most Amish families have gardens and preserve large quantities of food—often by canning. Yet, not all food is home-grown. Prepared foods such as instant pudding, snack foods, pizza, and soft drinks may be purchased at stores.

In some regions of the country, favorite Amish foods include shoofly pie—eaten as coffee cake with breakfast—snitz (dried apple) pie, applesauce, cornmeal mush, chicken pot pie, homemade noodles, and mashed potatoes smothered with gravy. Snitz pie is a staple at the fellowship meal following Sunday services in some regions. It is not unusual for a mother and her daughters to bake more than thirty pies for a fellowship meal. Noon meals during the week, often called "dinner," are the hearty meal of the day for farm workers.

Some Amish kitchens are equipped with fine cabinetry and have state-of-the-art stoves and refrigerators powered by bottled gas. In more conservative communities, cooking is done on wood stoves and ice is used for refrigeration. Generally speaking, the responsibilities for gardening, food preservation, and cooking fall to the women. Husbands sometimes help to prepare the garden for planting and help to harvest vegetables. Some men help to cook at large social gatherings like weddings or reunions, which may involve two large meals in a day. In recent years, some progressive families have begun hosting outside visitors in their homes for sumptuous Amish meals. This is often done to provide a sideline income as well as to extend a hand of hospitality to outsiders.

Occupations and the Future

Farming has long been the trademark of Amish life. This began to change in the last third of the twentieth century as farmland became more expensive and commercial agriculture became more competitive. Tourist markets and various business opportunities offered Amish people new ways of making a living. In some of the more rural areas, the bulk of Amish families are still tilling the soil. However, in many settlements the majority of households are no longer farming. Agriculture and sideline business are often mixed together. In some areas of Indiana, for example, Amish men work in large recreational vehicle factories.

In many settlements, the Amish have developed hundreds of small private businesses. These enterprises make fine indoor furniture, lawn furniture, gazebos, and storage sheds. Other Amish entrepreneurs operate greenhouses, construction crews, and machine shops. Amish women produce and sell lovely quilts, food preserves, and a wide assortment of handicrafts. Some of businesses are actually owned and operated by Amish women. The plentiful products of these shops are shipped and sold around the world by commercial distributors.

This growing Amish involvement in business signals an important social change that will likely alter Amish life and culture in

xvii

the years to come. Business involvements will impact child-rearing practices, gender roles, leisure activities, lifestyles, the use of technology, and the speaking of English. Such involvements will bring broader exposure to the outside world. All of these changes will likely modify the traditional understanding of what it means to be separate from the world as the Amish interact with their non-Amish neighbors more frequently.

Donald B. Kraybill
Messiah College
Grantham, PA

FOR FURTHER READING

Kraybill, Donald B. *The Riddle of Amish Culture, Revised Edition.* Baltimore, Md.: The Johns Hopkins University Press, 2001.

Kraybill, Donald B. and Carl Bowman. *On the Backroad to Heaven: Old Order Hutterites, Mennonites, Amish and Brethren.* Baltimore, Md.: The Johns Hopkins University Press, 2001.

Kraybill, Donald B. and Steve Nolt. *Amish Enterprise: From Plows to Profits.* Baltimore, Md.: The Johns Hopkins University Press, 1995.

Nolt, Steve. *A History of the Amish.* Intercourse, Pa.: Good Books, 1992.

Scott, Steve. *Why Do They Dress That Way?* Intercourse, Pa.: Good Books, 1986.

Breads, Pastries, Pancakes & Other Breakfasts

SUBSTITUTIONS

1 c. corn syrup = 1 c. sugar + ¼ c. of water or other type of
liquid called for in recipe

1 c. sugar = 1 c. powdered sugar

1 T. cornstarch (for thickening) = 2 T. flour

1 c. self-rising flour = 1 c. regular flour + ½ t. salt +
1½ t. baking powder

1 c. biscuit mix = 1 c. flour + 1½ t. baking powder + ½ t. salt +
1 T. shortening

1 t. baking powder = ¼ t. baking soda + ⅝ t. cream of tartar

1 sq. unsweetened chocolate = 3 T. cocoa + 1 T. fat

1 T. instant minced onion = 1 small to medium fresh onion

1 t. dry mustard = 1 T. prepared mustard

1 t. pumpkin pie spice = ½ t. cinnamon + ¼ t. ginger +
⅛ t. ground cloves + ⅛ t. nutmeg

1 t. allspice = ½ t. cinnamon + ⅛ t. ground cloves

1 c. ketchup or chili sauce = 1 c. tomato sauce + ½ c. sugar +
2 T. vinegar

15-oz. can tomato sauce = 6-oz. can tomato paste + 1 c. water

1 c. fine dry bread crumbs = 1 c. crushed cereal / cracker crumbs

Alice Moy (Administration)

BANANA BREAD

1 stick of butter, softened
1 c. sugar
2 eggs, beaten
1 t. baking soda
pinch of salt
2 c. flour
3 ripe bananas, mashed

Mix butter, sugar, and eggs together. Mix in the baking soda, salt, and flour. Add the bananas. Grease 3 mini loaf pans or 1 regular size loaf pan. Bake 45 minutes to 1 hour at 350°.

Makes 3 mini loaves or 1 regular loaf   Sharon Schlabach (Waitress)

BANANA OATMEAL BREAD

½ c. shortening
1 c. sugar
2 eggs
½ t. vanilla
1 c. flour
1 c. quick oatmeal
1 t. baking soda
½ t. salt, scant
½ t. cinnamon
1½ c. mashed bananas, 3 medium
¼ c. milk

Cream shortening and sugar together. Add eggs and vanilla and beat until fluffy. Sift dry ingredients together and add to mixture alternately with bananas and milk. Pour into greased 9"x5" loaf pan. Bake at 350° for 50–60 minutes. Cover 5 minutes after removed from oven to keep moist.

Makes 1 loaf   Danielle Yoder (Granddaughter of Bob & Sue)

 ## BLENDER BANANA BREAD

8 ripe bananas
1 c. vegetable oil
2 eggs
1½ c. flour
1 c. sugar
1 t. baking soda
½ t. salt

Blend bananas, oil, and eggs. Mix dry ingredients together. Mix everything together in blender. Put into bread pan and bake at 350° for 45 minutes.

Makes 1 loaf   Angela Miller (Daughter-in-Law of Bob & Sue)

BUBBLE BREAD

1 loaf white bread dough

Sauce:
1 box instant vanilla pudding
½ t. cinnamon
1 c. brown sugar
1 stick butter

Snip half of loaf of bread dough in small pieces, put in a 9"x13" cake pan. Mix pudding, cinnamon, and brown sugar together and then add just enough milk so it's a little runny. Pour half on top of first layer of bread. Melt butter and pour half over sauce. Snip up rest of bread then pour rest of sauce and then butter over it. Let rise until double in size. Bake at 350° until golden brown, about 20 minutes.

Serves 10–12   Louie Mast (Waitress)

CORN BREAD

1 c. cornmeal
1 c. flour
4 t. baking powder
3 T. sugar

1 t. salt
1½ c. milk
1 egg, beaten
2 T. shortening, melted

Combine cornmeal, flour, baking powder, sugar, and salt. Add milk, egg, and shortening. Mix well and pour into 9" square dish. Bake 25–30 minutes at 350°

Serves 9–12   April Ridenour (Waitress)

If a brother or sister is naked and destitute of daily food, and one of you says to them, "Depart in peace, be warmed and filled," but you do not give them the things which are needed for the body, what does it profit? Thus also faith by itself, if it does not have works, is dead.
James 2:15–17

CORNMEAL YEAST BREAD

2 pkg. yeast
½ c. lukewarm water
½ c. sugar
1½ t. salt
⅓ c. butter or margarine
¾ c. milk, scalded and cooled to lukewarm

1 egg
1 c. white flour
¾ c. cornmeal
3–3½ c. flour

Dissolve yeast and water. Combine sugar, salt, and margarine and mix well. Pour scalded milk cooled to lukewarm over sugar mixture. Stir in egg, flour, cornmeal, and yeast mixture. Beat well. Stir in enough additional flour to make a soft dough. Turn dough onto lightly floured board and knead until satiny, about 10 minutes. Place dough in greased bowl, cover and let rise in warm place until double in size, about 1 hour. Punch dough down and divide in half and place in 2 greased 8" loaf pans. Brush with melted margarine. Cover and let rise in warm place until nearly double, about 45 minutes. Bake at 350° for 30–45 minutes or golden brown. Tasty served with chili or any other soup.

Dorothy Miller (Waitress)

Worry does not empty tomorrow of its sorrow. It empties today of its strength.

EASY OATMEAL BREAD

2½ c. lukewarm water
2 pkg. yeast
2 c. oatmeal
¼ c. brown sugar

1 T. salt
2 T. shortening, softened
5½ c. flour

Mix together water and yeast and then add oatmeal, brown sugar, salt, and shortening. Then add enough flour to make dough stiff. Let rise until double, about one hour. Put in loaves and rise again. May be refrigerated overnight and made into two loaves of bread or dinner rolls. Let rise until double in size and bake at 400° for 15 minutes.

Makes 2 loaves

Connie Bowers (Kitchen)

I have been young, and now am old;
yet I have not seen the righteous
    forsaken,
nor his descendants begging bread.

Ps. 37:25

EASY CROISSANTS

1 pkg. yeast
1 c. warm water
¾ c. evaporated milk
½ t. salt
⅓ c. sugar
1 egg
1 c. flour
1 c. hard butter, cut till crumbly
4 c. flour

Dissolve yeast in water. Add to next five ingredients and beat until smooth. Stir in ¼ c. melted butter. Pour over flour and butter and carefully fold in. Cover with plastic and refrigerate. When cold, remove from refrigerator onto floured board. Press and knead six times to release any air. Cut into fours. Roll each ball into 16" circles. Cut into 8 pie shaped wedges. Roll wedge to point and curve into crescent. Let rise until double, approximately 2–4 hours. Brush with 1 egg and tablespoon of water. Bake at 325°–350° for 15 minutes.

Mary Stalter (Waitstaff)

DINNER ROLLS

2 T. dry yeast
¼ c. sugar
1½ c. milk, warm
1 t. salt
¼ c. margarine, softened
4 c. flour

Place yeast in a large bowl and add sugar and milk. Let stand for 5 minutes then add salt and butter. Mix well. Stir in flour until smooth. Cover bowl with cloth and place over another bowl filled with warm water. Let rise for 25 minutes. Do not stir dough again. Turn out onto a floured surface and shape into 18 balls. Place on greased pans. Cover and let rise 15 minutes. Bake at 375° for 15 minutes. Brush butter on rolls while hot.

Serves 18

Polly Miller (Bakery)

OVERNIGHT BUNS

1 cake yeast
2 c. sugar
4½ c. water
1 c. oil

1 t. salt
4–5 eggs, depending on size
16–18 c. flour

Soak yeast in ½ cup warm water. In a pan, boil 4 cups water and 2 cups sugar for 5 minutes. Cool until lukewarm and then add oil, salt, and eggs. Add dissolved yeast and enough flour to make dough soft. Punch down twice, then shape and put into pans. Leave set overnight, then bake at 350°–375° for 12–15 minutes.

Serves approx. 100   Leon Nafziger (Grounds Maintenance)

OVERNIGHT DINNER ROLLS

1 pkg. yeast
½ c. warm water
1 t. baking powder
1 c. milk
⅓ c. margarine

¼ c. sugar
⅛ t. salt
2 eggs, beaten
4½ c. flour

Dissolve yeast in warm water and then add baking powder. Let stand 20 minutes. Scald milk and then add margarine, sugar, and salt. Let cool and add eggs, yeast mixture, and flour. Cover and refrigerate at least 12 hours. Shape dough into balls and arrange in muffin pan, 2 small balls per muffin cup. Let rise for 2 hours. Bake 10 minutes at 400°. Spread butter over tops when done baking.

Serves 24   Doretta Wingard (Waitress)

MARILYN'S EASY WHITE BREAD

2 T. yeast
3 c. water, warm
8 c. flour

½ c. sugar
2 T. salt
½ c. vegetable oil

Dissolve yeast in one cup of warm water. Mix flour, sugar, salt, yeast, vegetable oil, and the rest of the water and knead. Let rise until double and punch down and let rise again until double. Divide into loaves. Bake at 350° for about 30 minutes. This dough can also be used for cinnamon rolls.

Susie Kauffman (Waitress)

MELT-IN-YOUR-MOUTH BISCUITS

2 T. white sugar
½ c. shortening
2 c. flour
2 t. baking powder

½ t. salt
½ t. cream of tartar
1 egg, unbeaten
⅔ c. milk

Mix sugar, shortening, flour, baking powder, and salt. Add tartar, egg, and milk. Mix well. Bake at 400° for 15 minutes. This is also good to use for pizza dough.

Norma Lehman (Bakery)

MOM'S HOMEMADE BREAD

3 pkg. yeast
3 c. warm water
⅓ c. brown sugar
1½ T. salt

3 T. flour
¾ c. vegetable oil
8 c. flour

Dissolve yeast in water. Mix sugar, salt, and 3 tablespoons flour. Add to yeast mixture. Stir, then add oil and gradually work in flour. Place in a lightly greased bowl; cover and let rise 30 minutes. Punch down then let rise another 30 minutes. Work dough again, then let rise for 1 hour. Punch down and form into 5 or 6 loaves. Put in greased pans and let rise approximately 1 hour or until raised ½ inch above pan. Bake at 325° for 30 minutes.

Serves 5–6

Lorene Miller (Busser)

PUMPKIN BREAD

4 eggs
1 c. oil
2 c. sugar
2 c. pumpkin
⅔ c. milk
3½ c. flour
1 t. salt

1 t. nutmeg
1 t. cloves
2 t. baking soda
1 t. cinnamon
1 t. ginger
1 t. all spice

Beat eggs, oil, and sugar together. Add pumpkin and milk. Add flour and remaining dry ingredients. Stir just until smooth. Bake at 350° until inserted toothpick comes out clean.

Serves 5 (small servings)

Suvilla Gingerich (Waitress)

SOFT PRETZELS

1½ c. warm water
1 T. yeast
2 T. brown sugar
½ t. salt
4 c. flour

Brine:
2 c. water
2 T. baking soda

Mix and let rise 30 minutes in a greased bowl. Then boil brine ingredients in a saucepan. Shape pretzel, dip in brine, and lay on greased cookie sheet. Salt pretzels and then bake at 450° for 10 minutes, brush with butter.

                        Jorgen Reimer (Grandson of Bob & Sue)

STRAWBERRY BREAD

3 c. flour
1 t. salt
1 t. baking soda
1 t. cinnamon
1½ c. sugar

3 eggs, well beaten
2 10-oz. pkgs. frozen strawberries,
   or 2½ cups fresh strawberries
1¼ c. cooking oil
1¼ c. pecans, chopped

Sift dry ingredients, flour, salt, baking soda, cinnamon, and sugar, into a large bowl and make a well in center. Mix eggs, strawberries, oil, and pecans and then pour into well. Stir enough to dampen all ingredients. Pour into greased and floured 8"x4" loaf pan and bake at 350° for 1 hour.

Makes 2 loaves   Joyce Miller (Sunshine Farm Manager)

Do not withhold good from those to
   whom it is due,
When it is in the power of your hand to
   do so.
Do not say to your neighbor,
"Go, and come back,
And tomorrow I will give it,"
When you have it with you.

                                    Prov. 3:27–28

TURTLE BREAD

2½–3 c. all-purpose flour
1 pkg. quick-acting active
   dry yeast
1 T. sugar
1 t. salt

½ c. water
⅓ c. milk
1 T. margarine or butter
1 egg
2 raisins

Mix 1½ cups of the flour, yeast, sugar, and salt in a large bowl. Heat water, milk, and margarine to 125°–130° and then stir into yeast mixture. Stir in egg, and enough of the remaining flour to make the dough easy to handle. Sprinkle a surface lightly with flour. Turn the dough onto the surface and knead until smooth and elastic, about five minutes. Cover and let rest 10 minutes. Lightly grease a cookie sheet. Shape a 2" piece of dough into a ball for the head. Shape four walnut-size pieces of dough into balls for feet. Shape one walnut-size piece of dough into balls for tail. Shape remaining dough into a ball for body and place on cookie sheet and flatten slightly. Attach head, feet, and tail by placing one end of each under edge of body to secure. Press raisins into head for eyes. Cover and let rise 20 minutes. Preheat the oven to 400°. Make crisscross cuts in body ¼" deep to look like a turtle's shell. Bake until golden brown, 20–25 minutes.

Makes 1 "turtle"   Courtney Reimer (Granddaughter of Bob & Sue)

WHOLE-WHEAT BREAD

1 c. mashed potatoes
1½ c. milk, scalded and cooled
½ c. honey
1 t. sea salt

1 pkg. Red Star® yeast (it contains
   no preservatives)
3 c. whole-wheat flour
finish with unbleached flour

Do not make as stiff as other bread doughs. Let rise, then knead, let rise again, and then shape into dinner rolls or small loaves. Bake in 425° oven for 15 minutes. Reduce heat to 350° and finish baking. For dinner rolls bake at 425° for 10–12 minutes or until done.

Sam Whetstone (Dishwasher)

Mother sets her pies on the windowsill to cool. Daughter sets hers there to thaw.

To prevent crust from becoming soggy with cream pie, sprinkle crust with powdered sugar.

It is easy to remove the white membrane from oranges by soaking them in boiling water for 5 minutes before you peel them.

APPLE DANISH

Pastry:
4½ c. all-purpose flour
¾ t. salt
1½ c. shortening
2 small eggs
¾ c. milk

Filling:
9 c. sliced, peeled apples
2¼ c. sugar
6 T. melted margarine or butter
3 T. flour
1½ t. ground cinnamon

Glaze:
1 egg white lightly beaten
¾ c. powdered sugar
2-3 t. water

In a mixing bowl, combine flour and salt, cut in shortening until mixture resembles coarse crumbs. Combine egg yolk and milk. Add flour mixture. Stir just until dough clings together. Divide dough in half on a lightly floured surface. Roll half of dough in a 15"x10" rectangle. Transfer to a greased 15"x10"x1" baking pan. Set aside.

In a bowl toss together filling ingredients, spoon over pastry in pan. Roll out remaining dough to another 15"x10" rectangle. Place over filling. Brush with egg white glaze.

Bake at 375° for 40 minutes or golden brown. Cool on wire rack. Serve warm or cold.

Serves 20–24   Mary K. Schmucker (Cook)

BEST BREAD PUDDING

1 loaf stale French bread
4 c. milk
3 eggs
1–1½ c. sugar
2 T. vanilla
1 c. raisins

Topping:
8 T. butter
1 c. 10x powered sugar
1 egg, beaten
3 t. orange extract

Break bread into large bowl. Pour milk over and set aside for one hour. Preheat oven to 325°. In a medium bowl, beat eggs, sugar, and vanilla. Stir into bread mixture, add raisins and mix well. Pour into buttered 9"x13"x2" baking dish. Bake in middle rack of oven until browned and set about 70 minutes. Cool to room temperature. For the topping, in a double boiler stir butter and sugar until sugar is dissolved and mixture is hot. Remove from heat. Wisk beaten egg into sugar mixture. Remove from water base and continue beating until sauce has cooled to room temperature. Stir in orange extract. Spread over bread and serve warm.

Note: For a low-fat, low-cholesterol pudding, use no-fat sour dough bread, skim milk, and non-cholesterol egg substitute. Spray baking dish with a butter-flavored vegetable spray and omit sauce.

Serves 8–10   Diane Butler (Bakery Sales)

BREAD PUDDING (BAKED FRENCH TOAST)

1 stick butter
2 loaves sweet Italian bread,
    cut into 1" slices
1 c. pecans or walnuts
3 c. milk or cream

½ t. salt
10 large eggs
½ t. nutmeg
1 t. cinnamon
¼ c. and 1 T. sugar

Melt ½ stick of butter in 13"x9" glass baking dish. Arrange bread over butter, sprinkle pecans over bread. Melt rest of butter; whip remaining ingredients together, including remaining butter. Pour egg mixture over bread. Prick bread to absorb egg mixture. Cover and refrigerate overnight. Preheat over to 325°, uncover and bake 45 minutes or until knife inserted comes clean. Serve with syrup.

Serves 12   Sharon McSorley (Supervisor)

MOM'S BREAD PUDDING

3 eggs
½ c. sugar
½ box raisins
½ c. milk
1–1½ t. cinnamon
5 slices of bread

Sauce:
4 T. vanilla
3 T. sugar
3 T. milk
3 T. cornstarch

Beat eggs and then add sugar, raisins, milk, and cinnamon. Mix well and pour over bread until gooey. Bake 20–30 minutes, cool. Break into pieces. Sauce: mix in double boiler vanilla, sugar, milk, and cornstarch. Cook until thickened. Remove from heat and pour over bread mixture. Let cool and refrigerate. Enjoy.

Serves 4–6   Diane Butler (Bakery Sales)

APPLE MUFFINS

1 c. sugar
½ c. shortening
2 eggs
1 t. vanilla

2 c. Gold Medal® self-rising flour
2 c. apples, chopped
½ c. nuts, chopped

Mix sugar, shortening, eggs, and vanilla. Stir in flour until smooth. Stir in apples and nuts. Put in baking cups. Mix 1 tablespoon of sugar and ¼ teaspoon cinnamon and then sprinkle on top. Bake at 350° until golden brown.

Esther Nisley (Bakery)

BLACKBERRY MUFFINS

1 egg
½ c. milk
¼ c. cooking oil
1⅓ c. flour
½ c. sugar

2 t. baking powder
½ t. salt
1 c. fresh chopped blackberries
    or ¾ c. well-drained canned
    blackberries

Beat egg slightly with fork. Stir in milk and cooking oil. Mix well. Sift together flour, sugar, baking powder, and salt and add to liquid mixture. Blend in blackberries carefully. Bake at 400° for 20–25 minutes.

Makes 12   Joyce Miller (Sunshine Farm Manager)

CHILI CHEESE CORN MUFFINS

2 c. cornmeal
½ c. flour
1 T. baking powder
1 T. sugar
1 t. baking soda
1 t. salt
½ t. cayenne pepper
⅓ c. red pepper

2 c. milk
2 eggs
2 T. butter, melted
2 T. onion, chopped
1½ c. cheese, grated
1½ c. canned or fresh corn
4 oz. can chili peppers

Combine first 8 ingredients. Beat together eggs, milk, and butter. Add to dry ingredients stirring just to blend. Fold in remaining ingredients. Do not over mix. Fill greased muffin pan ⅔ full. Bake at 375° or until firm.

Betty Miller (Waitress)

RAISIN BRAN® MUFFINS

10 oz. Raisin Bran® cereal
5 c. flour
3 c. sugar
2 t. salt
5 t. baking soda

1 qt. buttermilk
1 c. oil
4 eggs

Mix dry ingredients together. Mix buttermilk, oil, and eggs together. Add to dry ingredients and mix until well moistened. Bake at 400° for 15 minutes in muffin cups. Batter keeps in fridge for 6 weeks. Bake as needed.

Serves 48   Angela Miller (Daughter-in-Law of Bob & Sue)

ZUCCHINI MUFFINS

3 eggs beaten
2 c. sugar
3 t. vanilla
1 c. vegetable oil
1 t. baking soda
1 t. baking powder

1 t. salt
3 t. cinnamon
2½ c. flour
2 c. zucchini, shredded fine
1 c. nuts, optional
1 c. coconut, optional

Beat 3 eggs, add sugar, vanilla, vegetable oil, beat until creamy. Add baking soda, baking powder, salt and cinnamon. Mix well. Fold in flour, zucchini, nuts, and coconut. Bake at 375° for 20 minutes.

Esther Nisley (Bakery)

SCRAMBLED EGG MUFFINS

½ lb. bulk pork sausage
12 eggs
½ c. onion, chopped
¼ c. green pepper, chopped

½ t. salt
¼ t. pepper
¼ t. garlic powder
½ c. cheddar cheese, shredded

In a skillet, brown the sausage, drain. In a bowl, beat the eggs and then add onion, green peppers, salt, pepper, and garlic powder. Stir in sausage and cheese. Spoon by ⅓-cup measures into greased muffin cups. Bake at 350° for 20–25 minutes or until a knife inserted near the center comes out clean.

Serves 12

Jody Yoder (Waitress)

BUTTER BRIGHT PASTRIES

2 pkg. dry yeast
¼ c. warm water, 115°
½ c. sugar
⅛ t. salt
1 c. cold milk
4–4½ c. sifted flour
2 eggs
1 c. butter

Glaze:
1 c. sifted confectioners' sugar
2 T. butter
2 T. cream
½ t. vanilla

Dissolve yeast in warm water. Combine yeast mixture, sugar, salt, and milk. Beat in 2 cups of flour and then add eggs beating well. Stir in enough flour to make dough soft. Cover and refrigerate for 15 minutes. On a lightly floured surface, roll dough into a 18"x15" rectangle. Cut ⅓ c. butter into small pieces. Dot surfaces of dough with butter leaving a 1" margin. Fold 18" side into thirds and then fold 15" side into thirds. Wrap in floured aluminum foil. Chill 15 minutes. Repeat procedure twice using remaining butter. When you roll dough second and third times, turn dough so narrow side faces you. Chill 15 more minutes. Divide dough into fourths. Roll and cut into desired shapes. Let rise until doubled. Bake at 350° for 8 minutes or until golden brown. Cool. Glaze with an icing made by combining confectioners' sugar, butter, cream, and vanilla. Fill with jams or jellies or canned cherry, blueberry, or pineapple pie filling. To freeze, wrap in foil. To reheat, bake at 400° for 10 minutes.

Serves 24

Mary A. Bontrager (Waitress)

CINNAMON ROLLS

3½ c. flour
1 T. yeast
1¼ c. milk
1¼ c. sugar
½ c. shortening
1 t. salt
1 egg

Icing:
1 c. butter
2 c. brown sugar
⅔ c. milk
2–4 c. powdered sugar

In a large bowl combine 1½ c. flour and yeast. Heat milk, sugar, salt, and shortening until lukewarm. Add to flour mixture and add egg. Beat on low until blended then beat on high for 3 minutes. Stir in remaining flour and let rise until double. Punch down and let dough rest for 10 minutes. Roll out into a rectangle, spread lightly with butter, and sprinkle with brown sugar and cinnamon. Roll it up like a jellyroll and slice into 1½" pieces. Place cut side up in a 9"x13" pan. Let rise until double. Bake at 400° for 10–12 minutes.

For the icing, melt butter and then add sugar and milk. Heat just enough to dissolve sugar. Cool completely without stirring. Add powdered sugar and mix well. While rolls are still warm, frost with caramel icing.

Serves 12   Suvilla Gingerich (Waitress)

CINNAMON ROLLS

1 T. yeast
1 c. warm water
1 shortening
1 T. salt

1½ c. sugar
1 T. vanilla
4 eggs
4 c. warm water

Combine first two ingredients and then set aside. Combine shortening, salt, sugar, and vanilla. Beat all together, add eggs and beat again. Then add yeast mixture. Add enough flour to make a soft dough. Punch down every hour 3–4 times. Then roll out, spread with butter, sugar, and cinnamon, and roll up. Cut and then put in pans. Let rise overnight. Bake next morning at 350° for 15–20 minutes.

Millie Whetstone (Bakery)

DANISH ROLL GLAZE

3 c. powdered sugar
½ c. sour cream
1 t. clear vanilla

1 t. butter flavor
2 T. butter, softened

Stir together all ingredients and then beat or stir for 5 minutes. If too thick, add a little milk. Drizzle over Danish rolls.

Lena Bontrager (Bakery Sales)

MAPLE PECAN COFFEE RING

6 T. melted butter
6 T. maple syrup
½ c. brown sugar, packed
½ c. pecans, chopped

1 t. ground cinnamon
2 12-oz. tubes of refrigerated
    buttermilk biscuits

Brush a 10-inch fluted tube pan with 1 T. butter. Melt remaining butter in a saucepan and add syrup. Drizzle half of the mixture into pan. Combine brown sugar, nuts, and cinnamon. Divide mixture in half and sprinkle half over syrup and butter. Separate biscuits, place into the pan that is prepared, with the edges overlapping. Top with the remaining syrup and nut mixtures. Bake at 375° for 15–20 minutes or until golden brown. Cool 2–3 minutes and invert onto serving platter.

Serves 19–20

Norine Yoder (Restaurant Gifts)

BAKED FRENCH TOAST

1½ sticks butter
1 c. brown sugar
1½ t. cinnamon
thick sliced bread

6 eggs
2 c. milk
maple syrup

Melt butter and then add sugar and cinnamon. Spread mixture over bottom of 9"x12" baking dish and then layer 6 slices of bread over mixture and fill in. Beat eggs and add milk and then pour over top. Cover and refrigerate overnight. Bake at 350° for 25–30 minutes. Drizzle syrup on top and broil until brown and bubbly and then serve.

Serves 8

Mary K. Schmucker (Kitchen)

NUTTY FRENCH TOAST

12 slices French bread, 1" thick
8 eggs
2 c. milk
2 t. vanilla extract
½ t. ground cinnamon

¾ c. butter or margarine, softened
1⅓ c. brown sugar, packed
3 T. dark corn syrup
1 c. chopped walnuts

Place bread in a greased 13"x9"x2" baking dish. In a large bowl, beat eggs, milk, vanilla, and cinnamon. Pour over bread. Cover and refrigerate overnight. Remove from refrigerator 30 minutes before baking. Meanwhile, in a mixing bowl, cream butter, brown sugar, and syrup until mixture is smooth and then spread over bread. Sprinkle with walnuts. Bake uncovered at 350° for 1 hour or until golden brown.

Serves 6–8   Mary A. Bontrager (Waitress)

OVEN FRENCH TOAST WITH NUT TOPPING

12-oz. loaf French bread, cut in 1" slices
8 large eggs
2 c. milk
2 c. half and half
2 t. vanilla
½ t. nutmeg
½ t. cinnamon

Topping:
¾ c. butter, softened
1⅓ c. brown sugar
3 T. dark corn syrup
1⅓ c. chopped nuts

Heavily butter a 13"x9" baking pan. Fill pan with bread slices to within ½" of top. Set aside. In blender, mix eggs, milk, half and half, vanilla, nutmeg, and cinnamon. Pour over bread slices. Refrigerate, covered overnight. Make topping by combining all ingredients, set aside until time to bake toast. Spread topping over toast and bake at 350° for 50 minutes or until puffed and golden.

Serves 10   AnnaMary Yoder (Waitress)

Kind words can be short and easy to speak, but their echoes are endless.

SKIER FRENCH TOAST

2 T. corn syrup
½ c. butter
1 c. brown sugar
12 slices bread

5 eggs
1½ c. milk
1 t. vanilla
¼ t. salt

Combine corn syrup, butter, and brown sugar in saucepan. Simmer until syrup-like and then pour mixture in bottom of 9"x13" pan. Layer bread in pan. Beat together, eggs, milk, vanilla, and salt. Pour over bread. Cover and refrigerate overnight. Bake uncovered at 350° for 45 minutes.

Mary Schrock (Bakery)

MOM'S PANCAKES

4 c. flour
2 t. salt
6 T. buttermilk powder
4 T. baking powder
4 eggs, separated

¼ c. vegetable oil
1¾ c. milk
1 t. baking soda, dissolved in
    water
1¾ c. water

Combine flour, salt, buttermilk powder, and baking powder in a bowl, mix. Separate eggs, add yolks, oil, milk, baking soda, and water. Mix if batter is too thick. Add a bit more milk: beat egg whites and fold in last. Cook on a hot griddle or pan.

Serves 8–10

Martha Hochstedler (Cook)

OATMEAL BROWN SUGAR PANCAKES

2 eggs
2 T. vegetable oil
1 c. sour milk
⅓ c. brown sugar
¼ c. all-purpose flour

½ c. whole-wheat flour
½ t. baking soda
½ t. salt
½ c. and 2 T. quick oats

Beat together eggs, oil, sour milk, and then put together dry ingredients, except oatmeal. Add egg mixture last. Then add quick oats. Make on hot griddle.

Serves 8

Wanda Mullet (Waitress)

AMISH SCRAMBLE

8 eggs, beaten
3 c. potatoes, precooked and sliced

1½ c. sausage, ham, or bacon, precooked
2 c. shredded cheese

In sprayed oil hot skillet, add potatoes and meat and let cook for 3 minutes. Add egg mixture and cheese. Let cook until everything is thoroughly hot, 2–3 minutes. Serve.

BREAKFAST CASSEROLE

6 qt. potatoes
1 can cream of mushroom soup
1¼ c. milk
cheese, grated

1 lb. bacon
1½ doz. large eggs
3 lb. sausage

Cook, grate, and fry the potatoes. Mix together soup and milk. Fry bacon and sausage. Scramble the eggs with half amount of fried bacon. Stir in cheese, just as eggs are about done. May add some minced onion. Put together hot in order given in casserole dish. Bake at 350° for 30 minutes or more.

Fannie Yutzy (Bakery)

BREAKFAST CASSEROLE

9 eggs, beaten
3 c. milk
2 c. cheddar cheese, grated

9 slices bread, cubed
1½ lb. sausage, browned
salt and pepper to taste

Combine all ingredients and pour into a 9"x13" glass pan that has been sprayed with Pam®. Bake at 350° for 45 minutes.

Serves 12

Sharon McSorley (Management)

The seven ages of men: spills, drills, thrills, bills, ills, pills, wills. . . .

BREAKFAST HAYSTACKS

biscuits, crumbled
smokie links, heated, cut up
packaged french fries, heated
bacon, fried, cut up
eggs, scrambled

onions
bread, toasted, cubed
barbecue sauce
ketchup
cheese sauce

Serve buffet style, layer in order given to make haystacks. Enjoy!

Sue Miller (Owner)

BREAKFAST PIZZA

1½ lb. sausage
3 c. hash browns
4 eggs

2 c. pizza sauce
mozzarella or Velveeta® cheese

Brown sausage, drain, cool. Use your favorite pizza dough and put it on a cookie sheet. Put pizza sauce on crust, then add hash browns and sausage. Beat eggs and then pour over potatoes and sausage. Bake at 400° for 20 minutes. Remove and add the cheese and bake 5 minutes more or until cheese is melted.

Martha Hochstedler (Bakery)

 Godliness with contentment is great gain.
1 Tim. 6:6

CHEESE SOUFFLÉ

8 slices bread
1 lb. shredded cheese
6 eggs, beaten
2 c. milk

ham or bacon, cubed
salt
pepper

Cube bread and put in bottom of casserole dish. Combine cheese and meat and then sprinkle over bread cubes. Mix eggs, milk, and seasonings. Add over top of other ingredients. Refrigerate overnight. Bake at 325° for 45 minutes. Great for overnight company.

Serves 4–5

Marlys Pletcher (Waitress)

CRESCENT BREAKFAST PIZZA

2 pkgs. crescent rolls
1 c. peppers
½ c. onions
3 c. tater tots, sliced
1 lb. sausage, fried
1 pkg. smokies

1 lb. shaved ham
12 eggs beaten
¼ t. pepper
1 t. salt
½ c. milk

Put crescent rolls in 17"x12.5"x1" pan. Add following ingredients on top of crescent rolls, peppers, onions, tater tots, sausage, smokies, and ham. Beat eggs, pepper, salt, and milk together and pour over pizza, then top with cheese. Bake at 350° for 30 minutes.

Serves 12   Darlene Schmucker (Bakery)

EGG AND SAUSAGE BREAKFAST CASSEROLE

12 slices bread, cubed
1½ lb. sausage
½ c. onion, chopped
⅓ c. green peppers, chopped

6 eggs
3 c. milk
1 t. salt
½ t. pepper

Put the bread cubes into a greased 13"x9" pan and set aside. In a skillet, brown the sausage with the onions and the green peppers and drain the grease off. Sprinkle the sausage mixture over the bread. In a bowl, beat together the remaining ingredients and pour this egg mixture over the sausage mixture. Cover the pan and refrigerate the casserole overnight. Bake the casserole at 325° for 1 hour and 10 minutes.

Luan Westfall (Purchasing Manager)

[God] had commanded the clouds above,
And opened the doors of heaven,
Had rained down manna on them to eat,
And given them the bread of heaven.
Men ate angels' food;
He sent them food to the full.
                              Ps. 86:23–25

WINTER GARDEN SCRAMBLED EGGS

8 eggs
1 c. fully cooked ham,
    finely chopped
¼ c. sweet red pepper, chopped
¼ c. green pepper, chopped
¼ c. canned mushrooms, sliced

¼ c. onion, chopped
¼ c. butter or margarine
¼ t. garlic salt
pinch of pepper
pinch of celery seed

In a bowl, beat eggs. Add ham, peppers, mushrooms, and onion. Melt butter in a large skillet and add egg mixture. Cook and stir gently over medium heat until eggs are completely set. Add garlic salt, pepper, and celery seed.

Serves 4

Esther Wenger (Corporate Office)

BAKED OATMEAL

1 c. vegetable oil
1½ c. white sugar
4 eggs
6 c. quick oats

4 t. baking powder
1 t. salt
3 c. milk

Mix oil, sugar, and eggs until yellow and glossy. Add remaining ingredients and beat until blended. Put in 9"x13" greased pan and bake at 350° for 30–40 minutes. Optional: Add 2 apples chopped and 1 teaspoon of cinnamon on top.

Wanda Mullett (Waitress)

HOT PORRIDGE

3 c. milk
3 T. flour, rounded

pinch of salt

Heat 2½ cups milk. In mixing bowl add flour, salt, ½ cup cold milk. Mix well and then add to hot milk, stirring constantly with wisk until thickened. Serve while hot. Put as much brown sugar on top as desired.

Norma Lehman (Bakery)

Soups, Salads & Dressings

UNITS OF VOLUME

1 bushel = 4 pecks

1 peck = 8 quarts

1 gallon = 4 quarts

1 quart = 2 pints

1 pint = 2 cups

1 cup = 16 tablespoons

½ cup = 8 tablespoons

⅓ cup = 5⅓ tablespoons

¼ cup = 4 tablespoons

1 jigger = 12 ounces

2 tablespoons = 1 ounce

THREE BEAN SALAD

1 c. sugar
⅓ c. water, hot
⅓ c. cider vinegar
½ t. salt
1 t. vegetable oil
1 can green beans
1 can yellow wax beans
1 can kidney beans
1 t. chopped onion
1 t. celery

Dissolve sugar and hot water. Add vinegar, salt, and salad oil. Drain all cans of beans and then pour into dish. Add celery and onions. Pour sugar water mixture over all. Let marinate and serve.

KIDNEY BEAN SALAD

2 cans dark or light kidney beans, drained and rinsed
3 hard boiled eggs, chopped
¼ c. celery, chopped
1 T. onion, chopped
salt to taste

Dressing:
¾ c. Hellman's® mayonnaise or Miracle Whip® salad dressing
1 t. mustard
2 T. sugar

Mix together dressing ingredients until well mixed. Then mix with all other ingredients and mix well. Chill before serving.

Serves 8–10   Rosalie Bontrager (Country Inn Manager)

COTTAGE CHEESE SALAD

1 lb. marshmallows
½ c. milk
8 oz. cream cheese
1 pt. cottage cheese
#2 can crushed pineapple
½ c. nuts, chopped
1 c. cream, whipped

Melt together in double boiler, marshmallows and milk. Add cream cheese and melt in milk. Add cottage cheese and stir a little and cool. Add well drained pineapple and nuts. Chill. Fold in whipped cream. Pour in dish and let set.

Sam Whetstone (Dishwasher)

 FROZEN FRUIT SALAD

8-oz. pkg. cream cheese
⅔ c. sugar
10-oz. pkg. frozen sliced
   strawberries

1 large can crushed pineapple
   with juice
½ c. pecans, chopped
2 bananas, small chunks
19 oz. Cool Whip®

Cream together cream cheese and sugar. Add strawberries, pineapple with juice, pecans, and bananas. Mix carefully as you fold in Cool Whip®. Pour into a 9"x13" pan and freeze.

Serves 18–20   Brandie Leonard (Village Shops)

Things You Just Can't Do
Sow bad habits and reap good character.
Sow jealousy and hatred, and reap love
   and friendship.
Sow dissipation and reap a healthy body.
Sow deception and reap confidence.
Sow cowardice and reap courage.
Sow neglect of the Bible and reap a
   well-guided life.

AUNT RUTH'S STRAWBERRY SALAD

1 large box strawberry gelatin
1½ c. hot water
1 pt. frozen strawberries
1 c. crushed pineapple,
   not drained

1 c. 7-Up®
1 c. celery, diced
1 c. nuts, chopped

Dissolve gelatin in hot water. Add strawberries and pineapple. Stir in 7-Up®, celery, and nuts. Pour in mold and chill.

Serves 10   Joyce Miller (Sunshine Farm Manager)

FLUFFY FRUIT SALAD

2 20-oz. cans crushed pineapple
⅔ c. white sugar
2 T. flour
2 eggs, lightly beaten
¼ c. orange juice
3 T. lemon juice
1 T. vegetable oil
2 17-oz. cans fruit cocktail, drained
2 11-oz. cans mandarin oranges, drained
2 bananas, sliced
8-oz. tub Cool Whip®

Drain pineapple, reserving 1 cup of the juice in a small saucepan. Set pineapple aside. To saucepan, add sugar, flour, eggs, orange juice, lemon juice, and oil. Bring to a boil, stirring constantly. Boil for 1 minute longer and then remove from heat and let cool. In a salad bowl, combine pineapple, fruit cocktail, oranges, and bananas. Fold in Cool Whip® and the cooled sauce. Chill for several hours.

Serves 12–16   Norma Lehman (Bakery)

MELON SALAD WITH ORANGE LIME DRESSING

2 limes
¼ c. frozen orange juice
    concentrate, thawed
½ t. vanilla
1 cantaloupe
1 honeydew melon
2 c. (32 oz.) seedless red grapes

Squeeze 6 tablespoons lime juice. Combine lime juice, orange juice concentrate, and vanilla in small mixing bowl. Set aside. Cut cantaloupe in half, slice each half in 1" wedges and trim away rind. Cut melon into ¾" pieces. Combine fruit on platter. Pour dressing over fruit and combine.

Jennifer Leatherman (Hostess/Cashier)

A sharp tongue and a dull mind are often found in the same head.

FESTIVE CRANBERRY SALAD

14-oz. can sweetened condensed milk
¼ c. lemon juice
20-oz. can crushed pineapple, drained
16-oz. can whole-berry cranberry sauce
2 c. miniature marshmallows
½ c. pecans, chopped
8-oz. carton whipped topping

In a bowl, combine milk and lemon juice and mix well. Stir in pineapple, cranberry sauce, marshmallows, and pecans. Fold in whipped topping and then spoon into a 9"x13" baking dish. Freeze until firm, 4 hours or overnight. Cut into squares.

Serves 12–16   Martha Coblentz (Bakery)

PUDDING FRUIT SALAD

1 large can crushed pineapple
2 cans mandarin oranges
1 large can sliced peaches
3-oz. pkg. vanilla pudding, not instant
3-oz. pkg. tapioca pudding, not instant
bananas

Drain fruit. Use 3 cups fruit juice and mix with both pudding mixes and cook until thickened. Add fruits and sliced bananas when cool.

Katie Hochstedler (Bakery)

 ## QUICK APPLE SALAD

2 apples, cubed
2 bananas
⅓ c. celery
⅓ c. nuts
⅓ c. coconut
3 T. Cool Whip®
1 T. peanut butter
1 T. mayonnaise

Mix together first 5 ingredients and set aside. Mix together Cool Whip®, peanut butter, and mayonnaise and then add to apple mixture.

Serves 6   Sue Miller (Owner)

SUNSHINE FRUIT SALAD

5 navel oranges
½ c. sugar

8-oz. pkg. cream cheese, softened
½ c. pecans

Cut up oranges into bite size pieces. Mix sugar in softened cream cheese and add oranges and pecans. Mix well. Chill and serve.

Serves 8   Carol Detweiler (Administration)

ALMOND CRUNCH SALAD

½ c. almonds, sliced
3 T. sugar
½ head lettuce
bunch of romaine lettuce or fresh spinach
1 T. celery, sliced
3–4 T. onion, diced
11-oz. can mandarin oranges, chilled

Dressing:
¼ c. vegetable oil
2 T. sugar
2 T. white vinegar
½ t. salt
dash of pepper
dash of Tabasco®, optional
1 T. fresh parsley, chopped

Mix almonds and sugar in a small heavy skillet. Place over medium heat, stirring constantly until caramelized. Cool and set aside. When ready to serve toss vegetables, caramelized almonds, mandarin oranges and dressing.

Marlys Pletcher (Waitress)

CASHEW SALAD

1 head lettuce, chopped or torn
4 green onion, chopped
1 c. chow mein noodles
3 T. sunflower seeds
6 oz. cashews, chopped
4–6 strips bacon, cooked

Dressing:
4 T. sugar
1 t. salt
½ t. pepper
½ c. oil
6 T. tarragon vinegar

Toss lettuce, onions, chow mein noodles, sunflower seeds, cashews, and bacon in large bowl. For dressing, mix sugar, salt, pepper, oil, and vinegar until well blended. Pour dressing over salad and toss. Mix salad just before serving.

Serves 8–10   Anita Yoder (Daughter of Bob & Sue)

CARMEL APPLE SALAD

8 apples, diced
2 small boxes instant butterscotch pudding
2 c. dry roasted peanuts
2 16-oz. containers whipped topping
2 20-oz. cans crushed pineapple, well drained
3 c. mini marshmallows

Dice apples into large bowl. Add peanuts. In another bowl, mix together whipped topping, pineapple, and dry pudding mix. Pour over apples and peanuts and stir well. Stir in marshmallows.

Cassie Berney (Village Shops)

FRUIT SALAD

1 can pineapple chunks, drained
2 eggs, whipped
2 oranges, peeled and diced
2 T. flour
40 large marshmallows, cut
1 T. butter
1 c. fruit juice
1 c. whipped cream

Cook eggs, flour, and fruit juice over low heat. Cook until thick. Cool and add one cup of whipped cream. Combine dressing with fruit and let stand several hours.

Serves 6   Tracy Robinson (Country Inn)

CRANBERRY SALAD

16 oz. whole cranberry sauce
1 c. tropical fruit trail mix
2 oz. pecans or walnuts, chopped
12 oz. whipped topping

Break up cranberry sauce with fork and stir in fruit mix and nuts. Carefully fold in whipped topping. Best if prepared and served the same day.

Serves 4–6   Elizabeth Miller (Kitchen)

The best way to remember people is through prayer.

TAFFY APPLE SALAD

½ c. sugar
1 T. cornstarch
2 T. lemon juice
1 egg, beaten
20-oz. can pineapple chunks

8-oz. tub Cool Whip®
3 medium apples, cored and chopped
2 c. miniature marshmallows
1½ c. salted peanuts

In heavy bottomed saucepan, mix sugar, cornstarch, lemon juice, egg, and juice from pineapple. Cook over low heat, stirring constantly until mixture thickens, about 5 minutes. Allow to cool, stir in whipped topping. In large bowl, mix apples, pineapple chunks, marshmallows, and peanuts. Toss with dressing and refrigerate 2–3 hours before serving.

Serves 16   Sue McDowell (Housekeeping – Country Inn)

FROZEN GRAPE SALAD

2 3-oz. pkgs. cream cheese
2 T. mayonnaise
2 T. pineapple juice
24 large marshmallows, quartered

2½ c. pineapple tidbits, drained
1 c. heavy cream, whipped
2 c. seedless Tokay® grapes, cut in half

Soften cream cheese and blend in mayonnaise. Add pineapple juice and mix well. Add marshmallows and pineapple tidbits. Fold in whipped cream, add grapes, and place in freezer.

Serves 10–12   Rosalie Bontrager (Country Inn Manager)

CHERRY APPLE SALAD

3-oz. pkg. cherry-flavored gelatin
1 c. hot water
¼ c. red cinnamon candies
½ c. boiling water

1 c. apples, chopped and pared
1 c. celery, chopped
½ c. walnuts, chopped

Dissolve gelatin in one cup of hot water. Add cinnamon candies to half a cup of boiling water and stir to dissolve. Add enough water to make one cup liquid. Add to dissolved gelatin. Cool until partially set. Add remaining ingredients. Pour into 6 individual molds. Chill until firm and serve on crisp lettuce.

Serves 6   Sylvia Smith (Bakery Sales)

BEST EVER SALAD

4 c. hot water
2 pkgs. lime Jell-O®
1 large pkg. cream cheese
18 large marshmallows
1 can crushed pineapple, drained
1 c. pecans
4 c. whipped topping

Dissolve Jell-O® in hot water, along with cream cheese and marshmallows. Beat mixture until smooth. When semi-thick add nuts, pineapple, and whipped cream. Nuts and pineapple may be left out. Chill.

Lloyd Yoder (Meat Room)

If it is possible, as much as depends on you, live peaceably with all men. . . .
"Therefore, if your enemy hungers,
    feed him;
If he thirsts, give him a drink;
For in so doing you will heap
    coals of fire on his head."

Rom. 12:18, 20

EMERALD ISLE MOLD

Layer 1:
3-oz. pkg. lime-flavored gelatin
1 c. boiling water
¾ c. juice from grapefruit
8-oz. pkg. cream cheese

Layer 2:
3-oz. pkg. lime flavored gelatin
1 c. boiling water
1 c. ginger ale
1 c. grapefruit sections cut in half
1 c. diced apples
¼ c. walnuts, chopped

Dissolve one package lime gelatin in boiling water and then add grapefruit juice. Gradually add to cream cheese, mixing until well blended. Pour into 1½-quart mold and chill until firm. Then dissolve remaining pkg. lime gelatin in boiling water and add ginger ale. Chill until lightly thickened. Fold in fruit and nuts. Pour over molded gelatin layer. Chill until firm. Unmold on lettuce.

Serves 6–8   Sylvia Smith (Bakery Sales)

GLASS BOWL SALAD

1 medium head lettuce, shredded
1 c. carrots, shredded
10-oz. pkg. frozen peas, thawed
5 green onions, sliced
1 medium green pepper, chopped

1 c. Miracle Whip® salad dressing
⅔ c. sour cream
6 strips of bacon, cooked and crumbled

In a 3-quart clear glass bowl, layer the first 6 ingredients in order given. Combine Miracle Whip® and sour cream until smooth and spread evenly over salad. Cover and chill overnight. Sprinkle with bacon before serving.

Serves 8–10   Martha Coblentz (Bakery)

EGGNOG MOLDED SALAD

1 t. unflavored gelatin
¼ c. water
16-oz. can sliced pears
6-oz. pkg. lemon gelatin

8-oz. pkg. sour cream
¾ c. eggnog
1 can mandarin oranges, drained

In a small bowl, combine gelatin and water, set aside. Drain pears, reserving juice and add enough water to juice to measure 2 cups. Pour into a saucepan and bring to a boil. Remove from the heat. Stir in gelatin mixture and lemon gelatin until completely dissolved. Cool for about 15 minutes. Stir in sour cream and eggnog until well blended. Chill until partially set. Cut the oranges and pears into chunks and add to eggnog mixture. Pour into an oiled 6-cup mold or a serving dish. Chill until firm.

Serves 10–12   Martha Coblentz   (Bakery)

CRANBERRY GELATIN SALAD

6-oz. pkg. cherry gelatin
1½ c. boiling water
20-oz. can crushed pineapple, undrained

16-oz. can whole berry cranberry sauce
1½ c. seedless red grapes, halved
¼ c. chopped pecans, optional

In a large bowl, dissolve gelatin in water. Stir in pineapple and cranberry sauce. Refrigerate for 30 minutes. Stir in grapes and pecans. Pour into a 2-quart serving bowl.

Serves 8–10   Martha Coblentz (Bakery)

 Joys shared are multiplied.

RASPBERRY LAYER JELL-O® SALAD

First Layer:
1 small box raspberry Jell-O®
1 c. boiling water
1 c. cold water

Second Layer:
1 small box raspberry Jell-O®
1 c. boiling water
1 c. cold water
8-oz. pkg. cream cheese
8-oz. container Cool Whip®
½ c. sugar

Third Layer:
1 small box raspberry Jell-O®
1 c. boiling water
1 c. cold water

Combine ingredients for the first layer and mix until dissolved. Let harden in refrigerator. For the second layer, combine Jell-O® and boiling water, then cold water. Let cool, but not harden. Beat the cream cheese, Cool Whip®, and sugar together until smooth. Mix with the Jell-O® mixture. Pour on top of the first layer and let set. For the third layer, combine ingredients and mix until dissolved. Pour on top of other layers and let harden in refrigerator.

Mary Stalter (Waitress)

JELL-O® SALAD

2 3-oz. pkgs. Jell-O®
1 can pineapple
2 small pkg. cream cheese

1 T. mayonnaise
milk
2 c. whipped topping

Dissolve 2 packages of Jell-O® (your choice of flavor) in boiling water, add pineapple, and chill until partly set. Cream together cream cheese, mayonnaise, and add a little milk to make smooth mixture. Add 2 cups of whipped topping and mix with Jello® and pineapple. Let it set again. It's very quick and easy to make.

Elizabeth Miller (Kitchen)

APPLE JELL-O® SALAD

6-oz. box cherry Jello®
2 c. boiling water
1¾ c. cold water
4 c. apples, peeled and sliced

Dissolve Jell-O® in boiling water and then add cold water. Add apples to Jell-O® when it starts to set. Chill. Simple but good.

Serves 8–10   Mary K. Schmucker (Kitchen)

BLUEBERRY GELATIN SALAD

6-oz. pkg. cherry-flavored gelatin
2 c. boiling water
15-oz. bag blueberries, frozen
8-oz. pkg. cream cheese, softened
½ c. sugar
1 t. vanilla
1 c. sour cream
¼ c. chopped pecans

In bowl, dissolve gelatin in boiling water. Stir in blueberries. Pour into 12"x8"x2" dish. Chill until set. In a mixing bowl, beat cream cheese and sugar until smooth. Add vanilla and sour cream. Mix well. Spread over the gelatin layer. Sprinkle with pecans and chill several hours or overnight.

Serves 12   Doretta Wingard (Waitress)

Lettuce and celery keep longer if you store them in paper bags instead of plastic.

A dampened paper towel or terry cloth brushed downward on a cob of corn will remove every strand of corn silk.

CHEESY JELL-O® FRUIT SALAD

2 c. boiling water, divided
3-oz. pkg. lemon Jell-O®
2 c. ice cubes, divided
20-oz. can crushed pineapple, drained and liquid reserved
3-oz. pkg. orange Jello®
2 c. miniature marshmallows
3 large bananas, sliced
½–1 c. shredded cheddar cheese

For Cooked Dressing:
1 c. reserved pineapple juice
½ c. sugar
1 egg, beaten
2 T. cornstarch
1 T. butter
1 small tub Cool Whip®

In mixing bowl, combine 1 cup of boiling water with lemon Jell-O®. Then add 1 cup ice cubes and stir until melted and then add pineapple. Pour mixture into a 9"x13" pan and refrigerate until set. Repeat with orange Jell-O®, remaining water and ice cubes. Stir in marshmallows. Pour over lemon layer, refrigerate until set. For dressing, combine pineapple juice, sugar, egg, cornstarch, and butter in saucepan. Cook over medium heat, stirring constantly until thickened. Cover and refrigerate overnight or until completely cooled. The next day, arrange bananas over Jell-O®. Combine dressing and Cool Whip® and then spread over bananas. Sprinkle with desired amount of cheese.

Serves 12   Carol Detweiler (Administration)

APRICOT FLUFF SALAD

1 large box apricot Jell-O®
2 c. boiling water
2 c. cold water
2 bananas, sliced
2 c. crushed pineapple drained, reserve juice

Second Layer:
1 egg, beaten
½ c. sugar
2 T. flour
1 c. pineapple juice
2 T. butter
3 oz. cream cheese
1½ c. Cool Whip®

Combine first three items. After it has jelled, add bananas and pineapple. Reserve pineapple juice for second layer. Combine egg, sugar, flour, and pineapple juice. When thickened, add butter and cream cheese. When cool, add Cool Whip® and then put second layer on top of first when set.

Pam Frey (Bakery)

ORANGE JELL-O® SUPREME

1 large box orange Jell-O®
2 c. boiling water
6 oz. frozen orange juice concentrate
1 large can crushed pineapple, undrained
1 large can mandarin orange, drained
8-oz. tub Cool Whip®
1 small vanilla pudding
1 c. milk

Dissolve Jell-O® and orange juice concentrate in boiling water. Add pineapple and mandarin oranges. Pour into a 9"x13" pan and refrigerate. When set combine milk and pudding until mixed and stir in Cool Whip®. Top the Jell-O® mixture and refrigerate.

Serves 12   Fran Blough (Waitress)

Anxiety in the heart of man causes depression,
But a good word makes it glad.

Prov. 12:25

TACO SALAD

½ lb. hamburger
½ pkg. taco mix
½ head lettuce
1 small onion
2 tomatoes
6 oz. cheddar cheese
5 oz. Doritos® chips
½ c. red kidney beans
1 8-oz. Western® salad dressing

Brown the hamburger in a skillet and drain the fat. Add the taco mix and stir well. Set aside. Dice the onion, shred the lettuce, and cut up the tomatoes. Put them into a large bowl. Break up the Doritos® chips and add them to the bowl. Add the red kidney beans, taco meat, and cheese to the mixture. Pour the dressing over the salad and mix well. Serve immediately.

Luan Westfall (Purchasing Manager)

TACO SALAD MEAT

1 c. water
1 lb. ground chuck hamburger
1 T. dehydrated onions
1 t. salt

1 pkg. taco seasoning mix
1 can refried beans
pinch pepper

Fry hamburger with dehydrated onions, salt, pepper, and water until brown. Add refried beans and taco seasoning and mix well. Break up nacho chips on bottom layer. Add lettuce, onion, and tomato as desired. Add taco meat and top with cheese, sour cream, and salsa.

SEAFOOD SALAD

16-oz. box seashell pasta, cooked
4 c. Hellmann's® mayonnaise
1 c. sugar
1 jar pimentos

2 c. cheddar cheese
16 oz. imitation crabmeat
2 c. celery

Mix all together and leave half a cup of the cheddar cheese for the top. Put in refrigerator overnight or a few hours.

Sharon Schlabach (Waitress)

PEPPERONI CAESAR SALAD

8 c. romaine lettuce
1 c. pepperoni
¾ c. Parmesan cheese, grated
¼ t. black pepper
1½ c. croutons

Caesar Dressing:
6 T. olive oil
2 T. red wine vinegar
1 T. Miracle Whip® salad dressing
2 cloves garlic
½ t. Dijon mustard
¼ t. Worcestershire sauce

Combine salad ingredients and toss. For the dressing, blend on high until well blended and then top salad with dressing.

Serves 6–8

Mary Stalter (Waitress)

COMPANY SPECIAL CHICKEN SALAD

1 qt. chicken salad
1 c. white rice, cooked
1 c. small green grapes
13.5-oz. can pineapple tidbits, drained
1 c. pecans
11-oz. can mandarin oranges, drained

Gently toss together all ingredients, but reserve a few nuts, oranges, and pineapple tidbits for decorations on top. You can refrigerate mixture overnight. When ready to serve, serve on a bed of lettuce.

Joyce Miller (Sunshine Farm Manager)

FRUITED PASTA SALAD

1½ c. spiral pasta, uncooked
8-oz. can unsweetened pineapple chunks
8-oz. carton nonfat peach yogurt
2 T. sour cream
1½ c. cubed cantaloupe
1 c. halved seedless grapes
1½ c. sliced fresh strawberries

Cook pasta according to package. Rinse in cold water and drain. Cool completely. Drain pineapple, reserving 2 tablespoons of juice. Set pineapple aside. In a small bowl, combine the yogurt, sour cream, and reserved pineapple juice until smooth. Cover and refrigerate. In a large bowl, combine pasta, pineapple, cantaloupe, and grapes. Just before serving, stir in strawberries, and drizzle with yogurt mixture.

Serves 13   Martha Coblentz (Bakery)

 RAMEN® SALAD

1 medium head lettuce
3 eggs, cooked and sliced
2 green onions, sliced
1 small pkg. toasted almonds
1 pkg. Ramen® chicken noodles

Dressing:
½ c. oil
1 T. vinegar
2 T. sugar
flavor pkg. from noodle pkg.

Mix lettuce, eggs, onions, and almonds together. To make salad dressing, mix oil, vinegar, sugar, and flavor packet together. When ready to eat, pour dressing on salad, toss, and add crushed noodles.

Serves 8–10   Anita Yoder (Daughter of Bob & Sue)

PRETZEL CRUST SALAD

2½ c. pretzels, unsalted and crushed
3 t. sugar
¾ c. butter or margarine
1 c. sugar
8-oz. pkg. cream cheese
20-oz. pkg. frozen strawberries, partially thawed
16-oz. can crushed pineapple
6-oz. pkg. strawberry Jell-O®
1 small tub Cool Whip®

Combine first three ingredients and press into 13"x9" pan. Bake 10 minutes at 350°. Beat together sugar and cream cheese and then fold in Cool Whip®, then add to top of crust. Boil 2 cup water and combine with Jell-O®. Stir, then add strawberries and pineapple. Put in refrigerator to partially settle for approximately 1 hour. Pour on top of cream cheese mixture and chill overnight.

Sue Meeks (Kitchen)

DANISH POTATO SALAD

¼ c. vinegar
¼ c. water
¼ c. sugar
¼ t. salt
dash of pepper
1 t. prepared mustard
2 eggs, well beaten
1 c. salad dressing
4 c. potatoes, cooked and cubed
2 eggs, hard cooked and chopped
½ c. cucumber, chopped
1 T. minced onion
1 T. green onion, chopped

Combine first six ingredients. Bring to a boil. Reduce heat, and gradually beat in well-beaten eggs. Cook stirring constantly until slightly thickened, about 5 minutes. Beat in salad dressing. Toss together remaining ingredients. Pour on dressing and toss gently. Adjust seasoning if necessary. Best if made several hours or overnight before serving.

Serves 6

Leon Nafziger (Grounds Maintenance)

When you don't know what to do, pray. You'll be surprised at how much it will help you decide.

GRANDMA'S OLD-FASHIONED COLESLAW

1 head cabbage
½ c. grated carrots
1 c. salad dressing
½ c. sugar

dash salt
½ t. mustard
⅓ c. milk
1 medium apple
¼ pkg. miniature marshmallows

Shred cabbage and carrots or use one bag of shredded cabbage and carrots. Mix together: salad dressing, sugar, salt, mustard, and milk. Let it set while coring and dicing apple, leaving the peeling on for color. Stir cole slaw and mixture together. Add apple and marshmallows. Stir till all is coated with dressing mixture. Refrigerate till ready to eat.

Serves 8   Connie Bowers (Kitchen)

BROCCOLI SLAW

1 lb. bag broccoli slaw mix
2 pkgs. Ramen® noodles
1 c. almonds, sliced
1 c. sunflower seeds

Dressing:
1 c. oil
2 pkgs. seasoning from Ramen® noodles
½ c. sugar
⅓ c. vinegar

Break up Ramen® noodles in package. Open and mix with slaw mix, almonds, and sunflower seeds. Combine dressing ingredients and mix well. Store in refrigerator until ready to serve. Pour over slaw mix and serve.

Serves 6–8   Dave Wenger (Grounds Maintenance)

 ## COLESLAW

2 lbs. cabbage (1 large head
    or 2 bags pre-shredded
1 large carrot, shredded
1 c. sugar

⅓ c. cider vinegar
⅓ c. hot water
⅔ t. salt
¼ t. celery se3d

In a small bowl, dissolve sugar in hot water and then add salt, celery seed, and vinegar. Cool. Pour over cabbage and carrots. Mix well.

HOMESTEAD SALAD

¾ c. sugar
1 t. flour, heaping
½ c. vinegar
1 T. prepared mustard
1 large pkg. mixed frozen
    vegetables

1 can red kidney beans
3–4 stalks of celery, diced
½ c. onion, chopped
½ green pepper, chopped

Combine sugar, flour, vinegar, and mustard in saucepan and cook until clear. Let cool. Cook frozen vegetables as directed and let cool. Drain red kidney beans and rinse well. Then mix all ingredients together and let set overnight. Keeps for at least a week.

Esther Cross (Accounting)

PEA AND PEANUT SALAD

2 lbs. frozen peas
1 c. celery, diced
¼ c. onion, chopped

½ lb. salted spanish peanuts
½ c. mayonnaise
1 c. sour cream

Bring peas to boil and then put in ice cold water. Drain. Mix all ingredients just before serving.

Pam Frey (Bakery)

SURPRISE CABBAGE SALAD

3-oz. pkg. lime Jell-O®
3-oz. pkg. lemon Jell-O®
2 c. boiling water
1 c. miniature marshmallows
1 c. mayonnaise

1½ c. cabbage, shredded
1 c. pineapple juice
1 c. pineapple, crushed
1 c. cream, whipped
1 c. nuts

Dissolve lime and lemon Jello® in boiling water in a 9"x13"pan. Add miniature marshmallows and stir until dissolved. Add mayonnaise, cabbage, pineapple juice, and crushed pineapple. Refrigerate until it starts to set. Then add whipped cream and nuts.

Becky Helmuth (Waitress)

LETTUCE SALAD

1 pkg. Ramen® Oriental chicken-flavored noodles
½ cup nuts, chopped
1 T. butter
1 head lettuce
1 bunch broccoli
1 c. celery, chopped
green onion, optional
green peppers, optional
cucumbers, optional

Dressing:
⅓ c. vegetable oil
¾ c. sugar
¼ c. vinegar
1 T. soy sauce
pinch salt and pepper
½ c. salad dressing

Brown butter on low heat and add crumbled noodles and nuts. Sprinkle package of seasoning mix over mixture. Toast until brown, stirring constantly. Cool. Cut up lettuce, broccoli, celery, and whatever vegetables you wish to use. Mix dressing ingredients in blender and pour over greens when ready to serve. Add noodles and nuts and mix well.

Ellen Mishler (Administration)

BROCCOLI SALAD

1 head cauliflower, chopped
2 heads broccoli, chopped
¼ c. red onion, chopped
¼ c. shredded carrots, chopped
¼ c. sunflower seeds or to taste
1 c. cheddar cheese, shredded
2 lbs. bacon bits

Dressing:
1 c. real mayonnaise
⅓ c. sugar
2 T. vinegar

Combine salad ingredients and mix well. Combine ingredients for the dressing and mix well. Add to salad and mix.

Grace & Bob Carpenter (Accounting)

Better is the one who is slighted but
    has a servant,
Than he who honors himself but
    lacks bread.

Prov. 12:9

BROCCOLI DELIGHT SALAD

5 c. fresh broccoli, chopped
½ c. raisins or dates
¼ c. red onion, chopped
10 bacon slices, cooked and crumbled
1 c. sunflower seeds
2 T. sugar
3 T. vinegar
1 c. mayonnaise

In a large salad bowl, combine broccoli, raisins, and onion. In a small bowl, combine sugar, vinegar, and mayonnaise. Pour over broccoli and toss to coat. Refrigerate. Just before serving, sprinkle with bacon and sunflower seeds and toss.

Serves 6–8   Verna Lickfeldt (Restaurant Administration)

ORIENTAL CABBAGE SALAD

1 head cabbage, shredded
1 bunch broccoli, chopped
1 c. celery, chopped
6 green onions, sliced
1 cucumber, sliced
1 green pepper, chopped
¾ c. slivered almonds, toasted in the oven until brown
3-oz. pkg. Ramen® noodles, beef

Dressing:
1 c. olive oil
¾ c. sugar
½ c. vinegar
1 T. soy sauce
pinch of salt and pepper
seasoning pkg. from Ramen® noodles

Put everything together in airtight bowl, except dressing ingredients. Can be put together the night before. Combine dressing ingredients, mix well, and let set. Add the dressing just before serving.

Serves 10–12   Linda Miller (Cashier/Hostess)

Doctors will tell you that if you eat slowly you will eat less. This is particularly true if you are a member of a large family.

MIXED VEGETABLE SALAD

16-oz. pkg. frozen mixed
   vegetables
1 can kidney beans
1 c. green peppers, chopped
1 c. onion, chopped
1 c. celery, chopped

Dressing:
1 c. sugar
2 t. flour
1 t. mustard
½ c. water
½ c. vinegar

Cook frozen vegetables and drain. Add green peppers, onion, and celery. For the dressing, stir together all dressings ingredients and boil until thick. Cool slightly. Pour over vegetables and chill several hours before serving.

Brandie Leonard (Village Shops)

LETTUCE SALAD FAVORITE

1 head lettuce
1 small head cauliflower
2 c. cheddar cheese
1 pkg. bacon, fried

Dressing:
½ c. sugar
1 c. salad dressing
1 T. vinegar

Chop lettuce, cauliflower, and bacon. Top with cheese. Mix dressing in bowl and wait to put on salad just before serving.

Jeanie Mast (Bakery Sales)

CABBAGE SALAD

1 head cabbage, chopped fine
1 bunch green onions, chopped
1 pkg. chicken flavored Ramen®
   noodles, broken
2 T. sesame seeds
2 oz. slivered almonds

Dressing:
3 T. sugar
1½ t. season salt
¾ c. vinegar
¾ t. black pepper
⅔ c. vegetable oil
1 t. chicken base
1 pkg. chicken seasoning in
   Ramen® noodles

Mix dressing well and set aside. Chop cabbage fine, but do not shred. Toast almonds and sesame seeds. Break noodles. Combine ingredients no more than 20–30 minutes before serving. Mix well and serve.

Arlene Miller (Waitress)

I would rather be a doorkeeper
  in the house of my God
Than dwell in the tents of wickedness.
For the LORD God is a sun and shield;
The LORD will give grace and glory;
No good thing will He withhold
From those who walk uprightly.

Ps. 84:10b–11

COLORFUL VEGGIE SALAD

6 c. broccoli florets
6 c. cauliflower florets
2 c. cherry tomatoes, halved
1 large red onion, sliced
1 can pitted ripe olives, drained and sliced
1 envelope ranch salad dressing mix
⅔ c. oil
¼ c. vinegar

Toss the first five ingredients in a large bowl. Combine the last three ingredients together and shake well. Pour over salad and toss. Works well to put the salad in a marinating container. Refrigerate at least 3 hours. It is real good to do overnight.

Serves 20   Martha Coblentz (Bakery)

BROCCOLI SALAD

1 bunch broccoli, washed and sliced
1 medium onion, chopped fine
10 strips of bacon, fried crisp and crumbled
1 c. sunflower seeds, optional

Dressing:
1½ c. real mayonnaise
4 T. vinegar
½ c. sugar

Mix together first four ingredients. For the dressing, combine all dressing ingredients and mix well. Add to broccoli mixture and mix.

Norma Velleman (Bakery Sales)

SPINACH SALAD

spinach
raisins
sunflower seeds
orange sections

Dressing:
½ c. sugar
¾ t. dry mustard
½ t. paprika
½ t. celery seed
1 t. salt
¼ c. vinegar
1½ t. onion, finely chopped
1 c. salad oil

Measure all ingredients together except oil. Add oil last, adding very slowly while mixing with mixer until oil is all and mixture becomes thicker.

Harriet Miller (Marketing)

DUTCH BOY LETTUCE

4 slices bacon
1 egg, slightly beaten
⅓ c. sour cream
¼ c. vinegar
2 T. sugar

½ t. salt
3 c. torn lettuce
6 c. torn spinach
4 green onions, sliced
tomatoes, sliced

Cook bacon until crisp. Reserve 3 tablespoons of bacon grease. Stir egg, sour cream, vinegar, sugar, and salt into bacon grease. Cook and stir until thickened. Pour over greens and vegetables. Serve immediately. Crumble bacon on top.

By the time we realize our parents were right, we have children who think we are wrong.

CHINESE CABBAGE SALAD

Salad:
1 head celery cabbage, shredded
8 green onions, sliced thin
8 T. blanched almonds, slivered
8 T. sesame seeds
2 pkg. Ramen® noodles

Dressing:
4 T. sugar
1 t. pepper
2 t. salt
2 t. accent salt
1 c. salad oil
6 T. rice vinegar

Toast almonds and sesame seeds until brown, approximately 10-15 minutes. Mix the cabbage and the onions. Add the almonds, sesame seeds and noodles. Break the noodles up into small pieces. Put all the dressing ingredients into a bowl and mix well. Pour the dressing over the cabbage mixture and lightly toss the salad. Do not pour the dressing over the salad until you are ready to serve. Otherwise, the salad will become soggy.

Luan Westfall (Purchasing Manager)

TALLY HO SALAD DRESSING

1 c. salad oil
1 c. sugar
½ t. garlic salt

1 c. ketchup
2 T. vinegar

Mix all ingredients together with an electric mixer or blender. This must be beaten very well so the oil won't separate later. Then shake well before serving.

Marlene Lehman (Busser)

ZESTY FRENCH DRESSING

½ c. sugar
1½ t. salt
1 t. dry mustard
1½ t. paprika

1 c. oil
1 medium onion, grated fine
6 T. vinegar

Mix dry ingredients. Stir in oil and then add onion and vinegar. Beat well with eggbeater or electric mixer for 2 minutes. Dressing may be mixed in blender until smooth.

Makes 1½ Cups

Norine Yoder (Restaurant Gifts)

RANCH DRESSING

1 c. mayonnaise
1 c. buttermilk
1 T. parsley flakes
½ t. onion powder
¼ t. garlic powder
¼ t. pepper
⅛ t. salt

Combine all ingredients and mix thoroughly. Chill at least 4 hours before serving.

Betty Miller (Waitress)

OIL AND VINEGAR DRESSING

½ c. water
1½ c. sugar
1 T. ground mustard
1 t. salt
½ t. pepper
½ t. paprika
¼ c. vinegar
2 garlic cloves, halved
¼ c. vegetable oil

Combine first 6 ingredients in a 1-qt. jar with a tight-fitting lid. Add vinegar and garlic and shake until sugar is dissolved. Add oil. Shake well. Store in the refrigerator. Just before serving remove garlic from the dressing. Drizzle over salad greens or red cabbage.

Makes 2 cups

Mary K. Schmucker (Kitchen)

HOT BACON DRESSING

4 slices bacon
1 egg, beaten
½ t. salt
1 c. water
1 T. cornstarch
¼ c. vinegar

Fry bacon until crisp. Remove, drain, and crumble. Mix remaining ingredients. Pour over warm drippings and heat until thick. Combine bacon into dressing. Serve over fresh spinach or leaf lettuce salad.

Makes 1½ Cups

Arlene Miller (Waitress)

Most of us can keep a secret. It's the people we tell it to who can't.

FRENCH DRESSING

2 c. salad dressing
½ c. vinegar
¼ c. vegetable oil
½ t. salt
1 t. paprika

1 c. sugar
½ c. catsup
1 T. mustard
½ t. pepper
garlic, to taste

Mix together all ingredients well with a blender. Store in an airtight container in refrigerator. Will keep for weeks when in refrigerator.

Jeanie Mast (Bakery Sales)

SALAD DRESSING

1 c. oil
1 c. white sugar
1 onion, grated
½ t. season salt
1 T. mustard

½ t. salt
1 c. Miracle Whip®
¼ c. vinegar
½ t. celery seed
½ t. celery salt

Mix all ingredients together. Serve on any salad.

Effie Mast (Essenhaus Foods)

AMISH BEAN SOUP

1 qt. navy beans, partially cooked
¼ lb. butter
½ c. onions, chopped

½ c. celery, chopped
2 T. seasoning

Put butter in a large kettle and melt it. Then add onions, celery, and seasoning. Stir until all is mixed well. Add beans and enough water to cover all. Cook on slow heat until beans are soft. This can be kept in a covered container in refrigerator for a short length of time. Heat the amount of milk needed. Add beans to the milk. Bring to a boil. Pour over cubed homemade bread.

Sue Miller (Owner)

With God nothing shall be impossible.
Luke 1:37

BROCCOLI SOUP

⅓ c. margarine
½ c. flour
1 can chicken broth
pinch pepper
2 t. salt

2 t. Essenhaus® chicken base
3 c. milk
¾ c. American cheese
2 T. onion, chopped
1 bag frozen broccoli

Melt margarine in large pan. Add flour and mix well. Add broth and seasonings. Cook until thick, about 10 minutes. Heat milk and cheese until the cheese is melted. Add milk mixture to flour mixture. Continue to cook but turn heat down. Watch closely to prevent scorching. Last, microwave broccoli and onions for about 5–6 minutes and add to rest of mixture. Enjoy.

Serves 4

The ideal summer vacation spot is one where the fish bite and the mosquitoes don't.

CACTUS SOUP

2–3 lb. pork
3 cloves of garlic
1 onion

8–10 green chilies
10–12 green tomatoes, (tomatillos)
6–8 cactus leaves

Brown pork. Add garlic and half of the onion. Simmer until pork is tender. Strain broth and shred the meat. Seed chilies and add tomatoes and remaining onion. Cover with water and simmer until tender. Blend in blender and add it to the broth. Add finely diced cactus leaves and bring to a boil. If cactus is not available, substitute green beans.

Betty Miller (Waitress)

CHEESY POTATO SOUP

4 c. pared potatoes, diced
½ c. celery, diced
½ c. onion, diced
1½ c. water
2 bouillon cubes, chicken

2 c. milk
½ c. sour cream
4 T. flour
8 oz. Velveeta® cheese
¼ t. pepper

Combine potatoes, celery, onion, water, bouillon cube, and pepper in large saucepan. Cover and cook 10 minutes or until potatoes are tender. Add 1 c. milk and heat. Mix sour cream, flour, and remaining milk together. Gradually stir into soup base. Cook over low heat, stirring constantly until thickened. Add cheese and stir until melted. Variation: Add whatever frozen vegetables you have on hand, such as corn or lima beans.

Serves 8   Anita Yoder (Daughter of Bob & Sue)

COLD SOUP

bread crumbs
½ c. sugar
½ t. vanilla
milk

any kind of fresh fruit such as
    strawberries, bananas,
    peaches, or cherries

Put enough bread crumbs in a bowl to suit the size of your family. Make plenty this is a deliciously refreshing soup. Add fruit and sugar, more or less can be used, what ever you desire. Add milk with vanilla just before ready to serve.

Sue Miller (Owner)

CORN CHOWDER

3 medium potatoes
1 small onion
1 c. water
¼ c. butter

1½ c. whole kernel corn, cooked
4 c. milk
4 slices bacon, fried and crumbled
salt and pepper to taste

Pare potatoes and dice. Grate onion. Add water and butter and then simmer until tender. Add corn, milk, and bacon. Simmer 15 minutes. Season with salt and pepper if you desire.

Serves 4–6   Leon Nafziger (Grounds Maintenance)

CREAM OF ASPARAGUS SOUP

1 lb. asparagus
4 c. milk, scalded
2 T. butter
2 T. flour
1/8 t. pepper

Wash asparagus and cut off tips 1½" from top, cover with boiling water and cook uncovered until tender, approximately 15 minutes. Remove the tips and add rest of asparagus to water and cook until tender, approximately 20 minutes. Drain this asparagus and rub through a sieve and add to milk. Melt butter. Blend in flour, salt, and pepper. Then add sieved asparagus mixture and heat to boiling, stirring constantly. Add the asparagus tips and serve hot.

Serves 6   Sylvia Smith (Bakery Sales)

CHICKEN NOODLE SOUP

8 c. chicken broth
1 T. chicken base
1 t. salt
1 t. parsley flakes
1½ c. cooked chicken, chopped
12-oz. bag Essenhaus® noodles

Bring broth, chicken base, salt, and parsley flakes to a boil. Add noodles and chicken and bring to a boil again. Turn heat down and simmer for 20 minutes.

GRANDMA'S SOUP

2 medium potatoes, diced
1 lb. hamburger
2 T. onion
2 c. peas, canned or frozen
5 c. milk

Cook potatoes until done. Fry hamburger and onion until brown and drain. Add hamburger and peas to potatoes and then add milk. Heat but do not boil. Add salt and pepper to taste.

Martha Hochstedler (Bakery)

GRANDMA'S SOUR EGG SOUP

1 medium onion, chopped fine	⅛ c. bay leaf
2 T. butter	¼ c. lemon juice or white vinegar
2 T. flour	¾ c. sour cream
1 t. salt	4–6 poached eggs
3 c. water or chicken stock, hot	paprika to taste

Brown onion in butter and then add flour to make gravy light brown color. Add chicken broth or water. Add bay leaf and lemon juice or vinegar. Simmer until nearly boiling. Blend in sour cream. Add poached eggs one at a time. Serve, sprinkle with paprika. You may eat this soup over cooked noodles.

Serves 4–6 Diane Butler (Bakery Sales)

MARY'S CHILI

3 lb. hamburger	46-oz. can tomato juice
2 large onions, chopped	2 T. chili powder
2 14-oz. cans tomatoes, diced	½ T. salt
3 15-oz. cans kidney beans	¼ c. brown sugar

Brown hamburger with onion and drain. Combine all ingredients and heat slowly for 30 minutes.

Serves 10–12 Cletus Miller (Grounds Maintenance)

TACO SOUP

26-oz. can tomato soup	tortilla chips, crumbled
1 soup can full of water	chedder cheese, grated
½ c. salsa	1 container sour cream

In a 2-quart saucepan combine tomato soup and water. Add salsa and heat through top with tortilla chips, cheese, and sour cream. You can also can at 10 pounds pressure for 30 minutes.

Lorene Mast (Kitchen)

TACO SOUP

1½ lb. ground beef
½ c. onion, chopped
28-oz. can whole tomatoes w/juice
14-oz. can kidney beans w/juice
17-oz. can corn with juice
1–2 c. water
2 t. chili powder
1 t. garlic salt
salt and pepper to taste

Brown the beef in a heavy kettle, drain and add onions. Cook until onions are tender. Add remaining ingredients. Simmer for 15 minutes. Ladle into bowls, top with grated cheese if desired. Try using different vegetable especially beans and add spices to taste.

Serves 6–8   Alice Moy (Administration)

LINDA'S TACO SOUP

1 lb. hamburger, browned with onion, drained
15 oz. chili beans
1 pint corn
1 c. rice, cooked
1 pkg. taco seasoning
⅓ c. sugar
1 qt. tomato juice

Mix all ingredients together. Simmer 30 minutes to blend flavors. Serve with taco chips, sour cream, and grated cheese.

Serves 6   Linda Miller (Cashier/Hostess)

TOMATO SOUP

1 lb. hamburger
1 small onion, diced
2 c. potatoes, diced
1 pint tomato juice
1 c. water
salt and pepper to taste
chili powder, optional

Fry the hamburger and onions in a skillet. Cook the diced potatoes. Combine the hamburger, onions, and diced potatoes in kettle and mix well. Then add juice and water and heat until boiling point. I also like to add a little chili powder, along with salt and pepper.

Serves 6   Mary K. Schmucker (Cook)

TOMATO HAMBURGER SOUP

2 medium potatoes, diced
1 c. tomatoes, diced
½ lb. hamburger

2 T. onion
2 c. tomato juice
3 c. milk

Cook potatoes until done. Add diced tomatoes. Fry hamburger and onion until brown and then drain. Add to potatoes. Mash with potato masher. Then add tomato juice and milk, heat, do not boil and add salt and pepper to taste.

Martha Hochstedler (Kitchen)

CREAM OF TOMATO SOUP

2 T. margarine
2 T. onion, chopped
3 T. flour
2 t. sugar
1 t. salt
⅛ t. black pepper
dash of garlic salt

dash of basil
dash of oregano
dash of thyme
dash of rosemary
2 c. tomato juice
2 c. cold milk

Heat margarine in large skillet. Saute onion and then blend in flour, sugar, salt, and seasonings. Remove from heat and gradually stir in tomato juice. Bring to a boil, stirring constantly. Boil for one minute. Stir hot tomato mixture into cold milk. Heat, but do not boil. When heated it's ready to serve.

Norine Yoder (Restaurant Gifts)

TOMATO SOUP

32-oz. can tomatoes, diced
9-oz. can chicken broth
1 oz. butter
2 T. sugar

2 T. onion, chopped
pinch of baking soda
1½ c. cream

Mix tomatoes, broth, butter, sugar, onions, and baking soda. Simmer for 1 hour. Heat cream in double boiler. Add cream to hot tomato mixture. Serve.

Serves 5–6

Anne Yoder (Administration)

Pleasant words are like a honeycomb,
Sweetness to the soul and health
  to the bones.

Prov. 16:24

MULLIGAN SOUP

1 lb. ground beef
4 medium potatoes, peeled and cubed
4 medium carrots, peeled and sliced
1 small pkg. frozen peas
2 small cans tomato soup
4 cans water
salt and pepper to taste

Brown ground beef and drain. Cook potatoes and carrots in water until almost tender, drain. Combine hamburger and all vegetables in large soup pan. Add tomato soup and water. Cook until vegetables are tender. Add salt and pepper to taste.

Serves 4–6   Tonya Penner (Kitchen)

NEW ENGLAND CLAM CHOWDER

4 small cans chopped sea clams
4 small cans clam juice
3 c. diced potatoes, cooked
⅓ c. celery
⅓ . minced onions
⅓ c. fried chopped bacon
¼ t. salt
4 c. milk
½ pt. whipping cream
1 T. butter
1⅓ c. flour
1½ t. salt
¼ t. pepper
2 c. milk

Put clams, clam juice, diced potatoes, celery, onion, bacon, ¼ teaspoon salt, milk, whipping cream, and margarine in saucepans and cook approximately 10 minutes. Dissolve flour, salt, and pepper in milk using a mixer. Add the flour mixture to the large kettle and cook until it thickens. Watch the soup closely because it scorches easily.

RIVEL SOUP

2 qts. milk
1½ t. salt
a little pepper
1 c. self-rising flour, heaping

1 large egg
dash of salt
½ stick butter

Melt butter, than add milk to boiling point. To make rivels, rub egg, flour, and dash of salt. Drop rivels no larger than peas into milk. Simmer a few minutes. Serve with crackers and fresh chopped onions.

Serves 6–8   Sue Miller (Owner)

POTATO SOUP

¾ c. margarine
1⅓ c. flour
½ qt. ham broth
½ t. ham base
¼ t. salt

pinch pepper
1 t. Worcestershire sauce
6¾ c. milk
4 c. diced potatoes, cooked
½ c. ham, cooked

Melt margarine in large saucepan. Add flour and mix well. Add ham broth, salt, pepper, Worcestershire sauce, and onion. Cook until thick. Add milk, potatoes, and ham. Simmer on low heat for 30 minutes.

 POTATO SOUP

3 c. potatoes, diced
½ c. carrots, chopped
½ c. celery, chopped

¼ c. onion, chopped
4–5 slices Velveeta® cheese
2½–3 c. milk

Add just enough water to cover vegetables, cook until tender. Mash coarsely. Do not drain water off. Add Velveeta® cheese and milk, and heat thoroughly. Add salt, pepper, and seasoning salt to taste.

Serves 6   Dorothy Miller (Waitress)

POTATO SOUP

4 lbs. potatoes, peeled, quartered, and sliced
1 c. onion, chopped
1 c. celery, chopped
1 c. carrot, chopped
16-oz. can chicken broth
1 lb. cheese, Velveeta®
1 lb. sausage, browned, drained, and crumbled
1 stick butter or margarine
15.5-oz. can evaporated milk
salt and pepper, as needed

In large pot put potatoes, carrots, onions, celery, and broth, add water just so you can see it. Potatoes will not be completely covered. Add 1 teaspoon salt. Bring to boil, reduce heat, and gently boil until potatoes are tender, stirring occasionally. Then on low heat add cheese, sausage, margarine, and evaporated milk. Heat until cheese is melted. Add salt and pepper to taste. Serve.

Brandie Leonard (Village Shops)

PIZZA SOUP

¼ c. fresh mushrooms, sliced
½ c. onion, chopped
1 t. vegetable oil
2 c. water
15-oz. can pizza sauce
1 c. pepperoni, chopped
1 c. fresh tomatoes, chopped
½ c. Italian sausage, cooked
¼ t. Italian seasoning
¼ c. parmesan cheese, grated
mozzarella cheese, shredded

In large saucepan, sauté mushrooms and onion in oil for 2–3 minutes. Add water, pizza sauce, pepperoni, tomatoes, sausage, and Italian seasoning. Bring to a boil over medium heat. Reduce heat. Cover and simmer for 20 minutes, stirring occasionally. Stir in parmesan cheese and garnish with mozzarella cheese.

Serves 4

Jennifer Leatherman (Cashier/Hostess)

My help comes from the LORD,
Who made heaven and earth.
Psa. 121:2

VEGETABLE BEEF SOUP

3–4 lbs. beef, cubed
1 T. beef bouillon
1-lb. bag carrots, chopped
1 bunch celery, chopped
2 cans green beans
2 cans corn, use juice
2 large cans tomatoes
1 large head cabbage, chopped
salt and pepper as desired

Cook beef in slow cooker with water and bouillon 4 hours on high or 7–8 hours on low. When done and cooled, tear up beef. Put all broth from meat in 20-quart large cooker. Start cooking cabbage and carrots on high in this broth for 30 minutes. Now add rest of ingredients. You'll also need to add a lot of bouillon and water to get your desired thickness. Simmer for 1–2 hours.

Delora Harker (Bakery Production)

VEGETABLE BEEF SOUP

1 can tomato juice
1 small can tomato soup
1 small can tomato puree
2 c. beef broth
1 c. water
1 T. brown sugar
1 can Essenhaus® chunk cooked beef in broth
1 box frozen mixed vegetables

Mix all ingredients together and bring to a boil. Simmer for 20 minutes and serve.

ZUCCHINI SOUP

1 T. vegetable oil
1 c. onion, chopped
1 c. celery, thinly sliced
1 garlic clove, minced
¼ c. green pepper, chopped
2 lbs. zucchini, chopped
2 medium tomatoes, chopped
3 c. chicken broth
½ t. dried basil
¼ t. dried thyme
1 c. half and half cream or milk

In a large saucepan, sauté onion, celery, garlic, and green pepper in oil until tender. Add zucchini, tomatoes, broth, basil, and thyme. Bring to a boil. Reduce heat and simmer uncovered for 20-30 minutes or until the vegetables are tender. Stir in cream and heat through. Serve hot or cold.

Serves 8   Jennifer Leatherman (Cashier/Hostess)

Meats, Poultry & Main Dishes

HINTS FOR MEATS

Heat the frying pan before adding oil or butter to prevent sticking.

When you want a crisp, brown crust on chicken, rub mayonnaise over it.

Grate an apple into hamburger then shape into patties to add moistness.

A large roast or turkey can be carved easily after it stands for 30 minutes.

Use an ice cream dipper to make meat balls.

To make a fluffy meat loaf, beat an egg white stiff, and add it after all other ingredients have been mixed.

When making hamburgers, mix a little flour with the meat and they will stay together better.

For smooth brown gravy, brown the flour well in meat drippings before adding the liquid. Another way to brown flour is by placing it in a custard cup beside meat in oven. When meat is done, the flour will be brown and ready to make a nice, brown gravy.

To prevent splashing when frying meat, sprinkle a little salt into the pan before putting the fat in.

Have you ever tried to get roll sausage out of a package, only to find that half of it is stuck to the surrounding paper? Try running cold water over the paper before you remove the contents. Or let it stand in ice water for a while.

To keep fish from sticking to the pan, bake on a bed of chopped onion, celery, and parsley. This also adds a nice flavor to the fish.

For golden-brown fried chicken, roll it in powdered milk instead of flour.

Try using crushed corn flakes, cornbread, or onion-flavored potato chips instead of bread crumbs in a meatball recipe.

COMPANY ROAST BEEF

5–10 lb. beef roast
1 can French onion soup
1 pkg. dry onion soup mix

14 oz. beef broth
1 T. kitchen bouquet

Cut roast in half, dredge in flour and brown in oil. Combine soups, broth, and kitchen bouquet. Put browned roast in pan and cover with soup mixture. Cover and bake 12–24 hours at 200°. Take grease off before serving.

Charlotte Miller (Waitress)

SWISS STEAK

3 lb. Swiss steak
3 T. shortening
1 medium onion, diced
½ c. celery, chopped
¼ c. Worcestershire sauce

1 can tomato sauce
2 cans water
½ c. corn
½ c. peas
salt and pepper to taste

Cut steak into serving pieces. Cover with flour and pound well on both sides. Place shortening in large frying pan. Add meat and brown well. Add onion, celery and Worcestershire sauce. Simmer for 10 minutes. Place in baking dish. Add corn and peas, and pour tomato sauce and water over meat and vegetables. Bake for 1 hour 30 minutes at 375°.

Serves 5–6

Luann Cox (Waitress)

SALISBURY STEAK

2 lb. ground beef
2 c. cracker crumbs
2 eggs
½ c. ketchup
2 T. onions, grated

2 t. salt
1 t. Worcestershire sauce
½ t. pepper
2 T. parsley, chopped

Mix ground beef, cracker crumbs, and eggs together. Add remaining ingredients. When well mixed, mold into large patties. They will be large size and fairly thick. Place in a shallow baking dish and bake at 325° for 40–50 minutes or until done. Make gravy from drippings in pan. If desired, make a sauce and bake in the sauce. Sauce: 1 can cream of mushroom soup, 1 c. milk, 1 T. butter, ½ t. garlic salt.

Wilma Miller (Kitchen)

POOR MAN'S STEAK

3 lb. hamburger
1 c. cracker crumbs

1 can celery soup
1 soup can of milk

Mix hamburger, cracker crumbs, and milk. Pack down and cut in serving pieces, approximately 15. Refrigerate overnight. Brown in skillet, dip in flour, and put in a pan for roasting. Add celery soup mixed with one can of milk. Use more soup and milk for more gravy. Use a 10"x15" pan (foil works well). Bake at 350° for one hour or 325° for 1½–2 hours.

Serves 15   Barbara Stickel (Village Shops)

GLAZED MEAT LOAF

½ c. ketchup
⅓ c. brown sugar
¼ c. lemon juice, divided
1 t. mustard powder
2 lbs. ground beef

3 slices bread, broken in small
  pieces
¼ c. onion, chopped
1 egg, beaten
1 t. beef bouillon granules

Preheat oven to 350°. In a small bowl, combine ketchup, brown sugar, one tablespoon lemon juice and mustard powder. In a separate bowl, combine the ground beef, bread, onion, egg, bouillon, remaining lemon juice and ⅓ of the ketchup mixture from the small bowl. Mix well and put into a 5"x9" loaf pan. Bake for 1 hour, drain excess fat, coat with remaining ketchup mixture and bake 10 minutes more.

Sue Meeks (Kitchen)

MEAT LOAF

2½ lbs. hamburger
5 eggs
¼ lb. crackers, crumbled
¼ c. onions, diced
salt and pepper to taste

2 c. tomato juice
½ c. ketchup
1 T. prepared mustard
4 T. brown sugar

Mix thoroughly first six ingredients. Put in pan and bake 2–2½ hours at 325°. When nearly done pour off fat. Combine ketchup, mustard and brown sugar, pour over meat loaf, and bake until done.

Millie Whetstone (Bakery)

LI'L CHEDDAR MEAT LOAVES

1 egg
¾ c. milk
1 c. shredded cheddar cheese
½ c. quick cooking oats
½ c. onion, chopped
1 t. salt
1 lb. ground beef
⅔ c. ketchup
½ c. brown sugar, packed
1½ t. mustard

In a bowl, beat egg and milk. Stir in cheese, oats, onion, and salt. Add beef and mix well. Shape into eight loaves and place in a greased 13"x9" baking pan. Combine ketchup, brown sugar, and mustard and then spoon over loaves. Bake uncovered at 350° for 45 minutes or until the meat is no longer pink and a meat thermometer reads 160°.

Serves 8   Jeanie Mast (Bakery Sales)

TURKEY-STUFFED PEPPERS

2 large green peppers, tops and seeds removed
½ lb. ground turkey
1 small onion, chopped
1 garlic clove, minced
2 T. butter or margarine
1 T. all-purpose flour
½ t. salt
⅛ t. pepper
½ c. milk
½ c. tomato, chopped
4 T. shredded cheddar cheese, divided

In a large saucepan, cook peppers in boiling water for 3 minutes. Drain and rinse with cold water and set aside. In a skillet, cook the turkey, onion, and garlic over medium heat until meat is no longer pink, drain, and set aside. In the same skillet, melt butter. Stir in flour, salt, and pepper until smooth. Gradually add milk. Bring to a boil, cook and stir for 1–2 minutes or until thickened. Return turkey mixture to skillet. Stir in tomato and 2 tablespoons of cheese. Heat through. Spoon into peppers, sprinkle with the remaining cheese. Place in greased 1 quart baking dish. Cover and bake at 350° for 25–30 minutes or until peppers are tender and filling is hot.

Serves 2   Martha Coblentz (Bakery)

 Never let yesterdays use up today.

PARTY HAM CASSEROLE

10-oz. can mushroom soup
½ c. milk, scant
3 t. prepared mustard
1½ c. sour cram
3 c. cubed ham, fully cooked
6 oz. noodles, cooked
1–2 t. minced onion

Topping:
1 c. bread crumbs
2½ T. margarine
2 T. Parmesan cheese

Mix together soup, milk, mustard, and sour cream. Then mix with noodles, ham, and onion. Place in baking dish and bake at 325° for 25 minutes or until hot and bubbly. Brown bread crumbs in the margarine and then add Parmesan cheese. Top casserole with crumbs 10–15 minutes before taking it from the oven.

Serves 6–8   Ellen Mishler (Administration)

Be kindly affectionate to one another with botherly love, in honor giving preference to one another; not lagging in diligence, fervent in spirit, serving the Lord; rejoicing in hope, patient in tribulation, continuing steadfastly in prayer; distributing to the needs of the saints, given to hospitality.
Rom. 12:10–13

HAM SWISS CHEESE BAKE

2 c. ham, cubed
4 c. green beans, cooked
½ lb. grated Swiss cheese
Corn Flakes® cereal

Sauce:
¼ t. salt
1 t. grated onion
¼ c. margarine
¼ c. flour
1½ t. sugar
2 c. sour cream

In a 3-quart baking dish layer ham, green beans, cheese, and sauce. Sprinkle with crushed Corn Flakes® on top. Bake at 350° for 25–30 minutes.

Millie Whetstone (Bakery)

CHINESE PEPPER STEAK

1 lb. round steak, 1" thick	1 c. canned bean sprouts
¼ c. shortening	1 c. canned tomatoes
1 clove garlic, minced	2 green peppers, cut up in
½ t. salt	1" pieces
¼ t. pepper	½ T. cornstarch
4 T. soy sauce	4 green onions, sliced
½ t. sugar	2 T. cold water

Slice steak thinly in short crosswise pieces. Heat shortening, garlic, salt, and pepper in a skillet and cook until beef is brown on both sides. Add soy sauce and sugar and cook over high heat for 5 minutes. Add bean sprouts, tomatoes, and green peppers. Cover and soak 5 minutes. Then stir in cornstarch dissolved in cold water and cook until sauce is thickened. Sprinkle with green onions. Serve over cooked rice.

Serves 4   Sylvia Smith (Bakery Sales)

LAMB STEAKS WITH PEACHES

6 lamb shoulder steaks	1 c. water
2 T. vegetable oil	3 T. brown sugar, packed
1 onion, minced	1 t. salt
3 c. tomato sauce	1 T. Worcestershire sauce
1 c. vinegar	6 fresh peaches, peeled and sliced

In a large skillet brown steaks in oil on both sides, remove. Add onion and cook until soft. Add tomato sauce, vinegar, water, brown sugar, Worcestershire sauce, and salt. Stir to blend. Return steaks to skillet, spoon some sauce over meat. Cover and simmer for 1 hour, turning meat occasionally until tender. Add peaches and simmer for 5 minutes more. Serve at once with cooked rice.

Serves 6   Joyce Miller (Sunshine Farm Manager)

 Blessings are those things we are willing to count, anxious to multiply, and reluctant to divide.

Whoever has this world's goods, and sees his brother in need, and shuts up his heart against him, how does the love of God abide in him?

1 John 3:17

PORCUPINE MEAT BALLS

1½ lb. ground beef
½ c. rice, uncooked
1 t. salt
½ t. pepper

1 T. onion, minced
1 small can tomato soup or juice
1 c. water

Wash rice thoroughly. Combine meat, rice, salt, pepper, and onion. Heat tomato soup or juice and water in pressure cooker. Drop meatballs in soup mixture and close cover securely. Place pressure regulator on vent pipe and cook 10 minutes with pressure regulator rocking slowly. Let pressure drop of its own accord.

Wilma Miller (Kitchen)

HUNGARIAN MEATBALLS

1 lb. hamburger
1 clove garlic, minced
1 t. parsley flakes
1 t. salt
½ t. pepper
2 t. Parmesan cheese
¼ c. milk
½ c. bread crumbs

Sauce:
1 c. milk
1 can cream of mushroom soup
1 c. sour cream

Mix all ingredients together and form into small meatballs. Place on greased baking pan and bake at 350° for 20 minutes or until done. Or if desired, brown in ¼ c. hot oil and drain well. Combine sauce ingredients and pour over meatballs. Can be put into Crock-Pot® or baking dish and in oven until heated through, approximated 30 minutes. Works well over cooked rice or noodles. If desired for appetizer, double everything except milk, soup, and sour cream.

Serves 4–6

Carol Detweiler (Management)

LINDA'S MEATBALLS

3 lbs. ground beef
1 can evaporated milk
1 c. oatmeal
1 c. cracker crumbs
2 c. onion, chopped
2 t. minced garlic
2 t. salt
2 t. pepper
2 t. chili powder

Sauce:
4 c. ketchup
2 c. brown sugar
5 t. liquid smoke
4 t. garlic powder
22 c. onion, chopped

Mix meat mixture together and form into balls. Cover with sauce. Bake at 350° for 30 minutes. These can be made ahead and placed on cookie sheet and put in freezer. After frozen place in Ziploc® bags until ready to use. May be put in oven frozen, but allow extra baking time.

Makes 60 Meatballs   Pam Frey (Bakery)

HOT SPICY DOGS

3 lbs. wieners, cut into thirds
1 qt. water
¼ c. mixed pickling spices

3 c. vinegar
¼ c. sugar
3–4 drops Tabasco® sauce

Bring all ingredients to a boil except the wieners. When boiling, add wieners and bring to a boil again. Put into container, cool, cover, and refrigerate, stirring occasionally. Let set over night. Will keep at least 2 weeks in refrigerator. Good! Flavor improves with age.

Leon Nafziger (Grounds Maintenance)

ESSENHAUS® BARBECUED RIBS

3–4 lbs. pork ribs
1 t. salt

water
Essenhaus® barbecue sauce

Layer the ribs in a pan. Sprinkle salt over them and add just enough water to cover the ribs. Cover with foil and bake for 2 hours at 350°. Drain off water and cover ribs with Essenhaus® barbecue sauce. Put back in oven uncovered and let bake for another 30 minutes at 300°.

ESSENHAUS® BARBECUE SAUCE

4¼ c. catsup
1 T. salt
½ t. pepper
¼ c. Kraft® barbecue sauce
¼ c. water
1 T. onion salt
2⅓ c. brown sugar
1 t. mustard

Mix all ingredients together in a large bowl. Mix thoroughly. Can be used with ribs or any other meat, for grilling or other meat-baking recipes.

HAMBURGER BARBECUE

1 lb. hamburger
¾ c. onion, chopped
1½ c. celery, chopped
1 c. ketchup
2 t. vinegar
1 T. mustard
1 t. salt
1 T. brown sugar

Brown meat, onion, and celery, add all other ingredients and simmer for 30 minutes. Spoon into hamburger buns and enjoy.

Sharon Frye (Waitress)

CHICKEN NOODLE CASSEROLE

7 c. water
2 c. chicken broth
1 T. Essenhaus® chicken base
¾ t. parsley flakes
¾ t. yellow food coloring, optional
12-oz. bag Essenhaus® noodles
2¼ c. diced chicken cooked
1 can cream of mushroom soup
1 can cream of chicken soup
5 oz. American cheese

In a large saucepan, bring water, chicken broth, chicken base, parsley flakes, and food coloring to a boil. Add noodles and bring to a boil again. Then turn heat down and simmer for 15 minutes. Do not drain off the broth. When noodles are tender, add the rest of the ingredients and mix thoroughly. Simmer for 20 minutes or you can cover with foil and bake it in the oven for 30 minutes.

CHICKEN CASSEROLE

8 slices of bread, cubed
2–3 c. chicken, cooked and cut up
¼ c. onions, chopped
½ c. green pepper, chopped
½ c. margarine, melted
¾ t. salt

dash of pepper
2 eggs, slightly beaten
1½ c. milk
1 can cream of mushroom soup
½ c. cheese, grated

Combine half of the bread with chicken, vegetables, margarine, and seasonings. Mix together eggs and milk and pour over chicken mixture. Cover and chill. Top with the rest of bread, mushroom soup and cheese and bake at 350° for one hour.

Serves 4–6   Carol Detweiler (Management)

CHICKENETT FOR A BUNCH

5 1-lb. boxes of spaghetti
9–10 c. chicken, cooked and
    deboned
12 small cans cream of
    mushroom soup

6 c. chicken broth
1½ t. celery salt
1½ t. pepper
2–3 small onions, chopped
1 box Velveeta® cheese

Mix all ingredients together and cook for 1 hour at 350°.

Serves 50–60   Rosalie Bontrager (Country Inn)

SUPER CHICKEN CASSEROLE

2 c. chicken, cooked
2 c. macaroni, uncooked
2 c. milk
2 cans cream of mushroom soup
3 T. butter, melted

1 c. cheese, grated
½ c. onion, chopped
½ t. salt
½ t. pepper

Combine all ingredients and bake for 1½ hours at 350°.

Serves 8–10   Mary Stalter (Waitress)

BASIL CHICKEN AND DUMPLING CASSEROLE

½ c. onion, diced
½ c. celery, diced
2 garlic cloves, crushed
¼ c. margarine
½ c. flour
2 t. sugar
1 t. basil, dried
½ t. pepper
4 c. chicken broth, canned
4 c. chicken, cooked and chopped
5 oz. peas and carrots, frozen, optional

Dumpling Dough:
2 c. flour
1 t. salt
4 t. baking powder
2 T. butter, melted
2 t. basil, dried
milk

Sauté onion, celery, and garlic in margarine until just tender. Add flour, sugar, basil, and pepper. Mix well. Slowly pour in broth, stirring constantly until well blended. Cook until thickened, stirring occasionally. Add peas and carrots and cook five minutes more. Stir in chicken. Pour into a greased 9"x13" baking dish.

To make dumpling dough, sift together flour, salt, and baking powder. Add melted butter and enough milk to make dough that will drop from a spoon. Drop dumpling dough by spoonfuls on top of chicken mixture. Bake uncovered at 350° for 30 minutes. Cover and bake 10 minutes more or until dumplings are done.

Serves 6–8   Donna Matthews (Village Shops)

FAMILY FAVORITE CHICKEN CASSEROLE

2 pkgs. frozen asparagus or
    broccoli (or 3 c. fresh)
3 c. cooked chicken, diced
1 can cream of chicken soup

½ t. curry powder
½ c. mayonnaise
1 t. lemon juice
1 c. shredded cheese

Cook vegetables and put in buttered casserole. Next add chicken and remaining ingredients mixed as sauce. Top with cheese and garnish with some broccoli floretes. Bake at 375° for 30 minutes. This is very delicious served over baked potatoes.

Serves 8   Joyce Miller (Sunshine Farm Manager)

CHICKEN SUPREME

2 c. chicken, cooked
2 c. macaroni, uncooked
1 can cream of chicken soup
1 c. salad dressing
2 c. chicken broth
1 c. cheese, grated

2 c. mixed vegetables, optional
½ c. onion, chopped
½ t. salt
¼ t. pepper
bread crumbs

Combine all ingredients and put in greased casserole. Refrigerate overnight or a couple of hours before baking. Put buttered bread crumbs on top. Bake at 350° for 45–60 minutes. (Could also be done in a Crock-Pot®.)

Dorothy Miller (Waitress)

CRESCENT CHICKEN

2 9¼-oz. cans Swanson® chicken
1 c. cheddar cheese, grated
2 8-oz. pkgs. crescent rolls

¼ c. milk
1 can creamy chicken mushroom
   soup

Mix chicken with cheese. Place 1 tablespoon mixture in each crescent roll and roll up. Place in a greased 9"x13" baking dish. Mix milk and soup and pour over rolls. Sprinkle with remaining chicken mixture. Bake uncovered for 35 minutes at 350°.

Katie Hochstedler (Bakery)

CHICKEN CASSEROLE

½ c. instant rice
8 oz. can cream of chicken soup
¾ c. milk
1–1½ c. diced chicken, cooked
½ c. mayonnaise

1 pkg. dry onion soup mix, divided
2 hard-boiled eggs, diced
1 stalk celery, cut finely
¾ c. almonds, thinly sliced

Cook rice according to directions. Mix all ingredients, using only ¾ of the soup mix. Save some almonds to sprinkle on top with remaining soup mix. Put in casserole dish and bake at 325° for 30–40 minutes. Add salt and pepper to taste.

Serves 4–6

Gwen Linn (Restaurant Gifts)

CHICKEN CURRY

16-oz. can chicken
1 can whole tomatoes
1/3 c. onion, chopped
pinch crushed red pepper

1 t. chili powder
1/2 t. curry
1 can chicken broth
1 c. ketchup

Heat together chicken, tomatoes, onion, red pepper, chili powder, and curry in skillet. Add chicken broth and ketchup and mix well. Bring to a boil, then turn heat down and simmer for 20 minutes. Serve over white rice.

POPPY SEED CHICKEN

4 c. chicken breast, cooked and chopped
1 can cream of chicken soup
1 can cream of celery soup

1 c. sour cream
1 T. poppy seeds
1 sleeve Ritz® crackers
1 stick butter

Preheat oven to 350°. Mix chicken with soup, sour cream, and poppy seeds and then pour into greased 9"x13" baking dish. Melt butter in skillet and sauté crushed crackers until browned. Sprinkle on top of chicken mixture and bake for 30 minutes. Serve over rice or noodles.

Serves 6–8   Carol Detweiler (Management)

POPPY SEED CHICKEN CASSEROLE

7–8 c. chicken, chopped
1 can cream of chicken soup
1 c. sour cream

1/2 c. margarine, melted
2 c. crushed Ritz® crackers
2 T. poppy seeds

Lightly grease a 9"x13" pan. Place chicken over bottom of pan. Mix together soup and sour cream and pour over chicken layer evenly. Melt margarine in separate bowl. Add crushed crackers and poppy seeds. Mix together and top casserole with cracker mixture. Bake at 350° for 30 minutes. Delicious served over rice.

Serves 6–8   Sara Shetler (Busser)
                                                  Mary Schrock (Bakery)
                                                  Esther Nisley (Bakery)

POPPY SEED CHICKEN FOR A BUNCH

100 lbs. chicken breasts
50 cans cream of chicken soup
26 16-oz. containers sour cream
13 lbs. butter
13 boxes Ritz® crackers
1 c. poppy seeds

Melt butter and mix with cracker crumbs. Mix soup and sour cream. Put some in bottom of pan and then a layer of chicken and put rest of mixture on top. Then put cracker mixture on top and sprinkle with poppy seeds. Bake at 350° for approximately 30–45 minutes.

Serves approximately 250   Mary Schrock (Bakery)

CHICKEN ON SUNDAY

2–3 T. butter
2 c. rice, uncooked
1 chicken or boneless, skinless chicken breasts
1 can cream of celery soup
1 can cream of mushroom soup
1 c. milk
1 envelope Lipton's® dry onion soup mix

Melt butter in casserole dish that has a tight-fitting lid or cover it with foil. Add minute rice and then layer chicken on top of rice. On the stove, bring soups and milk to a boil. Pour over chicken. Sprinkle onion soup mix over all. Cover and bake 2 hours at 300°.

Serves 6   Mary Miller (Waitress)

Father and son went fishing all day and caught no fish. Father wrote in his journal, "Spent all day fishing—caught nothing—whole day wasted."

Later he noticed his son's diary said, "Spent all day fishing with Dad—greatest day of my life."

ORIENTAL CHICKEN WITH WALNUTS

1½ lb. whole chicken breasts, skinned, split, boned
3 T. soy sauce
2 t. cornstarch
1 t. gingerroot
1 t. sugar
½ t. salt
½ t. crushed red pepper
2 T. cooking oil
2 medium green peppers, cut into ¾" pieces
4 green onions, sliced into 1" lengths
1 c. walnut halves

Cut chicken into 1" pieces. Set aside. In small bowl, blend soy sauce into cornstarch. Stir in gingerroot, sugar, salt, and red pepper. Set aside. Preheat wok or skillet on high heat and then add oil. Stir fry peppers and onions 2 minutes and then remove from wok. Add walnuts to wok and cook 1–2 minutes or until just golden. Remove from wok, add more oil if necessary, add half of the chicken to wok and cook for 2 minutes and remove. Stir fry remaining chicken for 2 minutes. Return all chicken to wok. Stir soy mixture, stir into chicken. Cook and stir until thick and bubbly. Stir in vegetables. Cover and cook one minute longer. Serve at once, with rice.

Serves 4–6   Sharman Reimer (Daughter of Bob & Sue)

There is no want to those who fear Him.
The young lions lack and suffer hunger;
But those who seek the Lord shall not lack any good thing.
                                                    Ps. 34:9–10

SWISS CHICKEN

26-oz. can cream of chicken soup
6 boneless and skinless chicken breast
½ t. garlic salt
½ t. seasoning salt
bread crumbs
6 slices Swiss cheese

Cover bottom of cookie sheet with a thin layer of the cream of chicken soup. Layer the chicken breast singly out on top and then top with the seasoning. Cover with bread crumbs and bake for one hour at 350°. Take out and cover with cheese slices and put back into oven until cheese is melted.

Serves 6   Mary K. Schmucker (Kitchen)

15-MINUTE CHICKEN AND RICE DINNER

1 T. vegetable oil
4 boneless chicken breast halves
   or 1 can boneless chicken
1 can cream of chicken soup
1½ c. water
¼ t. paprika and pepper
1½ c. rice, uncooked
2 c. fresh or frozen broccoli

Heat oil in skillet. Add chicken and cook until browned. Remove chicken unless you use the can of boneless chicken. Add soup, water, paprika, and pepper. Heat to a boil and then stir in rice and broccoli. Top with chicken. Cover and cook over low heat 5 minutes or until done.

Rachel Yoder (Waitress)

BACON WRAPPED CHICKEN

6 boneless chicken breast halves
8-oz. container sour cream
1 pkg. onion soup mix
2 T. butter, cubed
6 bacon strips

Mix sour cream and onion soup mix together. If chicken breasts are large you may want to cut in half width-wise, this allows them to roll better. Spoon several spoonfuls of sour cream mixture onto chicken, dot with butter, and then wrap with bacon. Place seam side down in a greased 9"x13" pan and bake uncovered for 35–40 minutes or until juice runs clear at 400°. Broil for a few minutes if you desire the bacon to be crisp.

Serves 6   Anita Yoder (Daughter of Bob & Sue)

ZESTY ITALIAN CHICKEN BREASTS

16 oz. zesty Italian dressing
6 skinless, boneless chicken breast halves

Marinate chicken breast 24 hours or longer. Grill breast until the juices run clear, approximately 15–20 minutes, turning once.

Serves 6   Norine Yoder (Village Shops)

ITALIAN CHICKEN BREASTS

10 chicken breasts,
    skinless and boneless
¼ c. Morton's Tender Quick®

2½ c. water
2 c. creamy Italian dressing
2 T. Worcestershire sauce

Soak chicken breasts in a mixture of the Tender Quick® and water for 3 hours, then drain. Marinate with Italian dressing and Worcestershire sauce for one day. Grill until almost done and steam in covered roaster for 1 hour.

Luella Yoder (Kitchen)

CHICKEN PARMESAN

1 c. Miracle Whip®
½ c. Parmesan cheese
2 t. oregano

2–3 lbs. boneless, skinless chicken breasts

Mix together Miracle Whip®, parmesan cheese, and oregano. Grease 9"x13" dish and then place chicken in dish. Spoon mixture over chicken and bake 45 minutes at 375°.

Serves 5–6

Michele Shetler (Sunshine Farm)

CHICKEN MARSALA

4 boneless chicken breasts, split

10 chicken thighs

Marinating Ingredients:
1 head garlic, chopped
¼ c. oregano
½ c. red wine vinegar
½ c. olive oil
1 c. pitted prunes
½ c. pitted green olives
½ c. capers with some of the juices

Final Ingredients:
1 c. brown sugar
1 c. cooking sherry
¼ c. Italian parsley or cilantro, chopped as garnish

Preheat oven to 350°. Mix marinating ingredients in 9"x13" baking pan and then add chicken. Marinate, covered in refrigerator, several hours or overnight. When ready to bake, sprinkle with brown sugar and pour cooking sherry over top. Bake for 1 hour at 350°. Garnish and serve with rice.

Anne Yoder (Administration)

BARBECUED CHICKEN

1 chicken, cut up
flour to coat chicken
⅓ c. sugar
¼ t. pepper
½ t. chili powder

1 t. salt
4 T. flour
4 T. vinegar
4 T. ketchup
6 T. hot water

Dip chicken in flour and pan fry until brown on both sides. Place in a baking dish. Combine sugar, pepper, chili powder, salt, and 4 tablespoons of flour. Add remaining ingredients and pour over chicken. Bake at 300° for 1½ hours. Sauce makes delicious gravy on mashed potatoes.

Leon Nafziger (Grounds Maintenance)

SEASONED-SALT CHICKEN

2 c. flour
1 T. pepper
1½–2 lb. chicken, pre-cut

vegetable oil for frying
¼ c. seasoned salt

Preheat oven to 350°. Place flour and pepper in bowl and mix well. Rinse chicken in water. Heat ½″ of oil in large frying pan. Coat chicken in flour mixture and then place chicken in oil. Sprinkle with seasoned salt. Turn chicken when lightly browned. Sprinkle with more seasoned salt. Repeat until all chicken has been browned, adding oil as necessary. Place browned chicken in large baking pan in a single layer and add ½″ of water to the bottom of the pan. Cover tightly with aluminum foil. Bake at 350° for one hour.

Serves 4　　　　　　　　　　　　　　　　　Tonya Penner (Kitchen)

There is one who scatters,
　yet increases more;
And there is one who withholds
　more than is right,
But it leads to poverty.
The generous soul will be made rich,
and he who waters will also be
　watered himself.

Prov. 11:24–25

BAKED BARBECUED CHICKEN

3½ lbs. chicken
½ t. salt
¼ t. black pepper
olive oil

BBQ Sauce:
1 c. catsup
½ c. water
1 onion, chopped
¼ c. A-1® steak sauce
½ c. Worcestershire sauce
¼ c. cider vinegar
1 garlic clove, finely chopped

Put salt and pepper on chicken and refrigerate overnight. Brown in skillet with olive oil. Then put in a roaster or large casserole dish. Combine all ingredients to make BBQ sauce. Pour over chicken, cover, and bake at 325° for 1½ hours or until tender.

Katie Miller (Bakery)

 ## FRAN'S QUICK AND EASY CHICKEN BREASTS

4 chicken breasts with skin and with bone

Lawry's® seasoned salt
Miracle Whip® salad dressing

Rinse thawed chicken breasts. With pastry brush or by hand spread Miracle Whip® over entire chicken breast. Shake seasoned salt over chicken to desired taste. Bake approximately 45 minutes or until done at 350°.

Serves 4

Tammy Zeiger (Grill)

 ## CHICKEN & VEGETABLES

1 c. celery
1½ c. onion
2¾ c. chicken, cooked & diced
¼ c. soy sauce
1 t. salt

pinch pepper
¼ c. margarine
½ c. milk
1 can mushroom

Coarsely chop celery and onions and sauté in skillet until tender. Add chicken. Add rest of ingredients and simmer for 30 minutes. Great served over rice.

QUICHE CHICKEN AND ALMONDS

pie dough for 10" pie
6 eggs
3 c. half and half
1 t. salt
¼ t. sugar
½ t. cayenne pepper

6 oz. sharp cheddar cheese,
    shredded
6 oz. chicken, cooked & diced
⅓ c. green onion
6 T. almonds, sliced

Place pie dough in fluted pie tin and press into place. To make custard, mix eggs, half and half, salt, sugar, and pepper together. Place cheese, chicken, onions, and almonds into pie shell. Pour custard mixture over top. Bake at 350° for about 45 minutes.

Serves 6   Barbara Skarbek (Cashier/Hostess)

BEEF MACARONI AND CHEESE

2 cans beef broth
bouillon
4 c. water

2 c. macaroni, uncooked
2 c. Velveeta® cheese chunks
1 can cream of mushroom soup

Bring beef broth, bouillon, and water to a boil. Add macaroni and simmer until done. Stir in cheese and soup. Salt and pepper to taste.

Sue Miller (Owner)

BETH'S MEATZZIA PIE

1 lb. ground beef
½ t. garlic salt
½ c. bread crumbs
⅔ c. evaporated milk
⅓ c. ketchup

1 can mushrooms, drained
4 slices cheese
¼ t. oregano
2 T. grated cheese

Mix first four ingredients together, then arrange in 8" pie pan. Spread the ketchup over the mixture and then dot with mushrooms. Arrange the cheese slices on top and sprinkle with oregano and grated cheese. Bake at 400° for 20 minutes.

Geniese Trotter (Bakery Sales)

He who tills his land will be satisfied with bread.
But he who follows frivolity is devoid of understanding....
The recompense of a man's hands will be rendered to him.

Prov. 12:11, 14

HAMBURGER NOODLE CASSEROLE

3 c. water
¾ t. salt
½ bag Essenhaus® noodles
1 t. margarine
1 lb. hamburger
¾ t. salt

¼ t. pepper
1 T. minced onions
1 c. milk
5 oz. American cheese
1 can mushroom soup

Bring water and salt to a boil. Add noodles and margarine. Simmer for about 15 minutes. Don't need to drain noodles. In meantime fry hamburger, salt, pepper, and onions in a skillet. Drain off the grease. Add milk, cheese, and mushroom soup, mix well. Then add meat mixture with noodles and simmer for 10 minutes.

TUNA MACARONI CASSEROLE

2 qt. boiling water
2 c. macaroni
2 T. salt
4 T. butter or margarine
¼ c. milk

¾ c. shredded cheese
6.5-oz. can of tuna
1 c. frozen peas
2 T. onion, chopped
2 T. peppers, diced

Put macaroni and salt in boiling water. Cook for 8 minutes and drain. Add butter, milk, and ½ cup of cheese. Stir. Add tuna, peas, onion, and peppers and stir. Pour into greased baking dish. Top with remaining cheese. Bake at 350° for half an hour.

Serves 6–8   Esther Wenger (Corporate Office)

GRANDMA'S CASSEROLE

3 c. potatoes, peeled and
   sliced thick
onion to taste
2 c. carrots, sliced and parboiled
1 lb. lean hamburger, uncooked

1½ c. frozen or fresh peas
salt and pepper to taste
1 can mushroom soup or cheddar
   cheese soup
½ soup can of milk

Layer potatoes, onion, carrots, and hamburger twice. Top with peas and season with salt and pepper. Mix soup and milk and pour over casserole. Cover and bake at 350° for 1 hour. (Note: When I use mushroom soup I top the casserole with slices of cheese. You may also use ground turkey, chicken, or sausage instead of hamburger.)

Serves 12–14   Mary K. Schmucker (Kitchen)

Blessed are the meek,
   For they shall inherit the earth.
Blessed are those who hunger and thirst
after righteousness,
   For they shall be filled. . . .
Blessed are the peacemakers
   For they shall be called sons of God.
Blessed are those who are persecuted
for righteousness' sake,
   For theirs is the kingdom of heaven.
                              Matt. 5:5–6, 9–10

OVERNIGHT CASSEROLE

1 lb. hamburger or chopped
   chicken
½ lb. Velveeta® cheese, cubed
2 c. macaroni, dry
3 c. milk

1 c. cream of mushroom soup
   if using hamburger or
1 c. cream of chicken soup
   if using chicken

Fry or bake the meat. Then mix all ingredients together and let set 8 hours or overnight. Stir and bake for one hour at 350°, stirring halfway.

Serves 8   Judith Kauffman (Kitchen)

CHEESY BEEF SPIRALS

2 c. spiral pasta, uncooked
2 lbs. ground beef
2 small onions, chopped
1 garlic clove, minced
26-oz. jar spaghetti sauce
4.5-oz. jar sliced mushrooms, drained
½ c. sour cream
½ lb. processed American cheese, cubed
2 c. mozzarella cheese, shredded

Cook pasta according to package directions. Meanwhile in a large saucepan, cook the beef, onions, and garlic over medium heat until meat is no longer pink, drain. Stir in spaghetti and mushrooms, then bring to a boil. Reduce heat, cover, and simmer for 20 minutes. Place half a cup of meat sauce in a greased shallow 22-quart baking dish. Drain pasta and place half of the pasta over meat sauce. Top with remaining meat sauce and spread with sour cream. Top with American cheese and remaining pasta and meat sauce. Sprinkle with mozzarella cheese. Cover and bake at 350° for 25–30 minutes. Uncover and bake for 5–10 minutes longer or until bubbly.

Serves 8–10   Laura Lehman (Busser)

NIGHT BEFORE CASSEROLE

1¾ c. elbow macaroni, uncooked
2 c. cooked & diced chicken, turkey, ham, or tuna
2 cans mushroom soup
½ lb. soft yellow cheese, cut up
3 hard-boiled eggs
2 c. milk

Mix all ingredients together and let stand overnight. Bake at 350° for one hour and 15 minutes.

Serves 10   Vernon Roth (Van Driver)

Junk is something you keep a long time, then toss away a week before you need it.

DAD'S CASSEROLE

1 lb. hamburger
1 T. onion, diced
1 c. cottage cheese
2 c. noodles, uncooked
1 can cream of mushroom soup
1 T. salt
1 c. milk
1 egg
1 c. cheddar cheese, grated

Fry hamburger and onion until browned, drain. Mix in cottage cheese and set aside. Cook noodles until half tender. Put noodles and hamburger mixture in layers in casserole, starting and ending with noodles. Mix soup, salt, and milk together. Pour over mixture. Beat eggs and pour over top. Sprinkle cheese on top and bake for one hour at 350°.

Serves 6   Vernon Roth (Van Driver)

The LORD knows the days of the upright,
And their inheritance shall be forever.
They shall not be ashamed
    in the evil time,
And in the days of famine they shall
    be satisfied.
                                    Ps. 37:18–19

 ## HAM & GREEN BEAN CASSEROLE

⅔ c. margarine
½ c. flour
2¾ c. milk
5 oz. cheese
4 c. diced potatoes, cooked
1 can green beans, drained
2¾ c. diced ham

Melt margarine in a saucepan and stir in flour. Stir briskly over low heat until thickened. Microwave milk and cheese until the cheese melts and then add this mixture to the flour mixture. Then add potatoes, green beans, and ham. Simmer for about 20 minutes. Quick, easy, and delicious.

HOMESTEAD CHICKEN AND DRESSING

12 chicken drumsticks
½ t. salt
¼ t. black pepper
3 T. butter
¼ lb. pork sausage

½ c. onion
½ c. celery
½ c. green pepper
1 c. rice, uncooked
12 oz. corn

Sprinkle chicken parts with salt and pepper. In a large skillet, melt butter over medium heat. Brown chicken parts on all sides. Remove from pan, sauté sausage, onion, celery, and green pepper in pan until sausage is done and vegetables are tender. Add rice, corn, and broth to sausage mixture and bring to a boil. Place rice mixture in a greased 9"x13" pan. Arrange chicken on top, cover and bake at 350° for 45 minutes till chicken is tender.

SKILLET SUPPER

1 lb. bulk sausage
1 large onion, chopped
1 medium green pepper, chopped
1 pt. tomatoes
½ c. water or tomato juice

2 c. macaroni, uncooked
1 t. salt
2 t. chili powder
2 c. sour cream

Brown sausage in heavy skillet, pouring off fat as it accumulates. (This is an important step.) Stir in remaining ingredients, except sour cream. Simmer, stirring often to prevent sticking. Cook until macaroni is tender, 20–25 minutes. Blend in sour cream and reheat just to boiling.

Serves 6   Sam Whetstone (Dishwasher)

NOODLES

9 c. chicken broth
1 T. Essenhaus® chicken base
⅓ t. parsley flakes

¾ t. salt
2 drops yellow food coloring
1 bag Essenhaus® noodles

Bring broth, base, parsley flakes, salt, and food coloring to a boil. Add noodles and bring to a boil again. Turn heat down and simmer for 20 minutes.

DRESSING

1 c. rich chicken broth
2½ loaves bread, toasted and cubed
1 stick oleo or margarine
½ c. minced onion
1 c. raw potatoes
1 c. raw carrots, shredded
2½ c. celery, chopped, partially cooked, juice and all
2½ c. cooked chicken
15 eggs, whipped
1 qt. milk
salt, pepper, and chicken soup base to taste
½ lb. margarine

Bring chicken broth to boil and pour over bread. Brown 1 stick of margarine in roaster and then mix other ingredients together, except ½ pound margarine and seasoned salt. Pour dressing mixture into roaster. Brown ½ pound margarine, pour on top of dressing and sprinkle seasoned salt over top. Bake at 350° for 30–45 minutes. Stir, then bake until finished.

Luella Yoder (Kitchen)

DRESSING

2 pkgs. plain croutons
2 c. chicken broth
1½ c. milk
1¼ c. water
¼ c. margarine
3 eggs
½ c. chicken
⅓ c. chopped onions
⅓ c. chopped celery
1 t. parsley flakes
¼ t. celery seed
1 t. seasoned salt
¼ t. pepper
1 t. salt

Put croutons in large bowl. Add chicken broth, milk, water, margarine, and eggs. Mix thoroughly. Then add rest of the ingredients and mix well. Pour into 13"x9"x2" casserole dish. Cover with foil and bake at 350° for 1 hour. Serve with Essenhaus® Yellow Gravy.

Housework is something that nobody notices, until the day you don't do it!

MARY'S CASSEROLE

2 lbs. hamburger
1 medium onion, chopped
1 small can mushrooms
1 c. corn or peas
3 c. noodles, cooked and drained

1 can cream of chicken soup
2 cans cream of mushroom soup
2 c. sour cream
Velveeta® cheese slices

Fry hamburger with onions and drain. Add all other ingredients and place in a greased 9"x13" baking pan. Bake at 325° for 1 hour 30 minutes. May be topped with Velveeta® slices the last 10 minutes of baking.

Serves 6–8   Cletus Miller (Grounds Maintenance)

HUNGARIAN GOULASH

1 lb. hamburger
medium onion, diced
1 lb. noodles

26-oz. can tomato soup
1 lb. Velveeta® cheese

Brown hamburger with onion and drain. In large pan, boil noodles until tender and drain. Add hamburger and onions to noodles. Stir in tomato soup and cheese and heat until cheese is melted, stirring often. Mix well. Add salt and pepper to taste.

Serves 4   Brandie Leonard (Village Shops)

CHOP SUEY RICE CASSEROLE

1 lb. hamburger
1 medium size onion, chopped
½ c. celery, chopped
1 can cream of mushroom soup, undiluted
1 can cream of chicken soup, undiluted

1 can chop suey vegetables, with liquid
1 c. rice, uncooked
1 c. water
1 t. soy sauce to taste
1 T. Worcestershire sauce

Brown hamburger, onion, and celery. Combine all remaining ingredients in 2-quart casserole. Add meat and stir together. Bake covered in 350° oven for 1 hour.

Joyce Miller (Sunshine Farm Manager)

SAUSAGE CASSEROLE

2½ lb. sausage
5 diced onions
5 lbs. potatoes, diced or shredded
½ stalk celery, chopped
2 qts. frozen mixed vegetables
½ stick margarine
1 lb. Velveeta® cheese
2 cans mushroom soup
3 cans celery soup
2¼ c. milk

Brown and crumble sausage; drain. Mix all ingredients and bake at 350°.

Effie Mast (Essenhaus Foods)

TATER TOT® CASSEROLE

1 lb. hamburger
1 small onion, chopped
seasoned salt
garlic powder
½ c. instant rice
1 can cream of chicken soup
½ soup can of water
2 14-oz. cans green beans, drained
⅓ c. sour cream
1½ lb. Tater Tots®

Brown hamburger and onion in skillet, drain. Sprinkle with seasoned salt and garlic powder to taste, mix. In an 8"x11" baking pan combine all ingredients except Tater Tots®. Smooth out in pan. Cover the top of pan with Tater Tots®. Bake at 350° for 45 minutes.

Serves 6–8   Anita Yoder (Daughter of Bob and Sue)

UNDERGROUND HAM CASSEROLE

2 c. ham, cubed
¼ c. onion, chopped
2 T. margarine
½ T. Worcestershire sauce
1 can cream of mushroom soup
1 c. Velveeta®
½ c. milk
8 oz. sour cream
3–4 c. mashed potatoes
bacon bits

Cook first four ingredients together until onions are soft. Put in a 9"x13" baking dish. Melt together cream of mushroom soup, cheese, and milk. Pour over ham mixture. Mash the potatoes and add sour cream (do not add milk or salt to potatoes). Spread on top of other mixture. Sprinkle bacon on top and bake at 350° for 20–30 minutes.

Jody Yoder (Waitress)

BEEF WITH CAULIFLOWER AND SNOW PEAS

½ lb. boneless sirloin or top round steak
2 T. cornstarch, divided
3 T. soy sauce, divided
½ t. sugar
1 clove garlic
¼ t. red pepper
1 c. water
½ lb. fresh snow peas
3 T. olive oil, divided
1 small head cauliflower, separated
2 tomatoes, chunked
cooked rice

Cut beef across grain into thin slices. Combine 1 tablespoon each of cornstarch and soy sauce with sugar and garlic. Stir in beef and let stand 15 minutes. Meanwhile, combine remaining cornstarch and soy sauce with red pepper and half a cup of water, set aside. Remove tips and strings from snow peas. Heat 1 tablespoon of olive oil in wok or large skillet over high heat. Add beef and stir fry one minute. Remove. Heat 1 tablespoon of oil in same wok, add snow peas and stir fry for 2 minutes. If using frozen snow peas, add at the end. Remove. Heat remaining oil in same wok and add cauliflower and stir fry for 2 minutes. Add half a cup of water, cover and cook for 3 minutes. Stir in beef, snow peas, tomatoes, and soy sauce mixture. Cook and stir until sauce boils and thickens. Serve immediately with rice.

Serves 4   Anne Yoder (Administration)

Good character, like good soup, is usually homemade.

AMERICAN CHOP SUEY

2 lb. ground beef
1 c. onion, chopped
salt and pepper to taste
1 c. celery, chopped
1 can cream of mushroom soup
½ c. rice, uncooked
2 T. soy sauce
2 T. Worcestershire sauce
2 c. water
1 c. chow mein noodles

Brown in skillet: ground beef, onion, and salt and pepper. Add to this the rest of the ingredients except chow mein noodles. Mix well and place in baking dish. Top with chow mein noodles. Bake at 325° for 2 hours.

Serves 8–10   Esther Wenger (Corporate Office)

CHILIES RELLENNO

2 4-oz. mild green chilies, chopped
1 lb. Monterey Jack or Munster cheese, grated
1 lb. cheddar cheese, grated
4 eggs
⅔ c. evaporated milk
1 T. flour
½ t. salt
⅛ t. pepper

Stir chilies and cheese together and put in 12"x8" baking dish. Beat egg whites until stiff. Then combine egg yolks, milk, flour, salt, and pepper. Add to the egg whites and stir well. Pour over cheese and bake at 325°–350° for 30 minutes. You can slice tomatoes and put on the top and bake another 30 minutes if you desire.

Serves 10–12   Esther Thomas (Country Inn)

BEEF CRESCENT CASSEROLE

1½ lb. hamburger
½ c. onion, chopped
8-oz. pkg. cream cheese, may substitute sour cream
1 can cream of mushroom soup
¼ c. milk
¼ c. ketchup
1 tube crescent rolls

Brown hamburger with onion and drain. Add cream cheese, soup, milk, and ketchup and mix well. Pour into casserole and bake 10 minutes at 375°. Remove from oven and place unrolled crescent rolls on top. Return to oven and bake 15 minutes or until lightly browned.

Anita Yoder (Daughter of Bob & Sue)

MARY B. SPECIAL

2 slices of bread
1 T. butter, softened
2 slices of American cheese
2 T. sour cream
2 T. onion, chopped
1 hard-boiled egg, sliced
4 slices bacon, fried
seasoning salt

Butter one side of the bread slices. With the buttered sides down in the skillet, top each slice with cheese, sour cream onions, fried bacon, egg, and sprinkle with seasoning salt. Fry slowly until the bread is golden brown. Carefully fold the slices together to make a sandwich and then cut into four sections.

Mary A. Bontrager (Waitress)

FETTUCCINE ALFREDO

8 oz. fettuccine
2 T. flour
¾ c. milk
8 oz. cream cheese
¾ t. Italian seasoning

¼ t. garlic powder
⅛ t. pepper
½ t. salt
½ c. Parmesan cheese, grated

Cook pasta until done. In a medium saucepan, stir flour and milk until smooth. Add cream cheese and seasonings and bring to a boil. Cook and stir 1–2 minutes and then add Parmesan cheese. Toss pasta with cheese sauce. May top with grilled chicken breast cut in strips.

Serves 6   Mary Stalter (Waitress)

ITALIAN HERITAGE CASSEROLE

6 potatoes, peeled and cubed
1 red pepper, cut in strips
1 green pepper, cut in strips
1 t. oregano
1 t. paprika
½ t. salt

½ t. garlic powder
½ t. black pepper
chicken breast, cut in chunks
1 lb. Eckrich® smoked sausage,
   cut in 1–2" chunks

Spray 9"x13" pan and arrange veggies. Sprinkle ⅓ of the seasonings over veggies. Add meat and sprinkle with the rest of seasonings. Cover with foil and bake at 425° for 30 minutes, then 375° for 30–40 minutes.

Serves 6   Mary Stalter (Waitress)

QUICHE LORRAINE

1 Essenhaus® pie shell, unbaked
12 bacon strips
4 eggs
2 c. whipping cream

¾ t. salt
⅛ t. ground nutmeg
1 c. Swiss cheese, shredded

Heat oven to 425°. Fry bacon and drain. Crumble bacon and then spread in bottom of pie shell. With wire whisk beat eggs, cream, salt, and nutmeg. Stir in cheese. Pour egg mixture into crust. Bake for 15 minutes at 425°, then 35 minutes at 325°. Let set 10 minutes before serving.

Serves 6   Carol Detweiler (Management)

BAKED PINEAPPLE CASSEROLE

½ c. margarine
¾ c. sugar
4 eggs
pinch ground cinnamon

pinch nutmeg
5 slices bread, torn
20 oz. crushed pineapple,
   with juice

Preheat oven to 350°. Grease casserole dish. In mixing bowl cream margarine with sugar and then beat eggs, stirring in cinnamon and nutmeg. Stir bread and pineapple into the mixture. Pour into baking dish. Bake 60 minutes until bubbly and lightly browned.

Sue Meeks (Kitchen)

SCALLOPED PINEAPPLE

3 eggs
1 c. sugar
5 slices bread, cubed
½ t. salt

20-oz. can pineapple tidbits,
   undrained
½ c. butter, melted

Beat eggs and sugar together. Add other ingredients and mix together. Pour into a greased 8"x8" pan and bake at 350° for 30 minutes. This is a good side dish to serve with ham or other pork.

Serves 6   Dennis Risser (Country Inn)

SUMMER SKILLET

1 T. cooking oil
1 small onion
1–2 zucchini sliced ⅛" thick
1 clove garlic, crushed or
   ⅛ t. garlic powder

2 tomatoes, chopped
1 lb. ground beef
4 oz. cheese, shredded
salt and pepper to taste

Brown onion, zucchini, garlic, and tomato in oil, then add salt and pepper to taste. Stir lightly. Remove to dish. In the same skillet, brown the beef and season it with salt and pepper to taste. Pour off fat. Add first mixture to ground beef. Stir to mix. Sprinkle cheese on top and warm enough for cheese to melt.

Serves 4   Mary Miller (Waitress)

SAFFRON SEAFOOD AND RICE PAELLA

1 t. (10–12 threads) saffron,
    crushed
1 T. olive oil
1 lb. mixed seafood, shrimp,
    scallops, or firm white fish
1 c. onion, diced
1 c. red bell peppers, diced

1 t. garlic, minced
2 c. short grain rice
1¾ c. tomato, chopped
2 13¾-oz. cans chicken broth
6 oz. chorizo sausage, sliced
½ t. red pepper, ground

Fill half a cup with warm water and add saffron. Set aside for 10 minutes to get color and flavor. In large saucepan, heat oil over medium high heat. Add seafood and stir gently approx. 5 min. until opaque. Remove to a bowl. To saucepan, add onion, bell pepper, and garlic. Cook 2 min. until barely tender. Add rice and saffron, then cook 2 min. longer. Add tomato, chicken broth, sausage, and ground pepper. Bring to a boil. Reduce heat and cook uncovered approx. 15 min. until rice has absorbed liquid and is tender. Stir in seafood, reheat. Serve immediately.

Serves 6   Sylvia Smith (Bakery Sales)

HUSH PUPPIES

1 c. corn meal
½ c. flour
1 t. baking powder
1 egg

pinch of salt, to taste
pinch of baking soda
diced onions, if desired
1 c. milk or water

Blend all this together with milk or water and drop by spoonfuls into deep hot fat and fry. The onion in the batter gives a good flavor.

Sylvia Smith (Bakery Sales)

HUSH PUPPIES

2 c. cornmeal
1 T. flour
½ t. baking soda
1 t. salt

1 egg, beaten
3 T. onions, chopped
1 c. buttermilk

Mix dry ingredients. Then add egg, onions, and buttermilk. Mix thoroughly. Drop by teaspoonful into hot fat, around 300°.

Makes 3–4 Dozen   Sue Miller (Owner)

HEARTY ITALIAN SANDWICHES

1½ lbs. lean ground beef	1 t. pepper
1½ lbs. bulk Italian sausage	¼ t. crushed red pepper flakes
2 large onions, sliced	8 sandwich rolls, split
2 large green peppers, sliced	shredded Monterey Jack cheese,
2 large sweet red peppers, sliced	optional
1 t. salt	

In a skillet, brown beef and sausage and drain. Place a third of the onions and peppers in a Crock-Pot®, top with half of the meat mixture. Repeat layers of vegetables and meat. Then top with remaining vegetables. Sprinkle with salt, pepper, and pepper flakes. Cover and cook on low for 6 hours or until vegetables are tender. With a slotted spoon serve about one cup of meat and vegetables on each roll. Top with cheese if desired.

Sharman Reimer (Daughter of Bob & Sue)

Children disgrace us in public by behaving just as we do at home.

STROMBOLI SANDWICHES

1 lb. ground beef	½ t. fennel seeds
1 small onion, chopped	½ t. oregano
½ c. tomato sauce	4 slices mozzarella cheese
½ c. ketchup	4 kaiser rolls
2 T. Parmesan cheese	2 T. butter, soft
½ t. garlic powder	¼ t. garlic powder

Brown beef and onions, and then add tomato sauce, ketchup, Parmesan cheese, ½ teaspoon garlic powder, fennel seeds, and oregano. Simmer for 20 minutes. Split rolls, and then spread 1 teaspoon garlic powder spread on top half of each roll. To make garlic powder spread, mix butter and ¼ teaspoon garlic powder together. Spread ¼ of meat mixture on bottom half. Put one slice of mozzarella cheese over meat and then cover with top roll. Wrap each sandwich in foil and then bake at 350° for 15 minutes.

Serves 4

Sharon McSorley (Management)

SUPPER POPOVER

1 lb. ground beef
15-oz. can tomato sauce
¼ c. green pepper, chopped
2 T. flour
½ t. salt
½ t. pepper
1 t. parsley

2 c. cheddar cheese, shredded
2 eggs
1 c. milk
1 T. vegetable oil
1 c. flour
½ t. salt
2 T. green onion, chopped

Heat oven to 425°. Cook and stir ground beef in 10" skillet until brown, drain. Stir in tomato sauce, pepper, 2 tablespoons flour, salt, pepper, and parsley. Heat to a boil. Boil and stir for one minute. Pour into ungreased 9"x13" pan. Sprinkle cheese on top. Beat eggs, milk, oil, flour, and salt with hand beater until smooth. Pour over meat mixture and sprinkle with onions. Bake for 25–30 minutes or until puffy and golden brown.

Serves 6–8   Amanda Strebin (Bakery Sales)

SPAGHETTI PIZZA

8 oz. spaghetti
1 egg
¼ c. milk
½ c. mozzarella cheese
½ T. garlic powder
¼ T. salt

15 oz. pizza sauce
1½ c. mozzarella cheese
1 can mushrooms
pepperoni, ground beef, or ham
    as desired

Break spaghetti in half. Cook, drain, and cool. Preheat oven to 400°. In large bowl, beat egg slightly, then stir in milk, half a cup of cheese, garlic powder, and salt. Add spaghetti and mix well. Put mixture in a greased 9"x13" pan and bake 15 minutes. Remove and reduce heat to 350°. Spread sauce and add remaining ingredients. Bake about 30 minutes. Let stand at room temperature for 5 minutes.

Mary Oltz (Village Shops)

 People would learn from their mistakes if they weren't so busy denying them.

"The earth is the LORD's, and all its fullness." . . . Therefore, whether you eat or drink, or whatever you do, do all to the glory of God.

1 Cor. 10:28, 31

CHICKEN SPAGHETTI SUPREME

4 chicken breasts, boneless and skinless
8 oz. spaghetti, uncooked
2 4-oz. cans mushrooms
¼ c. onion, chopped
¼ c. celery, chopped
½ c. margarine or butter
1 can cream of mushroom soup
1 can cream of chicken soup
2 c. sour cream
grated Parmesan cheese
paprika to taste

Preheat oven to 350°. Cook chicken and chop into bite-size pieces. Break spaghetti in half. Cook per package directions and then spread in buttered 9"x13" baking dish. Saute mushrooms, onions, and celery in margarine in skillet. Stir in chicken, soup, and sour cream and then spoon over spaghetti. Top with cheese and paprika. Bake for 40 minutes.

Serves 6   Kathy Miller (Daughter-in-Law of Bob & Sue)

SPAGHETTI PIE

spaghetti noodles
1 egg
1 lb. hamburger, browned
spaghetti sauce
cheese

Cook noodles, drain and add egg. Mix well. Place in greased pie pan. Mix hamburger and sauce. Place on top of noodles. Top with cheese and bake at 325° for 20–30 minutes or until hot.

Serves 6   Angela Miller (Daughter-in-Law of Bob & Sue)

BAKED SPAGHETTI

1 c. onion, chopped
1 c. green pepper, chopped
1 T. butter or margarine
28-oz. can tomatoes with liquid, cut up
4-oz. can mushroom stems and pieces, drained
2¼-oz. can sliced ripe olives, drained
2 t. dried oregano
1 lb. ground beef, browned and drained, optional
12 oz. spaghetti, cooked and drained
2 c. shredded cheddar cheese
10¾-oz. can condensed cream of mushroom soup, undiluted
¼ c. water
¼ c. grated Parmesan cheese

In a large skillet, sauté onion and green pepper in butter until tender. Add tomatoes, mushrooms, olives, and oregano. Add ground beef if desired. Simmer, uncovered for 10 minutes. Place half of the spaghetti in a greased 13"x9"x2" baking dish. Top with half of the vegetable mixture. Sprinkle with 1 cup of cheddar cheese. Repeat layers. Mix the soup and water until smooth and pour over casserole. Sprinkle with Parmesan cheese. Bake uncovered at 350° for 30–35 minutes or until heated through.

Serves 12   Joyce Miller (Sunshine Farm Manager)

SPAGHETTI SAUCE

1 lb. ground beef or turkey
1 t. lard
1 medium onion
15-oz. can tomato sauce
1 can tomato paste
1 can tomato soup
1 small can mushrooms, optional

Brown ground meat and then drain. In large saucepan, melt lard and saute onion, sliced thin vertically, until glazed not brown. Do not drain lard. Add tomato sauce, paste, and soup, using one can of water to rinse cans, then add the water. Add ground beef and mushrooms. Stir and heat.

Tammy Zeiger (Cook)

Spend time with your children. It's the best investment you will ever make.

VIRGINIA'S EASY LASAGNA

1 lb. ground beef
32 oz. jar thick spaghetti sauce
1½ c. water
15-oz. container ricotta or small-
    curd cottage cheese
3 c. shredded mozzarella or
    Monterey Jack cheese
½ c. grated Parmesan cheese
2 eggs
¼ c. chopped parsley
1 t. salt
¼ t. pepper
8 oz. lasagna noodles, uncooked

Brown beef in 3-qt. saucepan and drain off excess fat. Add sauce and water. Simmer for about 10 minutes. Combine remaining ingredients, except noodles, for filling. Pour about 1 cup sauce on bottom of 13"x9"x2" baking pan. Layer 3 pieces of uncooked noodles over sauce. Cover with about 1½ cups sauce. Spread ½ of cheese filling over sauce. Repeat layers of noodles, sauce, and cheese filling. Top with layer of noodles and remaining sauce. Cover with aluminum foil and bake at 350° for 55–60 minutes. Remove foil and bake about 10 minutes longer. Allow to stand about 10 minutes before cutting for easier handling. Lasagna will expand to fill empty spaces.

Serves 8–10   Joyce Miller (Sunshine Farm Manager)

CROCK-POT® PIZZA

12-oz. pkg. bows noodles, wide
1½ lb. ground beef
1 medium onion
12- or 14-oz. jar of pizza sauce
16-oz. jar spaghetti sauce
8-oz. pkg. pepperoni, sliced
4-oz. can mushrooms, optional
1 c. green peppers, optional
8-oz. pkg. cheddar cheese, shred-
    ded
8-oz. pkg. mozzarella cheese,
    shredded

Cook and drain noodles and set aside. Brown beef and onions together, drain. Add sauces, meat, and optional ingredients and simmer well. Season meat sauce with salt and pepper if needed. Mix. Cut up pieces of pepperoni slices and add to sauce. Use a large Crock-Pot® or baking dish. Layer twice, first noodles, then meat sauce, and both cheeses. Turn crockpot on low for 2½–3 hours or set on high for 30–45 minutes, just until cheese is melted. You can add more cheese and meat to your liking if you wish.

Serves 8–10   Sharon Schlabach (Waitress)

 PIZZA BISCUIT BAKE

1 lb. ground beef
2 12-oz. tubes refrigerated biscuits
15-oz. can pizza sauce
¾ c. green pepper
½ c. onion
4-oz. can mushrooms
3½-oz. pkg. pepperoni
1½ c. mozzarella cheese, shredded
1 c. cheddar cheese, shredded

Cook beef and drain. Quarter the biscuits and place in a greased shallow 3-quart baking dish. Top with pizza sauce. Sprinkle beef over biscuits and sauce. Layer with green pepper, onion, mushroom, pepperoni, and cheeses. Bake uncovered at 350° for 30 minutes or until cheese is melted and biscuits are fully baked. Let stand five minutes before serving.

Serves 6–8   Anita Yoder (Daughter of Bob & Sue)

 A bathtub toy that provides great fun is an empty thread spool. Dampen it and rub one end on a soft bar of soap. Blow through the hole and see all the bubbles it makes.

PIZZA STICKS

11-oz. tube refrigerated breadsticks
24 pepperoni slices
2 T. grated Parmesan cheese
½ t. Italian seasoning
¼ t. garlic powder
½ c. pizza sauce, warmed

Unroll breadstick dough and separate into 8 pieces. Place 3 pepperoni slices on the bottom half of each breadstick, leaving about ¾ of dough at the end. Fold top of dough over pepperoni and pinch end to seal. Twist breadsticks and place on ungreased baking sheets. Combine Parmesan cheese, Italian seasoning, and garlic powder. Sprinkle over breadsticks and bake at 350° for 15–20 minutes or until golden brown. Serve with pizza sauce.

Serves 8   Mary K. Schmucker (Kitchen)

Whatever you do in word or deed, do all in the name of the Lord Jesus, giving thanks to God the Father through Him.... And whatever you do, do it heartily, as to the Lord and not to men....

Col. 3:17, 23

 PIZZA SANDWICHES

12 slices of bread
1 pkg. shredded mozzarella
   cheese

1 jar pizza quick sauce
butter
sliced pepperoni

Butter one side of each slice of bread. Place buttered side of bread down on hot frying pan. Spoon one tablespoon of pizza quick sauce on bread and spread, followed by a layer of pepperoni and mozzarella cheese. Cover with another slice of bread, buttered side up. Fry until golden on each side and cheese is melted in center.

Serves 6   Karen Arrington (Bakery Sales)

PIZZA HOT DISH

1½ lb. ground beef
¼ c. onions, chopped
16 oz. Ragu® spaghetti sauce
1 can cheddar cheese soup

mushrooms, drained
1 pkg. lasagna noodles
mozzarella cheese

Brown hamburger and onions together and drain. Add sauce, soup, and mushrooms. Cook noodles and put them into bottom of 9"x13" pan. Pour meat sauce over noodles and cover with mozzarella cheese. Bake at 375° for 30 minutes and then cut into squares.

Millie Whetstone (Bakery)

PIZZA ROUNDS

½ lb. ground beef
salt and pepper
16.3-oz. can Pillsbury®
    refrigerated buttermilk biscuits
1 egg yolk

¼ t. water
1 T. sesame seeds
14-oz. jar pizza sauce
1 c. cheddar cheese, shredded
1 c. mozzarella cheese

Brown ground beef, add salt and pepper. Separate dough, place 2″ apart on greased cookie sheet. Flatten each biscuit into a 3″ circle with a ¼″ rim around outside. Beat egg yolk and water. Brush on rim of biscuit and sprinkle with sesame seed. Add pizza sauce and cheddar cheese to ground beef. Spoon about ¼ cup beef mixture on each biscuit. Sprinkle with mozzarella cheese. Bake 12–17 minutes in a 375° oven until biscuits are golden brown.

Katie Hochstedler (Bakery)

PIZZA DOUGH

2 c. flour
3 T. baking powder
1 t. salt

⅔ c. milk
⅓ c. vegetable oil

Combine flour, baking powder, and salt in a bowl. Heat milk and vegetable oil until luke-warm. Pour over flour mixture and mix with fork. Then knead until smooth. Put on greased cookie sheet and then put your favorite recipe on top. Bake at 400° for 20–25 minutes.

Martha Hochstedler (Bakery)

BURRITO CASSEROLE

10 tortilla shells
2 lbs. hamburger
1 pkg. taco seasoning
2 cans refried beans

1 can cream of mushroom soup
10 oz. sour cream
shredded cheese

Brown hamburger and add seasoning. Drain. Mix refried beans, soup, and sour cream together. Place shells on bottom of pan and then put mixture on shells. Layer it twice, with the top layer being shells. Then put it in the oven for 45 minutes to 1 hour at 350°. The last 15 minutes cover it with the cheese. Serve with lettuce, tomato, salsa, and ranch dressing on the side.

Serves 10–12

Rachel Yoder (Waitress)

WET BURRITO CASSEROLE

1 lb. ground beef or chicken
¾ c. onion, chopped
½ c. green peppers, chopped
1 pkg. taco seasoning
¾ c. mushrooms, chopped
1 can refried beans

¾ c. water
1 can mushroom soup
1 c. sour cream
1 pkg. flour tortillas
3 c. cheddar cheese, grated
1 small can chilies, chopped

Fry hamburger, onion, and peppers. Drain and add taco seasoning, mushrooms, refried beans, and water to make a nice consistency. In another bowl, mix together mushroom soup and sour cream. Spread half of this mixture in the bottom of a 9"x13" pan. Reserve the rest for topping. Spoon taco mixture into flour tortillas, roll up and place in pan. Spread remaining soup mixture on top. Top with cheese and bake at 350° for 30 minutes or until warm and bubbly. Serve with lettuce, sour cream, taco sauce, and tomatoes.

Serves 8–10

Mary Stalter (Waitress)
Sara Shetler (Busser)

CHICKEN FAJITA PIZZA

Pizza Dough:
2 T. oil
1 t. sugar
½ T. salt
1 c. warm water
1 T. yeast
2 c. all-purpose flour
1 c. whole-wheat flour

Topping:
1–1½ lbs. boneless, skinless
    chicken breasts
1 medium onion, chopped
2 c. green peppers, chopped
1 t. chili powder
1 t. garlic powder
1 t. salt
1 c. salsa
3 c. mozzarella cheese, shredded
1 c. cheddar cheese, shredded

For the pizza dough, mix oil, sugar, salt, and warm water in a bowl. Sprinkle yeast over it and let set until yeast dissolves. Then stir in flours and let rise for about 30 minutes. Press into 13"x18" pan and let rise again 30 minutes. Bake for 10–15 minutes at 350°. For the topping, cut chicken into thin strips and sauté in oil until juices run clear. Add onions, peppers, salt, and spices. Cook until veggies are crisp and tender. Spoon onto crust and top with salsa and cheeses. Bake another 15 minutes or so.

Serves 4–6

Jan Bontrager (Waitress)

BEEF FAJITAS

1 lb. boneless beef plate skirt steaks, beef flank steak, or beef round steak
½ c. Italian salad dressing
½ c. salsa
2 T. lime or lemon juice
1 t. Worcestershire sauce
8 7" flour tortillas

1 T. cooking oil
1 medium onion, thinly sliced and separated into rings
1 medium green or sweet red or yellow pepper, cut into thin strips
1 medium tomato, chopped
optional toppings: shredded cheddar or Monterey Jack cheese, sour cream, guacamole, or salsa

Partially freeze beef. Thinly slice across the grain into bite-size strips. Place strips in a plastic bag and set into a deep bowl. In a mixing bowl. stir together salad dressing, salsa, lime or lemon juice, and Worcestershire sauce. Pour mixture over meat and seal bag. Marinate in the refrigerator for 6–24 hours, stirring occasionally. Wrap tortillas in foil and heat in a 350° oven for 10 minutes to soften. Meanwhile, preheat a large skillet over high heat and add oil. Cook and stir onion rings in hot oil for 1½-minutes or until crisp. Remove vegetable from skillet. Add half of the undrained beef strips to the hot skillet. Cook and stir for 2–3 minutes or until done. Remove beef and drain well. Repeat with remaining beef. Return all beef and vegetables to skillet. Add chopped tomato. Cook and stir for 1–2 minutes until heated through. To serve, fill warmed tortillas with beef mixture. If desired, add guacamole or avocado dip, sour cream, cheese, and additional salsa. Roll up fajitas.

Serves 4   Sharman Reimer (Daughter of Bob & Sue)

CHICKEN ENCHILADA CASSEROLE

4 chicken breasts, cooked and chopped
1 can enchilada sauce
1 can cream of chicken soup
1 can cream of mushroom soup
½ c. sour cream

1 onion, chopped
1 small can chopped chilies
1½ c. cheese, grated
1 T. cilantro, chopped
10–12 flour tortillas, cut in 1" squares

Stir everything together and bake in a casserole dish at 350° for 45–60 minutes. You can also cook this in a Crock-Pot®.

Serves 8   Mary Stalter (Waitress)

CHICKEN ENCHILADAS

2 c. cooked chicken, chopped
1 c. green pepper, chopped
8-oz. pkg. Philadelphia® cream cheese, cubed
8-oz. jar salsa, divided
8–6" flour tortillas
12 oz. Velveeta® cheese, cubed
¼ c. milk

Stir chicken, bell pepper, cream cheese, and ½ cup salsa in saucepan on low heat until cream cheese is melted. Spoon ⅓ c. chicken mixture down center of each tortilla and then roll it up. Place seam side down in lightly greased 12"x8" baking dish. Cut up the Velveeta® and combine with milk in saucepan on low heat until smooth. Pour cheese sauce over tortillas and cover with foil. Bake at 350° for 20 minutes or until thoroughly heated. Pour remaining salsa over tortillas.

Serves 4–6   Dorothy Miller (Waitress)

BEEF ENCHILADAS

½ stick butter
1 medium pepper, chopped
1 medium onion, chopped
fresh mushrooms, sliced
1 can cream of mushroom soup
1 can cream of chicken soup
½ can Rotel® tomatoes with chilies
1 lb. hamburger
1 pkg. taco seasoning
cheddar cheese

Melt butter and sauté the chopped pepper, onion, and sliced mushrooms. Add soups and Rotel® tomatoes. Fry hamburger and drain off grease. Then add taco seasoning to hamburger. Stuff hamburger into tortillas and place in cake pan. Pour gravy mixture over top and top with cheddar cheese. Bake at 350° until cheese is melted and hot all the way through, about 45 minutes.

Serves 12–15   Louie Mast (Waitress)

A child is a person who can clean out the frosting bowl without worrying about calories.

To know the will of God is the greatest knowledge. To find the will of God is the greatest discovery. To do the will of God is the greatest achievement.

ENCHILADA CASSEROLE

2 lbs. hamburger
1 onion, chopped
2 cans cream of chicken soup
2 8-oz. cans enchilada sauce
4-oz. can chopped green chilies
1 soup can water
1 pkg. grated cheddar or mixed blend cheese
1 pkg. soft flour tortillas, ripped into bite-size pieces

Brown meat and onion. Add soup, sauce, chilies, and water. Cook together for 3–5 minutes. In a 9"x13" pan, layer meat sauce, tortillas, and cheese. Bake at 350° for 45 minutes. This can be refrigerated overnight. Serve with lettuce, tomatoes, and sour cream.

Serves 10–12   Betty Miller (Waitress)

TACO CASSEROLE

1 lb. ground beef
2 c. Bisquick®
½ c. water
3 tomatoes
1 c. peppers, chopped
2 T. onion, chopped
⅔ c. Miracle Whip® or mayonnaise
1 c. sour cream
1 c. cheese, shredded
Doritos® tortilla chips

Preheat oven to 375° and grease baking dish. Brown beef and drain. Mix Bisquick® and water and put in pan ½" up the sides. Layer beef, tomatoes, peppers, and onions on top of Bisquick® and then spoon Miracle Whip® mixed with sour cream on next. Spread cheese on top and bake for 25–30 minutes. After baking, sprinkle crushed Doritos® on top.

Elizabeth Mae Knepp (Essenhaus Foods)

MEXICAN PIZZA

Crust:
2½ c. Bisquick® baking mix
½ c. yellow corn meal
¼ c. margarine, melted
½ c. water

Toppings:
1 lb. hamburger
1 onion
10-oz. can tomato sauce
4-oz. can green chilies
¼ t. cumin
1 t. chili powder
2 cubes beef bouillon
1 can refried beans
8 oz. cheddar cheese

Put all the crust ingredients into a bowl and mix well. Press the dough into a greased 10"x15" pan. Bake the dough at 425° for 10 minutes. Brown the hamburger and onion, drain fat. Add the tomato sauce, green chilies, cumin, chili powder, and beef bouillon cubes. Cook until bouillon cubes dissolve. When the crust is done, spread refried beans over it. Cover the refried beans with the meat mixture. Sprinkle the cheddar cheese over the entire pizza. Bake at 425° for 10 minutes. Serve.

Luan Westfall (Purchasing Manager)

CHEESE TACOS

1 medium onion, chopped
cooking oil
16-oz. can tomatoes, cut up
4-oz. can green chili peppers,
    rinsed, seeded, and chopped

1 t. crushed dried oregano
12 6" tortillas
8 oz. Monterey Jack or longhorn
    cheese
1 c. sour cream

Cook onion in 2 T. oil until tender, but not brown. Stir in undrained tomatoes, chili peppers, and oregano. Simmer for 20 minutes until very thick. In skillet, dip each tortilla in 2 T. hot oil for about 10 seconds or until limp. Set on paper towel to drain excess oil. Cut cheese into 12 strips. Place one strip of cheese and 2 T. sauce down center of each tortilla and roll up. Arrange on baking sheet, seam side up. Bake covered at 350° for 8 minutes. Uncover and bake 3–4 minutes more. Open tortillas and add sour cream and then roll up again.

Serves 6   Gloria Davila (Housekeeping at Country Inn)

Two marks of a Christian are giving and forgiving.

CHEESY POTATOES

24-oz. pkg. frozen hash browns, thawed
2 c. sour cream
1 can cream of mushroom soup
⅓ c. melted margarine
¾ c. onion, chopped
3 c. shredded cheddar cheese

Mix all ingredients in large bowl. Put into a 9"x13" dish and bake at 350° for one hour.

Norma Velleman (Bakery Sales)

SCALLOPED POTATOES

8 qt. potatoes, thinly sliced
3 cans cheddar cheese soup
1½ c. milk
4 T. butter
1 small onion
salt and paprika to taste

Arrange a layer of potatoes in baking dish. Mix cheese soup with milk and beat with egg beater to make smooth. Then top with butter, onion, salt, and soup and milk mixture. Continue to layer potatoes and other ingredients until all potatoes are used. Pour remaining soup and milk mixture over all. Season as desired. Bake for one hour at 375° or until tender.

Vernon Roth (Van Driver)

SCALLOPED POTATOES

2 cans cream of mushroom soup
½ c. milk
¼ t. pepper
½ t. salt
8 c. thinly-sliced potatoes, cooked
⅓ c. onions
2 c. shredded cheddar cheese
2 T. butter

Mix all ingredients together or layer them. Bake at 350° for 45 minutes.

Sue Miller (Owner)

 Don't find fault; find a remedy.

SCALLOPED POTATOES AND HAM

¾ lb. ham, cut into ⅛" cubes
6–8 medium potatoes
2 c. milk
1 t. salt
⅛ t. pepper

Brown ham cubes slightly in hot fat. Peel and slice potatoes. Heat the milk to boiling. Add ham and potatoes and again heat to boiling. Add salt and pepper. Put into a greased 2-quart casserole. Bake in slow oven at 325° for 30–45 minutes or until potatoes are tender.

Serves 6   Leon Nafziger (Grounds Maintenance)

 Don't ignore life's little joys while looking for the big ones.

EASY GOURMET POTATOES

2 lb. frozen hashbrowns, thaw for about 30 minutes
16 oz. sour cream
1 can cream of chicken soup
2 c. cheddar cheese, grated
¼ t. pepper
½ c. onion

Topping:
1 stick margarine, melted
2 c. Corn Flakes®

Combine all ingredients, except the toppings and mix well. Pour into glass bowl and then put toppings on top. Bake at 350° for 1 hour and 25 minutes. Variations: (1) Top with crushed potato chips, drizzle ½ c. melted margarine over top before baking. (2) Top with chopped green pepper. (3) May also be made without any topping. Looks like a popular side dish among our employees!

Serves 8

Mary Stalter (Waitress)
Norma Lehman (Bakery)
Elma Miller (Waitress)
Sharon McSorley (Management)
Carol Detweiler (Management)
Angela Miller (Daughter-in-Law of Bob & Sue)
Luan Westfall (Purchasing Manager)

MASHED POTATO CASSEROLE

8 c. cubed ham (approx. 4 lbs.)
3 cans mushroom soup
3 c. Velveeta® cheese, cubed
¾ c. onions, sautéed in ½ c. butter
2 T. Worcestershire sauce
¾ t. pepper

6 qt. mashed potatoes, do not add
   salt or milk
3 c. sour cream
1–2 lbs. bacon, if desired

Mix ham, soup, cheese, onion, Worchestershire sauce, and pepper. Place in large roaster. Mix sour cream and mashed potatoes and put on top of meat mixture. Fry bacon, cut up and put on top of potatoes. Bake at 350° for one hour.

Mary K. Schmucker (Kitchen)

BAKED MASHED POTATOES

6–8 c. mashed potatoes
8 oz. cream cheese
¼ c. butter
1 t. salt

¼ c. onion, finely chopped
½ t. garlic salt
1 c. sour cream
1 c. cheddar cheese, shredded

Beat all ingredients together, except cheddar cheese, until well blended. If needed add a little milk. Pour into a greased 2-quart casserole dish. Bake at 350° for 45 minutes or until hot. Remove from oven and sprinkle with cheese. Return to oven until cheese is melted. This dish can be refrigerated overnight and baked later if desired. Good for potluck dinners.

Anita Yoder (Daughter of Bob & Sue)

ROSEMARY RED POTATOES

6 red potatoes
3 T. butter
3 T. vegetable oil

1 t. rosemary
⅛ t. salt & pepper

Preheat oven to 375°. Scrub and cut potatoes into wedges. Melt butter and add vegetable oil, stir. Place potatoes into glass baking dish and pour the butter and oil mixture over the potatoes and stir until well coated. Sprinkle with rosemary, salt, and pepper. Cover the baking dish with foil. Bake for 30 minutes at 375°. Stir potatoes occasionally.

Sue Meeks (Kitchen)

KENTUCKY POTATOES

4 large potatoes
1 medium onion
3 eggs, well beaten

1 c. hot milk
6 T. butter
1½ t. salt

Peel and shred potatoes and onion and then add beaten eggs and milk, with the butter dissolved in it. Add salt and mix well. Pour into a shallow oiled baking dish and bake at 350° for 1½ hours.

Millie Whetstone (Bakery)

Love suffers long and is kind; love does not envy; love does not parade itself, is not puffed up; does not behave rudely, does not seek its own, is not provoked, thinks no evil; does not rejoice in inquity, but rejoices in the truth; bears all things, believes all things, hopes all things, endures all things.

1 Cor. 13:4–7

SWISS POTATO CASSEROLE

2-lb. pkg. frozen Southern-style hash brown potatoes
8 oz. Swiss cheese, shredded
¼ c. margarine or butter
3 T. flour

3 c. milk
1 t. salt
1 t. onion powder
½ t. white pepper
½ t. nutmeg

Preheat oven to 350°. Spray 13"x9" baking dish with nonstick cooking spray. In baking dish, combine potatoes and cheese and then toss to mix. Melt margarine in large saucepan. Stir in flour, cook over medium heat until bubbly, stirring constantly. Gradually add milk, stirring constantly. Add salt, onion powder, pepper, and nutmeg and mix well. Cook and stir mixture until it comes to a boil. Pour over potato mixture. Bake for 55–65 minutes or until mixture is set and top is lightly browned.

Serves 12   Archie Mundy (Material Handling)

POTATO PANCAKES

3 c. well drained raw potatoes, shredded
¼ c. peeled onion, grated
3 T. flour
½ t. salt to taste
¼ t. freshly ground pepper
2 eggs, room temperature and slightly beaten
3 T. cooking oil or butter

In a large bowl combine potatoes, onion, flour, salt, and pepper. Add eggs and mix well. In a large pan, heat a small amount of oil over moderate heat. Spoon ¼ cup potato mixture into frying pan for each pancake and then spread carefully to make a 3-inch cake. Prepare about three pancakes at a time. Cook until lightly browned on both sides, turning once, a total cooking time of 8-10 minutes. Add oil to pan as needed. Keep cooked pancakes warm in a preheated oven at about 200°. Note: Shred potatoes directly into ice water to prevent discoloration of potatoes and drain well before combining with other ingredients.

Serves 12   Barbara Skarbek (Cashier/Hostess)

 GARLIC FRIES

1 envelope Lipton® savory herb with garlic soup mix
⅓ c. butter or margarine, melted
1 c. plain dry bread crumbs
2 lbs. large red potatoes, cut lengthwise into wedges

In large bowl, place garlic soup mix with margarine. Place bread crumbs in a small bowl. Add potatoes to soup mixture and toss until evenly coated. Then put potatoes in bread crumbs and toss until evenly coated. Arrange potatoes in a single layer on a greased cookie sheet. Bake 40 minutes at 400° or until potatoes are done.

Serves 4   Sylvia Smith (Bakery Sales)

 Hospitality means treating your company like family and your family like company.

OVEN FRIED POTATOES

6 large potatoes
¼ c. oil
2 T. Parmesan, grated
1 t. salt

½ t. garlic powder
1 t. paprika
½ t. pepper

Scrub potatoes, cut into strips. Combine oil, cheese, salt, garlic powder, paprika, and pepper in plastic bag. Add potatoes and shake to coat. Spread in single layer on baking sheets. Bake at 400° for 20–30 minutes, stirring once, until golden brown. Serve with sour cream.

Serves 8   Zachary Reimer (Grandson of Bob & Sue)

PARSLEY POTATOES

3 c. potatoes
½ t. salt
½ t. parsley flakes
¼ c. margarine

¼ c. flour
1½ c. milk
4 oz. American cheese

Cut potatoes into bite-size chunks. Add salt and parsley flakes and boil about 20 min. until tender. Drain. Melt margarine, stir in flour and milk. Stir over low heat until thick and then add cheese; stir until melted. Add potatoes to sauce, stir and heat thoroughly. Serves 4–6

SWEET POTATO CASSEROLE

3 c. mashed yams
1 c. sugar
1 t. vanilla
½ c. butter
2 eggs beaten

Topping:
1 c. light brown sugar
1 c. pecans, chopped
⅓ c. flour
⅓ c. butter

Mix together yams, sugar, vanilla, butter, and eggs. Put mixture in a greased 8"x8"x2" dish. Then mix all the topping ingredients together and place on top of sweet potato mixture. Bake at 350° for 35 minutes. If you double recipe, bake in a 13"x9"x2" dish.

Serves 6–8   Connie Bowers (Kitchen)

SWEET POTATOES ON PINEAPPLE RINGS

2 c. mashed, canned, or cooked
    sweet potatoes, prepared
    without milk or butter
½ c. brown sugar, packed
3 T. butter, melted
¼ t. salt

¼ t. ground cinnamon
¼ t. ground nutmeg
10 miniature marshmallows
20-oz. can pineapple slices,
    drained

In a large bowl, combine the sweet potatoes, brown sugar, butter, salt, cinnamon, and nutmeg. Place pineapple slices in a greased 9"x13" baking dish. Top each slice with ¼ cup of sweet-potato mixture and a marshmallow. Bake uncovered at 400° for 10–15 minutes or until heated through.

Serves 10   Martha Coblentz (Bakery)

SWEET POTATOES WITH MARSHMALLOWS

6 sweet potatoes
¼ t. nutmeg
¼ t. salt
¼ t. cinnamon
1 c. water

1 t. vanilla
1¼ c. brown sugar
4 T. butter
1 c. miniature marshmallows

Cut sweet potatoes in thick slices and place in a large greased casserole dish. Sprinkle nutmeg, salt, and cinnamon on top. Mix water with vanilla and brown sugar and then pour on top of potatoes. Dot with butter and bake in a preheated oven at 400° until tender, about 30 minutes. Add marshmallows and bake for 5 minutes or until lightly browned.

Treva Yoder (Millers' Housekeeper)

CARAMEL SWEET POTATOES

5 medium sweet potatoes or
    1½ lbs. canned
1 t. salt
1 c. brown sugar

2 T. butter
3 T. flour
8 marshmallows
1 c. cream

Cook potatoes until tender and then cut in half lengthwise and arrange in a greased baking dish. Mix salt, sugar, and flour and pour over potatoes. Dot with butter and then add marshmallows. Pour cream over all and bake at 350° for 40–45 minutes.

Sylvia Smith (Bakery Sales)

SWEET POTATO SOUFFLÉ

4 c. mashed sweet potatoes
1 c. sugar
2 eggs
½ c. milk
½ t. salt
⅓ stick butter or margarine, melted
1 t. vanilla

Topping:
1 c. brown sugar
½ c. flour
⅓ c. butter or margarine, melted
1 c. pecans, chopped

Put first set of ingredients together and mix well. Pour mixture into buttered pan. Mix topping ingredients together. Crumble evenly over potato mixture. Bake at 350° for 35–45 minutes uncovered.

Serves 6–8

Lena Miller (Meatroom)

EASY SLOPPY JOES

3 lbs. hamburger
1 lb. onion
1½ c. celery
1½ t. garlic salt

2–3 T. Worcesteshire sauce
1½–2 c. ketchup
¼ c. brown sugar
½ c. mustard

Brown hamburger, onion, celery, and garlic salt. Add remaining ingredients. Simmer and serve.

Jennifer Leatherman (Hostess)

ZESTY TACO JOES

1 lb. hamburger
1 can Campbell's® tomato soup
1 c. salsa

1 c. cheddar cheese, shredded
8 sandwich buns

Brown hamburger in skillet and then add soup and salsa. Heat thoroughly and then top with cheese. Serve on buns. Also delicious served on rice.

Serves 8

Janelle Miller (Hostess)

SLOPPY JOE BAKE

1 lb. ground beef	2 t. mustard
½ c. onion, chopped	1½ c. Bisquick® baking mix
15-oz. can tomato sauce	1 c. milk
½ c. ketchup	2 eggs
⅓ c. brown sugar	2 T. sesame seeds, optional

Heat oven to 400°. Cook ground beef and onion in 10" skillet until beef is browned, drain. Stir in tomato sauce, ketchup, brown sugar, and mustard. Heat to boiling and then spoon into ungreased 13"x9"x2" pan. Stir baking mix, milk, and eggs with fork until blended. Carefully pour over beef mixture. Sprinkle with sesame seeds and then bake 20–25 minutes or until light golden brown.

Serves 10   April Ridenour (Waitress)

SWEET SLOPPY JOES

3–4 lbs. ground beef	¾ c. brown sugar
1 small onion, chopped	salt and pepper to taste
1 celery stalk, chopped	hamburger buns
28-oz. bottle ketchup	

Cook ground beef with onions and celery until done, drain. Stir ketchup and brown sugar together and heat in microwave for 3 minutes. Add to beef and cook 15 minutes on medium heat. Serve dill pickles and chips on the side.

Delora Harker (Bakery)

SLOPPY JOES

2½ lbs. hamburger	½ c. ketchup
1 t. salt	⅔ c. brown sugar
1 t. pepper	1 T. mustard
1 medium onion, chopped	1 can cream of mushroom soup
2½ T. Worcestershire sauce	

Fry hamburger with salt, pepper, and onions. Drain grease. Add remaining ingredients. Heat and serve on buns.

Serves 8–10   Diane Butler (Bakery Sales)

M.K.K.'S FISH BATTER

2 c. flour
2 c. crushed soda crackers
1 T. sugar
1 T. poultry seasoning
1 t. onion powder
1½ T. paprika
1 t. garlic powder
3–4 T. seasoned salt
1 T. seafood seasoning
1 t. black pepper

Mix all ingredients together. To use: beat 1 egg and ¼ c. milk. Dip fish in egg mixture then batter mix. Deep fry. Can also be used for chicken strips, except omit the seafood seasoning. Dip strips of chicken in milk, then coat with batter and fry.

Coats 3 lbs. of fish   Judith Kauffman (Kitchen)

So Far, So Good

Dear Lord: So far today, Lord, I've done all right. I haven't gossiped, lost my temper, been greedy, grumpy, nasty, selfish, or over indulgent. I am very thankful for that. But in a few minutes, Lord, I'm going to get out of bed and from then on, I'm probably going to need a lot more help. Amen.

FOIL BAKED FISH FILLETS

¼ c. regular or unsalted margarine
¼ c. green or sweet red pepper
¼ c. onion, chopped
10-oz. pkg. frozen corn, thawed
¼ t. dried thyme leaves
dash pepper
4 flounder fillets, approx. 1 lb. total

In skillet, melt 2 tablespoons of the margarine over medium heat. Add green peppers and onion, cook stirring one minute or until tender. Add next three ingredients, cook stirring 3 minutes or until heated. Place each fillet on a piece of foil. Divide corn mixture evenly among fish and then dot with remaining margarine. Wrap each tightly in foil. Place on cookie sheet and bake at 350° for 20 minutes or until fish flakes.

Serves 4   Sylvia Smith (Bakery Sales)

TUNA CHEESE TOASTIES

3 hamburger buns, split and buttered
9¼ oz. tuna, drained and flaked
3-oz. pkg. cream cheese, softened
2 T. mayonnaise or salad dressing
2 t. lemon juice
16-oz. can green beans, drained
1 c. American cheese, shredded

Set oven to broil or 550°. Broil bun halves with tops 4–5 inches from heat until light brown, about 2½ minutes. Remove from oven. Reduce oven temperature to 350°. Mix tuna, cream cheese, mayonnaise, and lemon juice, and then stir in green beans. Spoon scant ½ cup tuna mixture onto each bun half and then sprinkle cheese on top. Return to oven and bake approximately 10 minutes or until cheese is melted. These are very good sandwiches.

Serves 6   Leon Nafziger (Grounds Maintenance)

FISH STICK SUPPER

12 oz. pkg. hash browns
4 eggs
2 c. milk
1 T. dried minced onion
1¼ t. seasoned salt
1 T. snipped fresh dill or 1 t. dill weed
⅛ t. black pepper
1 c. shredded cheddar cheese
12 oz. pkg. fish sticks

Break apart hash browns with a fork. Set aside. In large bowl, beat eggs and milk. Add onions, seasoned salt, dill, and pepper. Stir in hash browns and cheese. Transfer to a greased 11"x7"x2" baking dish. Arrange fish sticks over the top. Bake uncovered at 350° for 50 minutes or until top is golden brown and eggs look done. Very good with applesauce.

Serves 6   Cheryl Lehman (Busser)

Just when you're successful enough to sleep late, you're so old you always wake up early.

TOUCHDOWN BEANS

1 lb. ground beef
chopped onion, to taste
salt and pepper, to taste
15- or16-oz. can kidney beans,
   drained
1 can lima beans, drained

16-oz. can pork and beans,
   undrained
½ c. brown sugar
¼ c. white sugar
½ c. ketchup
1 T. vinegar
1 t. dry mustard

Brown ground beef, onion, salt, and pepper. Mix all ingredients and put in baking dish that has been sprayed with Pam® or other oil. Bake at 350° for 1½ hours.

Serves 8–10   Esther Wenger (Corporate Office)

BAKED BEANS

1½ lb. beans, cooked
½ lb. bacon
1 c. brown sugar
onions, to your liking

1 T. mustard
small amount of molasses
1 medium bottle ketchup
pinch black pepper

Brown the bacon and then add brown sugar, onions, mustard, molasses, ketchup, and pepper to the grease and mix. Pour this mixture over the beans and bake for one hour at 350°.

Serves 21   Loranna Hochstetler (Kitchen)

VARIETY BAKED BEANS

2 14-oz. cans Campbells® baked
   beans
2 15-oz. cans Seaside® butter
   beans
16-oz. can green lima beans
16-oz. can dark red kidney beans

8–12 slices bacon
½ c. brown sugar
½ c. vinegar
2 small onions
¼ t. garlic salt
1 t. salt
1 t. dry mustard

Drain all beans and mix together. Fry bacon and set aside. Simmer the remaining ingredients. Pour over beans and add the crumbled bacon strips. Bake for 1½ hours at 350°.

Ellen Mishler (Administration)

NEW ENGLAND BAKED BEANS — CROCK-POT®

1½ lb. dry navy beans
1 medium onion, chopped
1 c. ketchup
1 c. brown sugar
1 c. water
2 t. dry mustard
2 T. dark molasses
1 T. salt
¼ lb. salt pork, ground or diced

Soak the navy beans in water overnight. Next morning cook until softened, approximately 30 minutes. Drain and put into a Crock-Pot®. Add all remaining ingredients and mix well. Cover and cook on low 10–12 hours or on high 4–6 hours. Make sure beans are soft before mixing with other ingredients.

Sylvia Smith (Bakery Sales)

BROCCOLI CASSEROLE

½ lb. Velveeta® cheese
1 can cream chicken soup
½ large can evaporated milk
1 medium onion
1 stick margarine
1 c. rice
1 large bag frozen chopped
    broccoli

Preheat oven to 350°. Sauté onion in margarine. Add soup, milk, and cheese and stir together. Add rest of ingredients and bake in a buttered casserole dish for 40–50 minutes.

Kathy Miller   (Daughter-in-Law of Bob & Sue)

 ## BROCCOLI AND CREAMED CORN CASSEROLE

1 lb. broccoli, chopped
1 can creamed corn
1 t. salt
½ t. pepper
1 small can French's® fried onion
    rings

Preheat oven to 350°. Cook broccoli in boiling water until tender and then drain. Place in casserole dish. Stir in creamed corn, salt, pepper, and half can of fried onion rings and then bake for 30 minutes. Add the remaining fried onion rings during the last 10 minutes of baking.

Serves 4–6   Tonya Penner (Kitchen)

BROCCOLI-HAM HOT DISH

2 10-oz. pkgs. frozen broccoli
2 c. cooked rice
6 T. butter
2 c. fresh bread crumbs
1 medium onion, chopped
3 T. flour

1 t. salt
4 t. pepper
3 c. milk
1½ lb. fully cooked ham, cubed
    cheddar or Swiss cheese

Cook broccoli and drain. Spoon rice into a 13"x9"x2" baking dish. Place broccoli over rice. Melt butter in large skillet, sprinkle 2 T. butter over bread crumbs, and set aside. Sauté onion in remaining butter until soft. Add flour, salt, and pepper. Stir constantly until sauce is thick and bubbly. Add milk and ham, heat thoroughly. Pour over rice and broccoli,then sprinkle with bread crumbs. Bake at 350° for 30 minutes. Sprinkle with cheese.

Serves 8   Joyce Schmucker (Kitchen)

BROCCOLI-CORN CASSEROLE

10-oz. pkg. frozen broccoli,
    thawed and chopped
16-oz. can cream-style corn
¼ c. cracker crumbs
1 egg, beaten
2 T. butter, melted

1 T. instant minced onion
½ t. salt

Crumb Topping:
¼ c. cracker crumbs
2 T. butter, melted

In a 1½-quart casserole dish combine first 7 ingredients. Combine cracker crumbs and butter, sprinkle on top. Bake at 350° for 45 min.

Serves 4–6   Glenda Koshmider (Village Shops)

BROCCOLI AND CAULIFLOWER CASSEROLE

1 pkg. broccoli, cooked
1 pkg. cauliflower, cooked
1 can cream of chicken soup

1 can cream of celery soup
1 jar Cheez Whiz® with pimento
1 can French's® fried onions

Placed the broccoli and cauliflower in a casserole dish. Heat the cream of chicken soup, cream of celery soup, and Cheez Whiz® together until well blended. Pour this mixture over the vegetables. Cover with the fried onions. Bake at 350° for 20–25 minutes.

Luan Westfall (Purchasing Manager)

CABBAGE CASSEROLE

1 large head cabbage, shredded (about 12 cups)
1 medium onion, chopped
6 T. butter, divided
1 c. cream of mushroom soup
8 oz. processed American cheese, cubed
salt and pepper to taste
¼ c. bread crumbs, dry

Cook cabbage in boiling salted water until tender. Drain thoroughly. In large skillet, sauté onion in 5 tablespoons of butter until tender. Add soup and mix well. Add cheese and heat until melted. Remove from heat and stir in cabbage, salt, and pepper. Pour into a greased 2-quart baking dish. In a small skillet, melt 1 tablespoon butter, add bread crumbs. Brown and sprinkle over cabbage. Bake at 350° for 20–30 minutes.

Serves 6–8   Carol Detweiler (Management)

Search me, O God, and know my heart;
Try me, and know my anxieties;
And see if there is any wicked way in me,
And lead me in the way everlasting.
                                        Ps. 139:23–24

CREAMED CABBAGE WITH CHEESE

1 medium head cabbage
1 c. cheese, grated
1½–2 T. flour
¼ t. salt
2 T. onion, minced
⅓ c. bread crumbs
2 T. butter
1 c. milk
⅛ t. paprika
2 T. parsley, minced

Shred the cabbage fine. Cook in salted boiling water until tender but still crisp (7–8 min.). Drain well. Place cabbage and cheese in layers in greased baking dish. Melt butter, blend in flour, and stir in milk slowly. Cook and stir until sauce comes to a boil. Add salt, paprika, onion, and parsley. Pour sauce over cabbage. Sprinkle with bread crumbs. Bake at 400° for 15–20 min. until crumbs are brown.

Serves 6   Esther Wenger (Corporate Office)

CABBAGE ROLLS

2–3 heads of cabbage
½ c. rice, uncooked
2 lbs. hamburger
1 egg
2 cans tomato soup
1 medium onion

salt to taste
pepper to taste
½ t. fresh dill, cut fine
1 pkg. sauerkraut
1 lb. Eckrich® kielbasa sausage

Put cabbage one head at a time into boiling water 5–6 minutes or until tender. Remove leaves from core. Set aside smaller leaves for later. Cook rice, rinse with cold water and let drain. Combine hamburger, egg, 1 can of tomato soup, chopped onion, salt, pepper, and dill if desired. Mix well in large bowl.

Take each cabbage leaf, cut stem thinner if needed. Put a large spoonful of meat on each leaf at stem end and fold in the sides as you roll it up. Lay the cabbage rolls next to each other in deep roaster pan. Cut kielbasa sausage into bite size pieces and lay over cabbage rolls. Take leftover precooked cabbage, cut it up fine and mix with squeezed out or rinsed sauerkraut; sprinkle over cabbage rolls. Mix tomato soup with about ¼ can of water, rinsing the can, and pour over the cabbage rolls. Bake at 350° for 1½ hours or until soft. Serve with rice. Enjoy!

Makes about 20 cabbage rolls   Tammy Zeiger (Grill)

SWEET AND SOUR CABBAGE

Syrup:
3 c. water
2–3 T. vinegar
½ c. sugar
1½ t. salt
pepper to taste
2 T. bacon grease

1 medium head of cabbage,
coarsely shredded or chopped

Bring syrup to a boil, add cabbage, turn heat down to simmer and cook 20–30 minutes or until tender. Variation: Try purple cabbage.

Serves 6   Mary Pinckert (Waitress)

CELERY CASSEROLE

2 c. celery, chopped
1 can cream of chicken soup,
    undiluted
1 can water chestnuts, drained,
    cut up
1 tube Ritz® crackers, crushed

1 stick margarine, melted
½ c. pecans or almonds

Layer the ingredients in the order listed. Do not stir. Bake at 350° for 30 minutes.

Pam Frey (Bakery)

CARROT CASSEROLE

3 c. carrots, sliced
4 slices bacon
1 T. onions, chopped
½ t. salt

¼ t. pepper
3 T. brown sugar
3 T. butter, melted

Cook carrots until tender, drain. Fry bacon, cool and crumble. In a greased casserole, place carrots, bacon, onion, salt, and pepper. Sprinkle brown sugar and butter on top. Cover and bake at 375° for 25 min.

Becky Helmuth (Waitress)

CREAMY CARROTS

3 c. carrots, sliced
1 c. green onions,
    coarsely chopped
¾ c. water
1 T. butter
½ t. salt

¼ t. sugar
⅛ t. or pinch pepper
1 T. flour
½ c. cream
2 t. dill weed

In 2-quart saucepan, combine everything except the flour, cream, and dill weed. Cover and simmer 10 minutes. Reserve liquid. Set carrots and onions aside and keep warm. In a small bowl, combine flour and cream until smooth, then add dill weed. Bring carrot water to a boil and slowly add cream mixture, stirring constantly. Simmer 10 minutes, stirring occasionally. Pour over the carrots and onions. Cover and let stand for 15 minutes before serving.

James Teall (Cook)

TRIPLE CORN SPOON BREAD

1 c. fat free sour cream
3 T. margarine, melted
1 large egg
½ c. onion, chopped

8½-oz. pkg. corn muffin mix
15-oz. can whole kernel corn, undrained
15-oz. can cream style corn

Preheat oven to 350°. Combine the sour cream, margarine, and egg in a large bowl. Stir well with a whisk. Stir in the onion, corn, and muffin mix. Pour the mixture into a greased 8" square baking dish. Bake 1 hour or until pudding is set and light brown.

Luan Westfall (Purchasing Manager)

SCALLOPED CORN

2 c. creamed style corn
2 c. milk
1½ c. cracker crumbs
6 t. butter, melted
¾ t. salt

dash pepper
2 T. sugar
4 eggs, beaten
⅛ c. minced onion

Combine all ingredients and place in a 2½- to 3-quart casserole dish. Bake at 350° for 45 minutes.

Serves 4–6   Leon Nafziger (Grounds Maintenance)

CORN BAKE

1 can creamed corn
1 can corn
8 oz. box corn muffin mix
1 c. sour cream

1 c. cheddar cheese, shredded
2 eggs
¼ c. butter, melted

Mix well and put in a greased 9"x13" baking dish. Bake at 350° for one hour. Stir and let set for 10 minutes before serving.

Eric Miller (Waiter)

 To belittle is to **be** little.

CALIFORNIA BLEND VEGETABLE CASSEROLE

1 bag California blend vegetables
8 oz. Velveeta® cheese
1 stick margarine
1 tube Ritz® crackers

Cook and drain vegetables. Put in casserole dish and add cubed cheese. Melt margarine in small pan and add in crushed cracker crumbs. Place on top of vegetables. Bake at 350° for 20–25 minutes.

Serves 6–8   Barbara Stickel (Village Shops)

 Kindness is one thing you can't give away. It always comes back.

SPINACH BALLS

2 boxes chopped frozen spinach
6 eggs
½ c. Parmesan cheese
⅔ c. margarine
1 T. garlic salt
1 t. pepper
8-oz. pkg. Pepperidge Farm® herb seasoned stuffing mix, crushed
2 large onions, minced

Cook the chopped spinach slightly. Beat the eggs well. Add all the ingredients to the eggs and mix well. Form the mixture into balls and bake at 350° for 20 minutes. Note: They may be frozen and baked later.

Luan Westfall (Purchasing Manager)

 ## SAUSAGE GRAVY

1 lb. bulk pork sausage
¾ t. salt
pinch pepper
⅔ c. flour
3⅔ c. whole milk

Brown sausage, salt, and pepper in large saucepan. Add flour and mix well. Add milk to sausage mixture. Cook until thick. Serve over biscuits and or home fries. Makes 5½ cups of gravy.

TOMATO GRAVY

1 c. tomato juice
½ c. water
3 T. flour

½ t. salt
½ c. cream
2 c. milk

Place juice and water in saucepan. Bring to a boil. Meanwhile, blend flour and salt with cream. Add the milk and mix well. Pour into the hot juice. Stir constantly until thickened.

Norma Lehman (Bakery)

SAUSAGE GRAVY

1 lb. sausage
2 T. onions, finely chopped
6 T. flour
1 qt. milk
½ t. poultry seasoning

½ t. nutmeg
¼ t. salt
dash Worcestershire sauce
biscuits

Crumble sausage into a large saucepan and cook over medium heat. Add onion and cook and stir until transparent. Drain, discarding all but 2 tablespoons of drippings. Stir in flour. Cook over medium heat for about 6 minutes or until mixture bubbles and turns golden. Stir in milk. Add seasonings and cook, stirring until thickened. To serve, slice biscuits and spoon gravy over halves.

Serves 4–6

Norma Lehman (Bakery)

YELLOW GRAVY

2 c. chicken broth
¾ T. Essenhaus® chicken base
3 T. cornstarch
2 T. flour

1 egg
½ c. milk
1 drop yellow food coloring

Heat chicken broth and chicken base to almost boiling. Meanwhile in a bowl, mix cornstarch, flour, egg, and milk together with a mixer. Add to hot broth, stirring constantly. Then add one drop of yellow food coloring if desired. Note: If broth is too hot, gravy might be lumpy.

Cakes & Frostings

HINTS FOR CAKES & FROSTINGS

Have all ingredients at room temperature.

Fill cake pans about ⅔ full and spread batter well into corners and to the sides, leaving a slight hollow in the center.

The cake is done when it shrinks slightly from the sides of the pan or if it springs back when toughed lightly with the finger.

After a cake comes from the oven, it should be placed on a rack for about five minutes. Then the sides should be loosened and the cake turned out onto a rack to finish cooling.

If eggs are not beaten well or ingredients not thoroughly mixed, a coarse-grained cake will result.

To keep chocolate cakes brown on the outside, dust the greased pan with cocoa instead of flour.

If a layer cake comes out lopsided, insert marshmallows between the bottom layer and the cake plate, or wherever they are needed.

When frosting a cake, place strips of waxed paper beneath the edges of the cake. They can easily be removed after frosting.

For a different frosting, mix 2 tablespoons of pineapple juice and 2 tablespoons of orange juice. Add enough powdered sugar to stiffen.

Sprinkle applesauce cake or banana cake generously with granulated sugar, coconut, and chopped nuts before baking. It makes a crunchy topping.

When you are creaming butter and sugar together, it's a good idea to rinse the bowl with boiling water first. They'll cream faster.

To prevent a freshly baked cake from sticking to the plate, sift some powdered sugar onto the plate.

To make powdered sugar, blend 1 cup granulated sugar and 1 tablespoon cornstarch in blender at medium speed for 2 minutes.

APPLE CAKE

4 c. apples, diced
2 c. sugar
2 c. flour
1 t. cinnamon
2 t. baking soda
2 eggs
1 c. nuts, chopped

Sauce:
1 c. brown sugar
1 c. white sugar
4 T. flour
½ c. butter
2 c. water, boiling
2 t. vanilla

Measure sugar, flour, cinnamon, and baking soda into sifter. Put diced apples into mixing bowl and sift dry ingredients over apples. Add eggs and nuts and mix thoroughly. Grease cake pan and bake at 375° for 35 minutes or until done. For the sauce, cook over heat until thick and then pour boiling hot on cake and bake for 5 more minutes. Cool and serve.

Marilyn Nisley (Bakery)

APPLE CAKE

1¾ c. sugar
3 eggs
1 c. vegetable oil
2 c. flour
1 t. baking soda

1 t. salt
1 t. cinnamon
½ c. nuts, chopped
3 c. apples, peeled and sliced

Cream together sugar, eggs, and oil and mix well. Add flour, baking soda, salt, and cinnamon, mix well. Stir in nuts and apples. Pour into a greased and floured 9"x13" pan and bake at 350° for 45 minutes. Good without icing or you can sprinkle with powdered sugar after cooled.

Dave Wenger (Grounds Maintenance)

You can live without music,
You can live without books,
But show me the one
That can live without cooks!

Sue Miller (Owner)

FRESH APPLE CAKE

3 c. flour
1 t. baking soda
1 t. salt
1 t. cloves
1 t. nutmeg
2 t. cinnamon

1½ c. oil
2 c. sugar
3 eggs
1 t. vanilla
3 c. fresh apples, chopped
1 c. pecan pieces

Sift together flour, baking soda, salt, and spices. Set aside. Combine in a large bowl, oil, sugar, eggs, and vanilla. Beat well. Add sifted flour mixture to oil combination in 3 portions along with half the chopped apples beating at medium speed. Fold in by hand the rest of the apples and pecans. Pour batter into greased and floured tube pan. Top with ⅓ cup brown sugar and 1 teaspoon cinnamon mixture before baking. Bake at 350° for 60–75 minutes. Let cool completely before removing from pan.

Serves 12–16   Verna Lickfeldt (Restaurant Administration)

BANANA CAKE

3 c. flour
2 c. sugar
1 t. baking soda
1 t. salt
3 eggs
1 8-oz. can crushed pineapple,
     drained
1 c. nuts
1½ c. vegetable oil

1 t. vanilla
2 c. bananas, mashed

Frosting:
½ c. margarine
1 c. brown sugar, packed
¼ c. milk
2 c. powdered sugar

Mix dry ingredients in a large bowl. Make a well in the center. Add eggs, pineapple, nuts, oil, vanilla, and mashed bananas. Stir, do not beat, will only take a few stirs. Pour into a greased and floured tube pan. Bake at 350° for 75 minutes. Frosting: in a saucepan, melt margarine add brown sugar, boil over low heat for 2 minutes, stirring constantly. Add milk and stir until mixture comes to a boil. Remove from heat and add powdered sugar. Beat until it reaches a spreading consistency. Frost cake when cake is cool.

Serves 10–12   Bob Kurth (Country Inn)

BANANA CAKE

1½ c. mashed bananas
½ t. baking soda
¼ c. sour milk
½ c. shortening
½ c. brown sugar
2½ c. sifted flour
½ t. salt
1 t. vanilla
1 c. white sugar
2 eggs, well beaten
1 t. baking powder

Mix bananas, baking soda, and milk together. Put together as for any other cake. Bake at 350° for 40–45 minutes.

Pam Frey (Bakery)

BLACK FOREST DUMP CAKE

20-oz. can crushed pineapple
    with juice
1 c. flaked coconut
3.5-oz. pkg. instant vanilla
    pudding mix
21-oz. can cherry pie filling
18.5-oz. pkg. chocolate cake mix
½ c. butter

Spread pineapple in a 9"x13" pan. Sprinkle a layer of flaked coconut on top of the pineapple and then a layer of dry pudding mix. Spread the cherry pie filling evenly over pudding mix and sprinkle dry cake mix over pie filling. Cut butter into thin slices and arrange on top of cake mix. Bake at 350° for one hour and cool.

Amy Batten (Country Inn)

BLACK FOREST CAKE

1 chocolate cake mix, devils food
    preferably
2 8-oz. pkgs. cream cheese,
    softened
4 T. sugar
½ t. vanilla
4 t. milk
large can cherry pie filling
1 tub Cool Whip®

Make chocolate cake according to directions on box. Spray 2 flan pans with non-stick cooking spray, pour cake mix into both pans, and bake according to directions on box. Blend together cream cheese, sugar, vanilla, and milk. Spread evenly on top of each cooled cake layer, then divide can of cherry pie filling and place on top of this. Top off with whipped topping.

Makes 2 Cakes

Linda Gubi (Waitress)

BLUEBERRY COFFEE CAKE

2 c. flour
¾ c. sugar
½ t. baking powder
½ t. salt
1 c. butter or margarine
2 eggs, beaten
½ c. orange juice

1 t. almond extract
1–2 c. blueberries (drain juice if
   frozen)

Glaze:
½ c. powdered sugar
⅓ c. milk

Sift dry ingredients together and cut in butter. Add eggs, orange juice, and almond extract. Spread half of the blueberries in bottom of a 9"x9" greased pan. Top with batter and spread remaining blueberries over top and mix. Bake at 350° for 40–45 minutes. Mix glaze ingredients and spread on top to cake while still warm.

Serves 12–15   Sharon Schlabach (Waitress)

CARROT CAKE

1½ c. salad oil
2 c. sugar
2 c. flour
2 t. baking powder
1 t. baking soda

2 t. cinnamon
1 t. salt
4 eggs
3 c. carrots, raw and grated

Mix all dry ingredients in a bowl. Mix salad oil and eggs, then add to dry ingredients. Put in a baking dish and bake at 325° for 35–40 minutes.

Susie Kauffman (Waitress)

TROPICAL CARROT CAKE

2 c. flour
½ t. salt
1 t. baking soda
1½ t. cinnamon
1½ c. brown sugar
3 eggs

1¼ c. vegetable oil
1 t. vanilla
2 c. carrots, finely grated
1 c. pineapples, crushed and
   drained
1 c. shredded coconut
1 c. nuts, chopped

Combine all ingredients. Bake in a greased and floured 13"x9" pan at 350° for 60 minutes or until done. Top with cream cheese frosting.

Clara Slabach (Kitchen)

COFFEE CAKE

1 white or yellow cake mix
1 pkg. instant vanilla pudding
⅔ c. oil
4 eggs
¼ t. salt
1 c. sour cream
1 t. vanilla

Sugar mixture:
½ c. brown sugar
3 t. cinnamon

Mix together all ingredients, except the sugar mixture. Pour half of the batter into an ungreased angel food pan. Sprinkle with half of the sugar mixture and cut through to make it swirl. Spread remaining batter on top of crumbs. Sprinkle with the remaining of the sugar mixture. Bake at 350° for 50–60 minutes.

Serves 10   Mary Stalter (Waitress)

CREAM FILLED COFFEE CAKE

½ T. yeast
¾ c. milk
1 stick margarine
½ t. salt
½ c. white sugar
2 eggs
4½ c. flour

Filling:
4 T. water
½ c. sugar
¾ c. Crisco®
4⅔ c. powdered sugar
2 egg whites
2 t. vanilla
½ t. salt

Crumbs:
½ c. brown sugar
¼ c. flour
little cinnamon and margarine

Dissolve yeast in half a cup warm water. Heat milk, add butter, salt, and sugar, stirring till butter has melted. Cool to lukewarm. Add egg-and-yeast mixture, then add flour as needed to make a nice dough. Let rise for one hour. Work out into 4 pans, put crumbs on top, and let rise again. Bake at 350° for 15–20 minutes. When cakes have cooled, cut off tops and spread filling on. For filling, boil water and sugar together for one minute. Mix Crisco®, powdered sugar, salt, and vanilla together. Then combine powdered sugar mixture and boiled sugar water. Fold in egg whites and put tops back on cakes.

Marilyn Nisley (Bakery)

Q EASY COFFEE CAKE

1 pkg. yellow cake mix
8 oz. sour cream
4 eggs
⅔ c. vegetable oil
1 c. brown sugar
1 T. cinnamon

Icing:
2 c. powdered sugar
¼ c. milk
2 t. vanilla

Mix cake mix, sour cream, eggs, and oil. Beat well and spread half of batter into greased 9"x13" pan. Combine brown sugar and cinnamon and sprinkle half over batter. Spread remaining batter on top of sugar and cinnamon and then sprinkle remaining sugar and cinnamon on top. Bake at 350° for 30–35 minutes or until toothpick comes out clean. Drizzle icing over warm cake. If using a glass pan, bake at 325°.

Angela Miller (Daughter-in-Law of Bob & Sue)

FRUIT SWIRL COFFEE CAKE

1½ c. white sugar
½ c. margarine
½ c. shortening
4 eggs
1½ t. baking powder
1 t. vanilla
1 t. almond extract
3 c. flour
21-oz. can cherry pie filling,
    or any flavor

Glaze:
1 c. powdered sugar
1–2 T. milk

Combine sugar, margarine, shortening, eggs, baking powder, vanilla, almond extract, and flour. Spread ⅔ of the batter in a cake pan. Spread pie filling over batter. Drop remaining batter by tablespoons onto pie filling. Bake until light brown at 300° for approximately 45 minutes. Beat powdered sugar and milk together to make glaze. Drizzle cake with glaze after baked and still warm.

Wanda Mullet (Waitress)

GRAHAM STREUSEL COFFEE CAKE

Cake:
18¼-oz. pkg. white cake mix with pudding
3 eggs, lightly beaten
1 c. water
¼ c. vegetable oil

Streusel:
1½ c. graham cracker crumbs
1 c. brown sugar
2 t. ground cinnamon
⅔ c. butter or margarine, melted
¾ c. pecans, chopped

Preheat oven to 350°. In a mixing bowl, combine cake mix, eggs, water, and oil. Beat on low speed until mixed, then beat on medium speed for another 2 minutes. Pour half of batter into a 9"x13" baking pan. For the streusel, mix graham cracker crumbs, brown sugar, and cinnamon together. Melt butter in a small saucepan and then add to crumb mixture. Stir together with a fork and then add pecans. Sprinkle half of streusel mix over first layer of cake mix. Carefully spread remaining cake mix batter over streusel. Top with remaining streusel and bake for 35–40 minutes or until cake is completely done.

Serves 14–18

Norine Yoder (Village Shops)

Before giving someone a piece of your mind, make sure you can spare it!

MARY EMMA'S COFFEE CAKE

½ c. shortening
1 c. sugar
1 egg
1 t. baking soda
1 c. buttermilk or sour milk
¼ t. salt
2 c. flour
1 t. baking powder

Crumbs:
1 c. brown sugar
3 T. butter
2 T. flour
1 t. cinnamon

Cream shortening, sugar, and egg. Add dry ingredients alternately with milk and baking soda. Pour half of batter in greased pan. Sprinkle half of the crumbs on top. Put remaining batter on and then the rest of the crumbs. Bake at 350° in a 9"x13" baking dish for approximately 40 minutes.

Marlys Pletcher (Waitress)

 CHOCOLATE CHIP PUDDING CAKE

1 small pkg. chocolate pudding mix, not instant
2 c. milk
1 pkg. chocolate cake mix
1 c. chocolate chips
1 c. nut meats

Cook milk and pudding mix according to box directions. Remove from heat and add dry cake mix. Fold in until mix is moistened. Pour into greased 9"x13" pan. Sprinkle with chocolate chips and nut meats. Bake at 350° for 25–30 minutes.

Katie Hochstedler (Bakery)

CHOCOLATE SALAD DRESSING CAKE

1 c. sugar
½ c. cocoa
1 c. salad dressing
2 t. baking soda
1 c. boiling water
1 t. vanilla
2 c. flour

Mix sugar, cocoa, salad dressing, and baking soda together. Add hot water and vanilla, mixing well. Then add flour and mix well. Bake at 350° for 30 minutes.

Elizabeth Miller (Kitchen)

The poor shall eat and be satisfied;
Those who seek Him will praise
the LORD.

Ps. 22:26

CHOCOLATE SNACK CAKE WITH VARIATIONS

1⅔ c. flour
1 c. brown sugar
¼ c. cocoa
1 t. baking soda
½ t. salt
1 c. water
⅓ c. vegetable oil
1 t. vinegar
½ t. vanilla

Mix flour, sugar, cocoa, baking soda, and salt in a bowl with a fork. Stir in water, vegetable oil, vinegar, and vanilla. Stir well. Pour into ungreased 8"x8" pan. Bake until toothpick comes out clean, approximately 35–40 minutes. (See the following page for variations.)

Chocolate Snack Cake with Variations (*continued*)

Applesauce Cake
Omit cocoa and vanilla. Stir 1½ teaspoon allspice into flour mix. Reduce water to ½ cup and stir in ½ cup applesauce.

Chocolate Cherry Cake
Omit water. Stir ⅓ cup chopped unblanched almonds into dry mix. Drain a 4-oz. jar marachino cherries, reserving syrup, chop cherries. Add enough water to syrup to measure one cup. Combine.

Double Chocolate Chip Cake
Sprinkle ½ cup chocolate chips over batter before baking.

Chocolate Mint Cake
Stir in ½ t. peppermint extract.

Chocolate Chip Nut Cake
Omit cocoa and vanilla. Stir in ⅓ c. chopped walnuts. Sprinkle with ⅓ c. mini-chocolate chips over batter.

Oatmeal-Molasses Cake
Omit cocoa and vanilla. Stir in ¾ cup quick oats and 1 teaspoon allspice. Stir in 2 tablespoons molasses with water.

Old-Fashioned Walnut Cake
Omit cocoa and vanilla. Stir in ⅓ c. chopped walnuts and 1½ teaspoon allspice.

Pumpkin Cake
Omit cocoa and vanilla. Stir 1 teaspoon allspice into flour. Reduce water to ½ cup and stir in ½ c. pumpkin pie mix.

Chocolate Spice Cake
Stir 1½ teaspoon allspice into the flour.

Maple Nut Cake
Omit cocoa and vanilla. Stir in ½ teaspoon maple extract with water.

Brown Sugar Nut Cake
Omit cocoa and vanilla. Stir in ⅓ cup chopped walnuts.

CHOCOLATE ZUCCHINI CAKE

½ c. oleo
½ c. oil
1¾ c. sugar
2 eggs
1 T. vanilla
½ c. sour milk
2½ c. flour
4 T. cocoa

½ t. salt
½ t. cloves
½ t. baking powder
½ t. baking soda
½ t. cinnamon
2 c. zucchini, shredded
¼ c. chocolate chips

Cream together oleo, oil, and sugar. Add eggs and sour milk and beat well. Stir in the rest of the ingredients. Pour batter into greased and floured bundt or loaf pan. Sprinkle chocolate chips on top. Bake at 350° for 40–45 minutes.

Luella Yoder (Kitchen)

DELICIOUS CHOCOLATE CAKE

German chocolate cake mix
1 c. chocolate chips
1 can Eagle® brand milk

1 jar ice cream fudge topping
1 small container Cool Whip®
2 crushed Heath® candy bars

Mix cake as directed on box. Fold in chocolate chips. Bake in a 9"x13" pan at 350°. While cake is hot, poke holes in top with end of a wooden spoon. Pour Eagle® brand milk over cake. When cake is cool, spread 2 jar of fudge topping on top, then 1 small container of Cool Whip® on top of the fudge. Pour crushed Heath® candy bars on top of whipped cream. Refrigerate and enjoy!

Luella Yoder (Kitchen)

CRUMB CAKE

4 c. flour
2 c. sugar
¾ c. butter
1½ c. buttermilk

1 t. nutmeg
1 t. cinnamon
1 t. baking soda
1 t. baking powder

Mix flour, sugar, and butter in crumbs. Reserve ½ cup of crumb mixture for topping. To remaining crumbs add buttermilk, nutmeg, cinnamon, baking soda, and baking powder. Pour batter into greased 9"x13" pan and sprinkle with crumbs on top. Bake at 350° until a toothpick comes out clean.

Esther Nisley (Bakery)

DUMP CAKE

1 pkg. yellow cake mix
20-oz. can crushed pineapple, undrained
22-oz. can cherry pie filling
butter

Dump pineapple into a greased 13"x9"x2" pan. Spread evenly, then dump pie filling on top and spread evenly. Dump dry cake mix over cherry layer, spread evenly, then sprinkle chopped pecans over cake mix. Put sliced butter over top. Bake 45–50 minutes at 350°. Serve warm or cold. Good warm with ice cream.

Lloyd Yoder (Meat Room)

EARTHQUAKE CAKE

1 c. nuts
1 c. coconut
1 pkg. German chocolate cake mix
1 stick butter
1 lb. powdered sugar
8 oz. cream cheese

Grease a 9"x13" pan. Mix nuts and coconut together and then spread into bottom of pan. Mix German chocolate cake mix together as directed and spread on nut mixture. Mix thoroughly butter, powdered sugar, and cream cheese. Spread on top of cake mixture. Bake at 350° for 45 minutes or until toothpick comes out clean. No need to frost because it's a moist cake.

Pam Frey (Bakery)

HEAVENLY HASH CAKE

1 lg. pkg. chocolate chips
4 eggs
2 t. salt
1 t. vanilla
1 pint whipped cream
1 c. pecans
1 lg. angel food cake

Melt chocolate chips over low heat. Beat egg yolks and add to chocolate chips. Beat egg white and add to chocolate chips mixture. Then add everything else but the cream. Fold in the whip cream last. Break cake in chunks and cover the bottom of the angel food pan. Cover with chocolate chip mix. Continue layering until the cake and the chocolate mix is all in the pan. Put in refrigerator over night. Slice and serve.

Luella Yoder (Kitchen)

MISSISSIPPI MUD CAKE

2 c. sugar
2 T. cocoa
2 sticks margarine
4 eggs
1 t. vanilla
pinch of salt
1½ c. flour
1 t. baking soda
1 c. coconut

1 c. nuts, chopped
1 small jar marshmallow crème

Frosting:
½ box powdered sugar
2 T. cocoa
¼ c. condensed milk
1 t. vanilla
1 stick margarine

Cream sugar, cocoa, and softened margarine. Add eggs, vanilla, and salt. Mix well. Add flour, baking soda, coconut, and nuts. Beat for 2 minutes. Bake in a greased 9"x12" pan at 350° for 30 minutes. While cake is still hot, top with a small jar of marshmallow crème. Let cool and frost. Swirl frosting over marshmallow crème for a muddy effect.

Sam Whetstone (Dishwasher)

ONE STEP ANGEL FOOD CAKE

1 pkg. of white angel food cake mix

16-oz. can crushed pineapple, undrained

Combine cake mix and pineapple in mixing bowl. Mix with a spoon and put into a 9"x13" cake pan or bundt pan. Bake at 350° for 30–35 minutes. Top with whipped topping if desired.

Serves 20

Martha Coblentz (Bakery)

OUR LORD'S SCRIPTURE CAKE

4½ c. flour (2 Sam. 13:8)
1 c. butter (Ps. 55:21)
2 c. sugar (Jer. 6:20)
2 c. raisins (1 Sam. 30:12)
2 c. figs (Judg. 9:11)
2 c. almonds (Num. 17:8)
2 T. honey (Isa. 7:15)

1 pinch salt (Jas. 3:12)
6 whole eggs, (Isa. 10:14)
½ c. milk (Ex. 3:8)
2 T. leaven–baking powder
   (Lev. 6:17)
season to taste with spices
   (2 Chron. 9:1)

Mix all ingredients together, bake at 325° for approx. 1 hr. and 15 min.

Mary Schrock (Bakery)

To make a fine-textured cake, add 2 tablespoons of boiling water or hot milk when creaming the butter and sugar. Adding 1 teaspoon of lemon juice to the butter and sugar will make it very light.

PAYDAY CAKE

1 yellow cake mix
⅓ c. oleo
1 egg
3 c. mini marshmallows
⅔ c. corn syrup
¼ c. oleo
2 t. vanilla
12 oz. peanut butter chips
2 c. Rice Krispies®
2 c. salted peanuts

Mix first 3 ingredients together and bake in 9"x13" pan at 350° for 12-18 minutes or until light brown. While still hot, put marshmallows on top. Melt corn syrup, oleo, vanilla, and peanut butter chips and stir until smooth. Remove from heat and add Rice Krispies® and salted peanuts. Pour over marshmallow topped cake.

Mary Miller (Waitress)

SOUR CREAM SPICE CAKE

1½ c. cake flour
1 t. baking powder
½ t. baking soda
½ t. salt
1¼ t. cinnamon
¾ t. cloves
¾ t. allspice
2 eggs
1 c. sugar
1 c. sour cream
1 t. vanilla
¼ t. lemon flavoring

Preheat oven to 350°. Grease and flour a 9"x9"x1¾" square pan. Blend flour, baking powder, baking soda, salt, and spices. Set aside. Beat eggs in small bowl until thick, approximately 5 minutes. Beat in sugar gradually. Transfer egg-sugar mixture to a large bowl. Stir in flour mixture alternately with cream and flavorings. Pour into pan and bake for 35-40 minutes. Cool.

Polly Miller (Bakery)

STRAWBERRY PECAN CAKE

1 box white cake mix
4 eggs
1 c. coconut
3-oz. box strawberry gelatin
½ c. oil
1 c. pecans, chopped
½ c. milk

Frosting:
1 box confectioners sugar
½ c. butter
½ c. strawberries, drained
½ c. pecans, chopped
½ c. coconut

Mix first 7 ingredients together for 3 minutes. Pour into 3 8-inch layer pans. Bake at 350° for 30 minutes or until done. For the frosting, cream together all remaining ingredients and spread between layers. Then spread over entire cake. Garnish with a few fresh strawberries.

Serves 12   Joyce Miller (Sunshine Farm Manager)

TEXAS SHEET CAKE

2 sticks butter
1 c. water
2 T. cocoa
2 c. flour
2 c. sugar
½ t. salt
1 t. baking soda
1 c. sour cream
2 eggs, beaten

Icing:
1 stick butter
6 T. milk
2 T. cocoa
1 lb. powdered sugar
1 t. vanilla
1 c. nuts, chopped

Preheat oven to 350°. Bring butter, water, and cocoa to a boil in large saucepan. Remove from heat. Stir all other dry ingredients together and add to boiled ingredients. Mix in sour cream and eggs and beat well. Pour into a greased jellyroll pan. Bake for 20 minutes or until toothpick comes out clean.

Meanwhile prepare icing as follows: Bring butter, milk, and cocoa to a boil. Remove from heat. Add powdered sugar and vanilla and nuts if desired. Spread on warm cake while icing is still very warm.

Serves 18   Tiffany Detweiler (Waitress)

TURTLE CAKE

14-oz. bag caramels
¾ c. butter
½ c. evaporated milk

German chocolate cake mix
1 c. chocolate chips
½ c. pecans

Melt caramels, butter, and milk over low heat. Mix cake mix as directed on box and pour half the batter into a greased 9"x13" pan. Bake at 350° for 15 minutes. Pour caramel mixture over baked cake. Top with chocolate chips, nuts, and then the rest of the batter. Bake for 20–25 more minutes. This cake is tasty, with or without frosting

Serves 15
Glenda Koshmider (Restaurant Gifts)
Sue Miller (Owner)

WHITE SHEET CAKE

1 c. butter
1 c. water
2 c. flour
2 c. sugar
2 eggs, beaten
½ c. sour cream
1 t. almond extract
1 t. salt
1 t. baking soda

Frosting:
½ c. butter
¼ c. milk
4½ c. powdered sugar
½ t. almond extract
½ c. sour cream
1 c. nuts, chopped, optional

Heat butter and water to boiling. Stir in remaining ingredients until smooth. Pour into greased 10"x15" pan. Bake at 375° for 20–25 minutes or until done. Cool for 20 minutes and then frost. Frosting: combine butter and milk, heat until butter is melted. Remove from heat and let cool to room temperature. Add powdered sugar, almond extract, and sour cream. Stir in chopped nuts and spread on warm cake.

Arlene Miller (Waitress)

"For who is greater, he who sits at the table, or he who serves? Is it not he who sits at the table? Yet I am among you as the One who serves."
Luke 22:27

WHITE TEXAS SHEET CAKE

1 c. butter or margarine
1 c. water
2 c. all-purpose flour
2 c. sugar
2 eggs, beaten
½ c. sour cream
1 t. almond extract
1 t. salt
1 t. baking soda

Frosting:
½ c. butter or margarine
¼ c. milk
4½ c. confectioners sugar
½ t. almond extract
1 c. walnuts, chopped

In a large saucepan, bring butter or margarine and water to a boil. Remove from heat. Stir in flour, sugar, eggs, sour cream, almond extract, salt, and baking soda until smooth. Pour into a greased 15"x10"x1" baking pan. Bake at 375° for 20–22 minutes or until cake tests done. Cool 20 minutes. For the frosting, combine butter and milk in saucepan and bring to a boil. Remove from heat and add confectioners sugar and almond extract and mix well. Stir in walnuts. Spread on cake while still warm.

Serves 16–20   Effie Mast (Essenhaus Foods)

ZUCCHINI CAKE

1 c. vegetable oil
4 eggs
2 c. sugar
2½ c. flour
1½ t. cinnamon
1 t. salt
1½ t. baking powder
½ t. baking soda
2 c. zucchini, shredded
½ c. walnuts, chopped

Frosting:
4 oz. cream cheese
¼ c. butter or margarine, softened
1 T. milk
1 t. vanilla
2 c. powdered sugar

Mix oil, eggs, and sugar. Add dry ingredients and mix well. Add zucchini and walnuts and stir by hand until thoroughly combined. Put in greased 9"x13" pan. Bake at 350° for 40–45 minutes. For the frosting, beat cream cheese, butter, milk, and vanilla until smooth. Add powdered sugar and beat until well mixed. When cool top with cream cheese frosting.

Dave Wenger (Grounds Maintenance)

BUTTERCREME ICING

2 lbs. powdered sugar
12 oz. Crisco® shortening
½ c. 2% milk, hot

1 t. butter
1 t. vanilla
⅛ t. salt

Cream all ingredients together until smooth. Makes enough to decorate one 9"x13" cake.

Dorothy Miller (Waitress)

CARAMEL FROSTING

2½ c. butter
5 c. brown sugar

1¼ c. milk
9 c. powdered sugar

Melt butter in saucepan and then add brown sugar and milk. Bring to a boil. Let cool and add to powdered sugar. Mix well.

Lesa Yoder (Waitress)

CARAMEL FROSTING

1 stick margarine or butter
¾ c. brown sugar
pinch of salt

¼ c. cream
1 box powdered sugar
1 t. maple flavoring

Melt butter and add brown sugar and cream. Mix thoroughly. Add powdered sugar, maple flavoring and salt. Mix well.

Sue Miller (Owner)

CREAMY FROSTING

12 c. powdered sugar
2 t. salt
1–1½ c. water
2 c. shortening

4 t. vanilla
2 t. butter flavoring
1 t. almond extract

Cream all ingredients together until smooth.

Lesa Yoder (Waitress)

CREAMY WHITE FROSTING

½ c. margarine
1–1½ c. Crisco® shortening
1 c. white sugar
⅔ c. milk

¾ t. salt
2 T. flour
1 t. vanilla
1½ c. powdered sugar

Cream together the margarine, Crisco®, and sugar, then add last 4 ingredients. Beat together for 12 minutes, the last 2 minutes are most important. When that's done add powdered sugar. You don't have to add powdered sugar if you don't want to. You can use this for whoopee pies, long john filling, and much more.

Becky Helmuth (Waitress)

FLUFFY FROSTING

¼ c. sugar
2 T. water
2⅓ c. powdered sugar
1 t. salt

1 egg, beaten
½ c. shortening
1 t. vanilla
¼ c. cocoa, optional

Boil water and sugar together for one minute. Mix powdered sugar, salt, and egg. Blend the two mixtures together. Add shortening and vanilla. Add cocoa if you want chocolate frosting. Beat until creamy.

Frosts 1 Cake   Norine Yoder (Village Shops)

GLOSSY CHOCOLATE ICING

3 T. shortening
3 oz. unsweetened chocolate
2 c. powdered sugar, sifted

¼ t. salt
⅓ c. milk
1 t. vanilla

Melt shortening and chocolate together over hot water. Blend in powdered sugar, salt, milk, and vanilla. Stir until smooth. Place bowl in ice water and continue stirring until thick enough to spread. It makes enough frosting for a 2-layer cake or a 13"x9" oblong cake.

Polly Miller (Bakery)

"PHILLY" FROSTING

3-oz. pkg. cream cheese
1 T. milk
2½ c. sifted confectioners sugar
your favorite flavoring

Blend cream cheese and milk together. Add sugar gradually, blending in well. Then add your favorite flavoring, approximately ½ teaspoon.

Frosts 2-layer 8" cake   Sylvia Smith (Bakery Sales)

Hey, diddle, diddle,
   I'm watching my middle.
I'm hoping to whittle it soon.

But eating's such fun
   I may not get done
Till my dish runs away with my spoon.

                    Marlys Pletcher (Waitress)

SOFT LEMON FROSTING

14-oz. can sweetened
   condensed milk
¾ c. lemonade concentrate
8-oz. carton frozen whipped
   topping, thawed

In a bowl, combine milk and lemonade concentrate. Fold in whipped topping. Store in refrigerator. Will frost 2 dozen cupcakes or a two-layer cake.

Makes 4 cups   Mary K. Schmucker (Kitchen)

SOUR CREAM FROSTING

¼ c. butter or margarine, melted
3 T. sour cream
2 t. vanilla
2¾–3 c. powdered sugar

Combine melted butter, sour cream, and vanilla. Mix well and gradually stir in sugar until frosting is smooth and reaches desired consistency.

                    Mary K. Schmucker (Kitchen)

MAHOGANY CHIFFON CAKE

¾ c. boiling water
½ c. cocoa
1¾ c. cake flour
1¾ c. sugar
1½ t. baking soda
1 t. salt

½ c. vegetable oil
7 medium egg yolks, unbeaten
2 t. vanilla
1 c. egg whites (from 7–8 eggs)
½ t. cream of tartar

Preheat oven to 325°. Combine boiling water and cocoa. Let cool. Blend flour, sugar, baking soda, and salt in bowl. Mix well and add oil, egg yolks, vanilla, and cocoa mixture. Beat until smooth. Measure egg whites and cream of tartar into large mixing bowl and heat until very stiff. Pour egg yolk mixture in thin stream over entire surface of egg whites, gently cutting and folding in with spatula until completely blended. Pour into ungreased 10" tube pan. Bake 55 minutes at 325° and then at 350° for 10–15 minutes or until done. Invert. Let hang until cold. Ice with chocolate icing.

Polly Miller (Bakery)

Rinse a saucepan in very cold water before scalding milk and the pan won't get coated with milk while heating. It will be much easier to clean.

Leftover egg yolks will keep for several days in the refrigerator. Cover them with cold water and drain off the water before using.

Egg whites are easiest to beat when at room temperature. Remove the eggs from your refrigerator at least 30 minutes before you're ready to beat them.

To keep cake icings moist and prevent them from cracking, add a pinch of baking soda to the icing recipe.

Cookies, Bars & Cupcakes

COOKIE HINTS

Grease the cookie sheet once (before you begin to bake) and there's no need to grease for the rest of the batch of dough.

Heavy, shiny cookie sheets are best for baking. When using lightweight sheets, reduce oven temperature slightly.

Before rolling, chill cookie dough in refrigerator for 30–60 minutes. Less dusting flour or powdered sugar will be needed. Too much flour rolled into cookies can cause them to be tough.

To cream butter or margarine, allow it to reach room temperature. While this requires planning ahead, melting the shortening would make the batter too liquid.

When baking cookies, use the center shelf of oven only. Sheets on two levels will cause uneven distribution of heat.

Place a piece of fresh baked bread in the cookie jar to keep the cookies soft and chewy.

When rolling out sugar cookies, use powdered sugar instead of flour.

Add 2 eggs and ½ cup cooking oil to any flavor cake mix and you have a quick batch of cookies. Raisins, nuts, or coconut can be added, if desired. Drop by teaspoonsful onto slightly greased cookie sheets. Bake at 350° for 8–10 minutes.

EASTER STORY COOKIES (TO BE MADE THE EVENING BEFORE EASTER)

1 c. whole pecans	tape
Ziploc® bag	pinch salt
1 t. vinegar	Bible
wooden spoon	1 c. sugar
3 egg whites	

Begin by preheating the oven to 300°. Place pecans in Ziploc® bag and let children beat them with the wooden spoon to break into small pieces. **Explain that after Christ was arrested, He was beaten by the Roman soldiers.** Read John 19:1–3. Let each child smell the vinegar. Put vinegar into mixing bowl. **Explain that when Jesus was thirsty on the cross He was given vinegar to drink.** Read John 19:28–38. Add egg whites to vinegar. Eggs represent life. **Explain that Jesus gave His life to give us life.** Read John 10:10–11.

Sprinkle a little salt into each child's hand. Let them taste it and brush the rest into the bowl. **Explain that this represents the salty tears shed by Jesus' followers, and the bitterness of our own sin.** Read Luke 23:27.

So far the ingredients are not very appetizing. Add the sugar. **Explain that the sweetest part of the story is that Jesus died because He loves us. He wants us to know and belong to Him.** Read Psalm 34:8 and John 3:16.

Beat with a mixer on high speed for 12–15 minutes until stiff peaks are formed. **Explain that the color white represents the purity of God's eyes for those whose sins have been cleansed by Jesus.** Read Isaiah 1:18 and John 3:1–3. Fold in broken nuts. Drop by teaspoon onto waxed-paper-covered cookie sheet. **Explain that each mound represents the rocky tomb where Jesus' body was laid.** Read Matthew 27:57–58.

Put the cookie sheet in the oven, close the door and turn the oven OFF. Give each child a piece of tape and seal the oven door. **Explain that Jesus' tomb was sealed. Read Matthew 27:65–66. GO TO BED! Explain that they may feel sad to leave the cookies in the oven overnight, as Jesus' followers were in despair when the tomb was sealed.** Read John 16:20, 22. On Easter morning, open the oven and give everyone a cookie. Notice the cracked surface and take a bite. The cookies are hollow! On the first Easter, Jesus' followers were amazed to find the tomb open and empty. Read Matthew 28:1–9. **HE HAS RISEN!!!**

AMISH COOKIES

1 c. Crisco® or shortening
⅔ c. hot water
3 c. brown sugar, unpacked
2 eggs, beaten
1 t. vanilla

4 c. flour
1 t. baking powder
1 t. baking soda
½ t. salt
jam, any flavor

Combine Crisco®, water, and brown sugar. Let cool for a few minutes. Add eggs and vanilla, beat together. Add dry ingredients and mix well. Drop by teaspoons onto ungreased cookie sheet. Put a dab of jam in center of dough (you can make a slight pocket with spoon for jam if preferred). Bake at 400° for 8 minutes. Watch closely because they will burn easily.

Michael Carrico (Essenhaus Foods)

100 GOOD COOKIES

1 c. white sugar
1 egg
1 t. cream of tarter
1 c. margarine
1 c. coconut
1 c. brown sugar

1 c. Rice Krispies®
1 t. baking soda
1 c. vegetable oil
1 c. quick oatmeal
3½ c. flour

Mix first six ingredients in order given. Then add last six ingredients. Drop by teaspoons on cookie sheet. Bake at 350° for 12–15 minutes.

Ellen Mishler (Administration)

BANANA CHOCOLATE CHIP COOKIES

⅔ c. shortening
2 eggs
1 c. sugar
2¼ c. flour
2 t. baking powder

¾ t. salt
¼ t. baking soda
1 c. mashed bananas
1 t. vanilla
1 c. chocolate chips

Cream together shortening, eggs, and sugar. Add dry ingredients, bananas, and vanilla. Mix well. Stir in chocolate chips. Drop by teaspoons on ungreased cookie sheet. Before baking sprinkle with mixture of cinnamon and sugar. Bake at 400° 8–10 minutes. Do not overbake; this is a soft cookie.

Makes 2 Dozen

Michael Carrico (Essenhaus Foods)

BROWN SUGAR COOKIES

2 c. brown sugar
2 c. butter flavored Crisco®
4 eggs
1 c. water
5 c. flour
1 t. baking soda
2 T. baking powder
1 T. nutmeg
2 T. cinnamon
1 t. salt

Frosting:
¼ c. brown sugar
1 stick butter
6 T. milk
powdered sugar

Cream brown sugar and Crisco® until smooth and then add eggs one at a time; then water. Mix dry ingredients together. Gradually add to sugar mixture. Drop by heaping teaspoon onto cookie sheet. Bake at 350° for 10 minutes or until edges of cookie are slightly brown. For the frosting, heat brown sugar and butter together to a light boil; remove from heat, add milk. Add powdered sugar until thick. Then frost cookies.

Makes 3–4 Dozen   Rosemary Thomas (Country Inn)

BROWN SUGAR COOKIES

⅔ c. butter
1½ c. brown sugar, packed
2 eggs, unbeaten
1 c. evaporated milk
1 t. vanilla
1 T. vinegar
2½ c. flour, sifted
1 t. baking soda
½ t. baking powder

½ t. salt
1 c. walnuts, chopped
5 doz. walnut halves or quarters

Brown Butter Frosting:
½ c. butter
3 c. powdered sugar
¼ c. boiling water

Cream butter and brown sugar until light and then add eggs. Beat well. Add vanilla and vinegar to milk. Sift dry ingredients and add alternately with milk to creamed mixture. Fold in walnuts. Drop by tablespoonfuls about 2″ apart on greased baking sheet. Bake at 350° until delicately browned, about 12 minutes. For the frosting, melt butter over medium heat until light golden brown. Add sugar, then water. Beat until frosting holds its shape. Spread and swirl frosting on each cookie and garnish each with nut halves or quarters.

Makes 5 dozen   Verna Lickfeldt (Restaurant Administration)

BUTTERMILK COOKIES

1 c. butter
3 eggs
2 c. sugar
1 t. baking soda
1 c. buttermilk
1½ t. vanilla
¼ t. salt
3 t. baking powder
5 c. flour

Frosting:
6 T. butter, browned
3 T. hot water
1 t. vanilla
powdered sugar

Cream butter, sugar, and eggs together and then dissolve baking soda in buttermilk. Add rest of cookie ingredients and mix well. Bake at 350° for 5 minutes on top rack and 5 minutes on bottom rack. For the frosting, combine all ingredients and mix well. Add powdered sugar to make desired consistency. Frost cookies when cooled.

Arlene Miller (Waitress)

CARROT COOKIES

¾ c. sugar
¾ c. Crisco® shortening
1 egg, beaten
1 c. cooked mashed carrots
1 t. vanilla
2 c. flour
2 t. baking powder
¼ t. salt

Frosting:
Juice from 1 orange
1 t. lemon juice
powdered sugar

Cream sugar and Crisco® and then add egg, carrots, and vanilla. Add flour, baking powder, and salt. Drop by teaspoonfuls onto greased cookie sheet and bake at 425° for 15 minutes. Mix frosting ingredients. Make very stiff and frost cookies while hot.

Makes 3 Dozen   April Ridenour (Waitstaff)

A smile is a light in the window of your face to show your heart is at home.

CHOCOLATE CHIP COOKIES

¾ c. sugar
¾ c. brown sugar
1 stick margarine, softened
1 stick butter, softened
1½ t. vanilla

2 eggs
2¾ c. flour
½ t. salt
1 t. baking soda
2 c. chocolate chips

Cream together sugars, margarine, butter, and vanilla and then add eggs and beat for 1 minute. Mix flour, salt, and baking soda together. Add to sugar and butter mixture. Add chocolate chips. Bake at 375° for 7–10 minutes. (I usually keep an extra bag of chocolate chips on hand so I can add an extra ½ cup to make cookies more chocolatey.)

Stephanie Yoder (Granddaughter of Bob & Sue)

CHOCOLATE PEANUT BUTTER CUP COOKIES

1 tube refrigerator chocolate chip
 cookie dough

48 mini Reeses® peanut butter
 cups

Divide cookie dough into 12 equal parts. Divide each part into 4 parts. Roll 4 parts into small balls. Drop into lined muffin pan. Bake at 350° for no longer than 8 minutes. Remove from oven and immediately push Reeses® cups into cookie. Let cool.

Makes 4 Dozen   Jennifer Leatherman (Hostess)

JUST RIGHT CHOCOLATE CHIP COOKIES

½ c. butter
½ c. shortening
¾ c. white sugar
¾ c. brown sugar
2 eggs
2 t. vanilla

1 small box vanilla instant
 pudding
3 c. flour
1 t. baking soda
12 oz. chocolate chips

Mix first four ingredients together and then blend in eggs and vanilla. Next add dry ingredients and then chocolate chips. Bake on an ungreased pan at 350° for 12–14 minutes. Remove from oven before they are quite done and let them set on cookie sheet for several minutes.

Loranna Hochstetler (Kitchen)

CHOCOLATE PEANUT BUTTER CUP COOKIES

1 c. semi-sweet chocolate chips
2 squares unsweetened baking chocolate
1 c. sugar
½ stick butter flavored Crisco®
2 eggs
1 t. salt
1 t. vanilla
1½ c. + 2 T. all-purpose flour
½ t. baking soda
¾ c. peanuts, finely chopped
36 miniature peanut butter cups
1 c. peanut butter chips

Preheat oven to 350°. Melt chocolate chips and chocolate squares in microwave until smooth. Cool slightly. Then combine sugar and Crisco® in large bowl and blend until crumbly. Beat in eggs one at a time and then add salt and vanilla. Add chocolate slowly at low speed. With spoon, stir in flour and baking soda until well blended. Shape dough into 1¼" balls and roll in nuts. Bake on ungreased baking sheet 8–10 minutes or until set. Press peanut butter cup into center of each cookie immediately after removing from oven. Press cookie against peanut butter cup and cool 2 minutes on baking sheet before removing. Cool completely.

Place peanut butter chips in a heavy resealable sandwich bag and seal. Microwave until smooth. Knead bag to mix. Cut tip off corner of bag and squeeze out the melted chips to drizzle over cookies.

Makes 3 dozen   Charlotte Miller (Waitress)

CHOCOLATE SANDWICH COOKIES

2 pkgs. devil's food cake mix
4 eggs, lightly beaten
⅔ c. vegetable oil
8 oz. cream cheese, softened
½ c. butter or margarine, softened
3–4 c. powdered sugar
½ t. vanilla

In large mixing bowl beat cake mixes, eggs, and oil. Batter will be very stiff. Roll into 1" balls and place on ungreased baking sheets and flatten slightly. Bake at 350° for 8–10 minutes. Cool. In another bowl, beat cream cheese and butter. Add powdered sugar and vanilla and mix until smooth. Spread on bottom of half the cookies. Top with remaining cookies.

Makes 4 dozen   Martha Coblentz (Bakery)

CLOTHESPIN COOKIES

3¼ c. sifted flour
1 t. salt
2 T. sugar
2 c. shortening, separated
1¼ c. warm water
2 egg yolks

Filling:
3 T. flour, heaping
1 c. milk
1 c. butter
1 c. granulated sugar
1 t. vanilla
paste food coloring (optional)

Blend together flour, salt, sugar, and ½ cup shortening as for pie dough. Stir in warm water and egg yolks beaten together. Cover bowl and chill for 1 hour. Remove dough from refrigerator and roll in rectangle ¼" thick. Spread with ½ cup shortening. Fold dough in half and refrigerate for 1 hour. Repeat process 2 more times using ½ cup shortening each time. Roll a fourth of dough at a time leaving rest of dough in refrigerator. Cut in strips ¾"x6". Roll each strip around a clean round wooden clothespin or ½" dowel. Lay on jelly roll pan. Bake at 425° for 10–12 minutes. Place on cooling rack and 2–3 minutes later strip clothespin out of cookie. When cool, fill with cream filling.

Cream filling:
Mix flour and a little milk to make smooth paste and add remaining milk in double boiler. Cook until thick; cool with lid on. Cream butter and sugar and beat until fluffy. Add cooled flour and milk mixture. Beat well. Add vanilla and food coloring if desired. Fill cookies with pastry bag or cookie press. Filling may have to be refrigerated before use.

Millie Whetstone (Bakery)

"What man is there among you who, if his son asks for bread, will give him a stone? . . .

"If you then, being evil, know how to give good gifts to your children, how much more will your Father who is in heaven give good things to those who ask Him!"

Matt. 7:9, 11

CREAM WAFERS

1 c. shortening
2 c. brown sugar
4 eggs, beaten
2 t. vanilla
4 T. cream or milk
2 t. baking soda in a little water
5 c. flour
1 t. salt
1 t. baking powder

Frosting:
8 T. butter
4 T. hot cream
4 c. powdered sugar
2 t. vanilla
1 t. maple flavor

Mix all wafer ingredients together and bake at 350° until slightly browned. Mix all frosting ingredients together. Put 2 cookies together with frosting in the middle. Very good!

Regina Gingerich (Village Shops)

The future lies before you
　like a field of driven snow,
be careful how you tread it,
　for every track will show.

FAVORITE PEANUT BUTTER OATMEAL COOKIES

1 c. margarine
1 c. peanut butter
½ c. sugar
1 c. brown sugar
2 eggs
1 t. vanilla

2 T. water
1½ c. flour
1 t. baking soda
1 t. salt
2½ c. quick oats
¾ c. chocolate chips

Cream together margarine, peanut butter, sugars, and then add eggs, vanilla, and water. Beat until fluffy. Sift together flour, baking soda and salt and add. Stir in oats and chocolate chips. Drop onto ungreased baking sheet and bake at 350° for 10–12 minutes.

Makes 5 dozen

Mary Stalter (Waitress)

FIRE TRUCK COOKIES

16 whole graham crackers, 4¾"x2½"
1 c. vanilla frosting
red paste or liquid food coloring
32 chocolate cream-filled sandwich cookies
black shoestring licorice
16 red gumdrops

With a serrated knife, cut one corner off of each graham cracker at a 45° angle. Tint frosting red and frost crackers. Place two sandwich cookies on each for wheels. For each truck, cut licorice into two 22" pieces. Place the large pieces parallel to each other above wheels with the small pieces between to form a ladder. Place the medium pieces at cut edge forming a windshield. Add a gumdrop for the light on top.

Makes 16   Mary K. Schmucker (Kitchen)

FUDGY BONBONS

12-oz. pkg. semi-sweet chocolate chips
¼ c. butter
14-oz. can of sweetened condensed milk
1 t. vanilla
½ c. nuts, finely chopped
2 c. all-purpose flour
55–60 Hershey's® hugs, unwrapped
2 oz. white baking bar or vanilla chocolate chips

Melt chocolate chips and butter over low heat or in microwave until chips are melted. Mix well and add sweetened condensed milk. Mix well then add vanilla, nuts if desired, and flour. Shape one tablespoon of dough around each candy hug covering completely and place on ungreased cookie sheet 2 inches apart. Bake at 350° for 6–7 minutes, no more. Do not overbake. Cookies will still look shiny, and will firm as they cool. Remove from cookie sheet. Cool. Then melt white chocolate and drizzle over cookies. Store in an airtight container.

Makes 5 dozen   Ellen Mishler (Administration)

God will either lighten our load or strengthen our backs.

GIANT SPICE COOKIES

18¼-oz. pkg. spice cake mix
½ t. ground ginger
¼ t. baking soda

¼ c. water
¼ c. molasses
6 t. vanilla extract

In a bowl combine the cake mix, ginger, and baking soda. Stir in water, molasses, and vanilla. Mix well. With floured hands roll into 10 balls and place 3" apart on greased baking sheets, flatten slightly. Bake at 375° for 13–15 minutes or until surface cracks and cookies are firm. Remove to wire racks to cool.

Makes 10 cookies   Laura Lehman (Busser)

GRANDMA'S SOFT BROWN SUGAR COOKIES

1 c. brown sugar
½ c. shortening
1 egg
½ c. milk
½ t. vanilla

1 t. baking soda
1½ t. baking powder
¼ t. salt
3 c. flour

Cream together brown sugar and shortening. Add egg, milk and vanilla; mix well. Add baking soda, baking powder, and salt. Blend well after each addition. Add flour, one cup at a time. Adjust flour amount, if necessary, to make batter a nice rolling consistency. Flour work surface and roll dough. Cut into desired shapes. Bake until slightly browned, about 10 minutes at 350°. Cookies can be sprinkled with colored sugar before baking or decorated with frosting after being baked.

Wendy Miller (Bakery Sales)

SUGAR COOKIES

1 c. sugar
1 c. brown sugar
1 c. oil
2 eggs
¼ t. salt
6 c. flour

2 t. baking soda
4 t. baking powder
2 t. vanilla
2 t. lemon extract
1 c. sour milk

Mix together and make balls. Press down with a glass dipped in sugar. Bake on cookie sheet at 375° for 8–10 minutes.

Esther Nisley (Bakery)

SUGAR COOKIES

5 c. white sugar
2½ c. corn oil
6 eggs
3 t. baking soda
1½ t. salt

2 t. vanilla
2 t. lemon flavoring
3 c. milk
6 t. baking powder
13 c. flour

Mix sugar and oil together; beat eggs and add. Add soda, salt, vanilla and lemon flavoring. Then add milk. Add baking powder and flour. Mix well. Drop dough onto cookie sheets, sprinkle with sugar. Bake at 350° for 8–10 min. You may sprinkle with sugar, dry Jell-O®, or frost the cookies.

Norma Lehman (Bakery)

HOLIDAY SUGAR COOKIES

¾ c. margarine
1 c. sugar
1 egg
¼ c. milk

1 t. vanilla
3 c. flour
2 t. baking powder

Cream margarine and sugar until light. Beat egg, add and mix well. Add milk and vanilla, mix well. Add dry ingredients. Chill dough for several hours and then roll out ¼"–⅜" thick and cut into desired shapes. Bake at 375° until done. Watch carefully, they brown fast. For crisp cookies, roll dough thinner.

Polly Miller (Bakery)

GUMDROP COOKIES

¾ c. brown sugar
½ c. white sugar
½ c. margarine
½ c. vegetable shortening
1 egg
1 t. vanilla
¼ t. salt

½ t. baking powder
1 c. gumdrops, chopped
2 c. flour
2 c. oatmeal
½ c. coconut
1 t. baking soda

Combine brown and white sugars with margarine and shortening. Mix well. Add egg and vanilla. Mix with the rest of ingredients. Drop by teaspoonsful and bake at 350° for 10–15 minutes.

Becky Helmuth (Waitress)

The only way to settle a disagreement is on the basis of what's right, not who's right.

KIEFLIES (HUNGARIAN CHRISTMAS COOKIES)

Cookie:
6 c. flour
1 lb. butter, softened
12 egg yolks
1 c. sour cream

Filling:
12 egg whites
1 lb. powdered sugar
3 lb. walnuts, ground fine
1 t. vanilla

Mix flour and butter like pastry. Add beaten egg yolks and sour cream to flour mixture. Work until dough is smooth. Roll dough into walnut-sized balls and chill overnight. Roll each ball thin on a board that has been sprinkled with half flour and half confectioner's sugar. For the filling, beat egg whites until stiff and then add sugar, nuts, and vanilla. Put one rounded teaspoon of nut filling on each piece of dough. Roll up crescent style and seal ends. Place on ungreased cookie sheet and bake at 350° for 20 minutes or until golden. Cool and sprinkle with powdered sugar.

Makes 10 dozen   Mary Pinckert (Waitress)

MOM'S OVERNIGHT COOKIES

2 eggs
2 c. brown sugar
½ c. shortening or margarine
2 c. flour

½ t. baking soda
½ t. cream of tartar
1 t. vanilla

Beat eggs, brown sugar, and shortening until fluffy. Add remaining ingredients and mix well. Roll into large stick or log and wrap in wax paper. Refrigerate overnight. Then slice ½" thick and bake at 350° for 10 minutes or until lightly browned.

Makes 4 dozen   Diane Butler (Bakery Sales)

MOM'S RANGER COOKIES

½ c. shortening
½ c. sugar
½ c. brown sugar, packed
1 egg
½ t. vanilla
1 c. flour

½ t. baking soda
¼ t. salt
2 c. cereal—Cornflakes®,
   Wheaties®, etc.
½ c. shredded coconut

Mix shortening, sugars, egg, and vanilla. Stir in remaining ingredients. Dough will be stiff. Drop 2 inches apart on ungreased cookie sheet. Bake at 375° for 9–10 minutes.

Makes 3 Dozen   Robyn Pippenger (Hostess/Cashier)

MONSTER COOKIES

1 lb. butter
4 c. sugar
1 doz. eggs
3 lbs. peanut butter
2 lbs. brown sugar
8 t. baking soda

1 t. vanilla
11 c. oatmeal
6 c. flour
1 lb. M&M's® candies
2 c. nuts

Combine above ingredients, drop by teaspoonful onto greased cookie sheets. Bake at 350° 10–15 min. Makes about 200 cookies.

Stephanie Yoder (Granddaughter of Bob & Sue)

NO-BAKE COOKIES

¼ c. cocoa
½ c. milk
2 c. sugar

½ c. butter
½ c. peanut butter
3 c. oatmeal, uncooked

Mix cocoa and milk in large saucepan. Add sugar and butter and boil for 3 minutes. Add oatmeal and peanut butter and stir until melted. Remove from heat and stir until mixture begins to thicken. Drop onto wax paper with tablespoon. Cool, eat, and enjoy.

Anita Wanamaker (Kitchen)

OATMEAL LACE COOKIES, NO FLOUR

2½ c. quick oats, uncooked
2 t. baking powder
1 c. dark brown sugar, packed
½ c. oil or melted margarine
1 egg, beaten
½ t. almond flavor

Blend dry ingredients and then add margarine or oil. Add beaten egg and mix well. Add flavoring. Drop from a teaspoon onto greased cookie sheet leaving plenty of room for them to spread. Bake at 350° for 10 minutes. Let stand a minute or so before removing from the pan.

Makes 6 Dozen   Sylvia Smith (Bakery Sales)

OATMEAL RAISIN COOKIES

1 c. shortening
2 c. brown sugar
2 eggs
1 t. vanilla
3 c. oatmeal
1½ c. flour
½ t. salt
1 t. baking soda
1 t. baking powder
1 c. chopped raisins
powdered sugar

Cream shortening and sugar and then add eggs, vanilla, and oatmeal. Combine dry ingredients and then add to other mixture. Add the chopped raisins. Form into balls and roll in powdered sugar. Bake at 375° for 10–12 minutes.

Makes 2½–3 Dozen   Sharon Schlabach (Waitress)

"Give, and it will be given to you: good measure, pressed down, shaken together, and running over will be put into your bosom. For with the same measure that you use, it will be measured back to you."

Luke 6:38

ORANGE COOKIES

2 c. brown sugar
1 c. shortening
2 eggs
2 oranges, put thru a grinder
1 c. sour cream
1 t. baking soda
2 t. baking powder

½ t. salt
5 c. flour

Frosting:
½ ground orange
2 T. butter
powdered sugar

Cream sugar and shortening together, add eggs. Beat well and then add 1½ oranges and sour cream with baking soda dissolved in it and stir. Add baking powder, salt and flour. Use scant flour as the cookies get dry easily. Bake at 400° for 15–18 minutes. For frosting: Mix rest of orange and butter together and then add powdered sugar until it's a good spreading consistency. Frost while still warm.

Makes 3 Dozen   Judith Kauffman (Kitchen)

PAN COOKIES

2¼ c. flour
1 t. baking soda
1 t. salt
1 c. margarine
¾ c. white sugar

¾ c. brown sugar
1 t. vanilla
2 eggs
1 pkg. chocolate chips

Mix all ingredients together and then spread on a cookie sheet. Bake for 20 minutes at 375°.

Mary Schrock (Bakery)

SANDWICH COOKIES

2 boxes cake mix
4 eggs
1 c. vegetable oil

Filling:
8 oz. cream cheese
¼–½ c. stick margarine

Combine cake mix, eggs, and oil. Dough will be very oily! Roll into 1" balls and bake for 18 minutes at 325°. Cookies will feel soft at first but will firm up when cool. For the filling, blend cream cheese and margarine and then add powdered sugar. Frost cookie and then put another cookie on top.

Makes 2 dozen   Polly Miller (Bakery)

 When the tip of a shoestring comes off, dip the end of the lace in clear fingernail polish and let dry. You will have a hard-tipped shoestring again for easier lacing.

SOUR CREAM COOKIES

3 c. white sugar
1¾ c. shortening
4 eggs, beaten
1 t. salt
2 t. baking soda
1 T. vanilla
1 T. lemon flavoring
1 c. sour milk*
1 c. sour cream
4 t. baking powder
6½ c. flour

Cream Cheese Frosting:
1 c. shortening
2 oz. cream cheese
½ stick butter
1 t. vanilla
powdered sugar

Mix sugar and shortening together. Add eggs, salt, baking soda, vanilla, and lemon flavoring, stir. Add sour milk and sour cream and mix well, add baking powder and flour. (The more sour cream, the better the cookie!) Bake at 350° for 8–10 minutes. For the frosting, combine all ingredients and mix until well blended. Add enough powdered sugar to make a good spreading consistency. Frost cookies when cooled.

*To make sour milk, mix 2–3 tablespoons lemon juice or vinegar to a cup of milk.

Norma Lehman (Bakery)

VANILLA NUT ICEBOX COOKIES

2 c. flour
1½ t. baking powder
½ t. salt
⅔ c. butter or Crisco®

1 c. sugar
1 egg
1 t. vanilla
½ c. pecans or almonds, chopped

Mix and roll up and refrigerate overnight. Slice and bake at 375° until done. Do not over-bake.

Mary Schrock (Bakery)

CAN'T LEAVE ALONE BARS

1 yellow or chocolate cake mix
⅓ c. vegetable oil
2 eggs

Filling:
½ stick margarine
1 c. milk chocolate chips
14-oz. can sweetened condensed
milk

Preheat oven to 350°. Mix cake mix, oil, and eggs. Mixture will be stiff. Keep 1 c. mixture out and spread the rest in a 9"x13" cake pan. Be sure to press it up the sides ½". For the filling, melt the margarine and add chocolate chips. Stir until melted. Add sweetened condensed milk. Pour on top of cake mixture, then put dabs of leftover dough on top. Bake for 25–30 minutes.

Mary Miller (Bakery)
Martha Miller (Hostess)

CHERRY FRUIT BARS

1½ c. sugar
1 c. butter
4 eggs
1 t. almond flavoring
1½ t. baking powder

3 c. flour
2 c. pie filling of choice
1 c. powdered sugar
2 T. milk

Mix first six ingredients together to make a batter. Pour half onto cookie sheet. Pour pie filling over top then spoon and drop rest of dough on top of filling. Bake at 350° until golden brown on top, about 30 minutes. Cool completely and mix powdered sugar and milk and drizzle on top.

Makes 15–20

Louie Mast (Waitress)

CHESS BROWNIES

1 box yellow cake mix
1 stick margarine
1 egg

Topping:
3 eggs
8 oz. pkg. cream cheese
1 lb. box powdered sugar

Mix first 3 ingredients and press into a 13"x9" pan. Mix topping and pour over cake mixture. Sprinkle with nutmeg. Bake at 325° for 1 hour.

Linda Miller (Waitress)

Q CHEWY DATE NUT BARS

1 pkg. yellow cake mix
½ c. brown sugar
¾ c. butter

2 eggs
2 c. chopped dates
2 c. chopped nuts

Combine cake mix and brown sugar. Add butter and eggs. Combine dates and nuts and stir into batter. Spread batter into a 9"x13" greased pan or cookie sheet. Bake at 350° until a toothpick comes out clean.

Makes 40–45   Martha Coblentz (Bakery)

CHOCOLATE CHEESE LAYERED BARS

½ c. butter, softened
1 c. sugar
2 eggs
1 oz. unsweetened chocolate, melted
1 t. vanilla extract
1 c. all-purpose flour
1 t. baking powder
½ c. pecans, chopped (optional)

Cheese Layer:
6 oz. cream cheese, softened
¼ c. butter, softened
½ c. sugar
1 egg
2 T. all-purpose flour
½ t. vanilla extract
¼ c. pecans, chopped (optional)
1 c. semisweet chocolate chips
3 c. miniature marshmallows

Topping:
¼ c. butter
2 oz. cream cheese
1 oz. unsweetened chocolate

2 T. milk
3 c. powdered sugar
1 t. vanilla extract

In a mixing bowl, cream butter and sugar. Add eggs, chocolate, and vanilla, mix well. Combine flour and baking powder. Stir into chocolate mixture; fold in pecans. Pour into a greased 13"x9"x2" baking pan. In a mixing bowl, combine cream cheese and butter. Beat in sugar, egg, flour, and vanilla. Mix well then fold in pecans. Spread over the chocolate layer and sprinkle with chips. Bake at 350° for 20–25 minutes or until edges pull away from sides of pan. Sprinkle with marshmallows and bake for 2 more minutes or until puffed. Spread evenly over cream cheese layer and cool on a wire rack. In a saucepan, combine first four topping ingredients. Cook and stir over low heat until smooth. Transfer into a mixing bowl. Add the powdered sugar and vanilla. Beat until smooth. Spread over cooled bars and store in the refrigerator.

Makes 2 dozen   Norma Hochstetler (Busser)

CHOCOLATE CHIP BARS

2 eggs
1½ c. brown sugar
⅔ c. oil
1 t. vanilla
1½ t. baking powder

1 t. salt
½ c. nuts
1 c. chocolate chips
2 c. flour

Cream together eggs, sugar, and oil. Stir in vanilla. Mix together the remaining ingredients. Stir together both mixtures and pat into greased 11"x15" pan and bake at 350° for 25 minutes or until light brown. Variation: Instead of 2 cups of flour, use 1 cup of flour and 3 cups of oatmeal.

Makes 30 Bars   Mary Pinckert (Waitress)

CHOCOLATE CHIP MARSHMALLOW BARS

1 c. shortening
¾ c. white sugar
¾ c. brown sugar
2 eggs
1 t. vanilla
2¼ c. flour

1 t. baking soda
1 t. salt
2 c. chocolate chips
1 c. pecans
2 c. miniature marshmallows

In large bowl, combine shortening and sugars. Beat till creamy. Beat in eggs and vanilla. Gradually add flour, baking soda, and salt. Stir in chocolate chips, nuts, and marshmallows. Spread in greased cookie sheet. Bake 35 minutes at 350°.

Wilma Miller (Kitchen)

He causes the grass to grow for
   the cattle,
And vegetation for the service of man,
That he may bring forth food from
   the earth,
And wine that makes glad the heart
   of man,
Oil to make his face shine,
And bread which strengthens
   man's heart.

Ps. 104:14–15

CHOCOLATE CHIP SQUARES

¾ c. margarine
½ c. white sugar
½ c. brown sugar
4 egg yolks
½ t. vanilla
¼ t. salt
½ t. baking soda

½ t. baking powder
2 c. flour
12 oz. chocolate chips

Topping:
4 egg whites
1 c. brown sugar

Cream together margarine, sugars, egg yolks, and vanilla. Mix in dry ingredients. Spread evenly in jelly roll pan or large cookie sheet. Sprinkle chocolate chips over top. Prepare topping by beating egg whites stiff. Beat in 1 cup brown sugar and then spread topping over top of squares. Bake at 350° for 30 minutes.

Makes 12   Mary Lewallen (Bakery Sales)

CHOCOLATE SCOTCHEROOS

1 c. sugar
1 c. light corn syrup
1 c. peanut butter

6 c. Rice Krispies®
1 c. semi-sweet chocolate morsels
1 c. butterscotch chips

Cook sugar and light corn syrup in a 3-quart saucepan over moderate heat until mixture begins to boil. Remove from heat and stir in peanut butter and Rice Krispies®. Press into buttered pan. Let harden. Melt semi-sweet chocolate morsels and butterscotch chips. Stir to blend and spread over mixture.

Elizabeth Mae Knepp (Essenhaus Foods)
Linda Miller (Waitress)

COWBOY BARS

2 c. brown sugar
2 c. white sugar
2 c. margarine
4 eggs, beaten
2 t. vanilla
½ c. milk

4 c. flour
3 t. baking powder
1 t. salt
3 c. oatmeal
1½ c. coconut
2 c. chocolate chips

Combine above ingredients and mix well. Place in two jelly-roll pans. Spread evenly and press lightly. Bake at 350° for 20–30 minutes.

Mary Schrock (Bakery)

EASY CHOCOLATE CHIP BARS

1 c. sugar
1 c. brown sugar
2 eggs
½ c. oil
½ c. milk

3 c. flour
1 t. baking soda
½ t. salt
16 oz. pkg. chocolate chips

Cream together sugars, eggs, oil and milk. Blend thoroughly. Add dry ingredients. Pour batter into 15"x10" cookie sheet. Sprinkle chocolate chips on top. Bake at 350° for 20 minutes or until toothpick inserted comes out dry.

Loranna Hochstetler (Kitchen)

 Kindness is the language that the deaf can hear and the blind can see.

FROSTED BANANA BARS

½ c. butter
2 c. white sugar
3 eggs
1½ c. mashed ripe bananas
1 t. vanilla
2 c. flour
1 t. baking soda
pinch of salt

Frosting:
½ c. butter, softened
8-oz. pkg. cream cheese, softened
4 c. powdered sugar
2 t. vanilla

Cream butter and sugar and then beat in eggs, bananas, and vanilla. Combine flour, baking soda, and salt and then add to creamed mixture and mix well. Pour into a greased 15"x10"x1" baking pan. Bake at 350° for 25 minutes or until bars look done. Cool. For frosting, cream butter and cream cheese in a mixing bowl. Gradually add powdered sugar and vanilla and beat well. Spread over bars.

Makes 3 Dozen

Norma Lehman (Bakery)

FROSTED CHOCOLATE CHIP BARS

½ c. brown sugar
½ c. white sugar
4 egg yolks
½ c. margarine
1 t. vanilla
½ t. salt
1 t. baking soda

1 T. water
2 c. flour

Topping:
6 oz. chocolate chips
4 egg whites
1 c. brown sugar

Mix all cookie ingredients together and spread on cookie sheet. Mixture may be crumbly. Use a spatula and press down well. Sprinkle top with chocolate chips. Beat egg whites and add brown sugar. Spread on top of chocolate chips 1 tablespoon at a time. Bake at 300° for 30 minutes.

Becky Helmuth (Waitress)

Happiness is like honey: You can pass it around but some of it will stick to you.

FROSTED RAISIN CREMES

2 c. raisins
1 t. baking soda
1½ c. white sugar
2 large eggs, beaten
3½ c. flour
1 c. margarine, softened
2 t. cinnamon
⅛ t. salt
1 t. vanilla

Frosting:
2 c. powdered sugar
¼ c. margarine
½ t. vanilla
enough water for good
    spreading consistency

Place raisins in a saucepan, cover with water and bring to a boil. Remove from heat. Cool 20 minutes, then drain raisins, saving the water. To raisin liquid, add enough water to make 1 cup of liquid. Then add baking soda to this. Combine all ingredients at once. Stir well. Spread very thinly on a greased 12"x17" cookie sheet and then bake at 350° for 15–18 minutes or until done. Combine frosting ingredients and frost while still hot. Cool and then cut into squares.

Makes 2 Dozen   Donna Matthews (Village Shops)

FUDGE NUT BARS

First Part:
1 c. butter
2 c. brown sugar
2 eggs
2 t. vanilla
2½ c. flour
1 t. salt
3 c. oatmeal
1 t. baking soda

Second Part:
16 oz. chocolate chips
2 T. butter
1 can Eagle® brand milk
1 t. vanilla
½ t. salt
1 c. nuts

Combine first part ingredients and spread ¼" thick in bottom of cookie sheet, keep remaining crumbs for top. For the second part, melt chocolate chips and butter together. Add remaining ingredients and mix well. Pour on crust and put remaining crumbs on top. Bake at 350° for 25–30 minutes.

Treva Yoder (Millers' Housekeeper)

FUDGY TOFFEE BARS

1¾ c. all-purpose flour
¾ c. powdered sugar
¼ c. baking cocoa
¾ c. cold butter or margarine
14-oz. can sweetened condensed milk
1 t. vanilla extract

2 cups semi-sweet chocolate chips, divided
1 c. coarsely chopped walnuts
½ c. flaked coconut
½ c. English toffee bits or almond brickle chips

In a bowl combine flour, sugar, and cocoa. Cut in butter until mixture resembles coarse crumbs. Press firmly into a 13"x9"x2" baking pan. Bake at 350° for 10 minutes. Meanwhile in a saucepan, heat condensed milk, vanilla, and 1 cup of chocolate chips, stirring until smooth. Pour over the crust. Sprinkle with nuts, coconut, toffee bits and remaining chocolate chips; press down firmly. Bake for 18–20 minutes.

Makes 3 dozen

Lorene Miller (Busser)

The fruit of the righteous is a tree of life,
And he who wins souls is wise.

Prov. 11:30

When a refrigerator cookie recipe calls for nuts, chop them finely so that no large chunks tear the dough when it's sliced.

To freeze cookie dough, use freezer wrap or aluminum foil. Waxed paper or plastic wrap alone will not protect the dough from absorbing the odor of other foods or drying out.

To thaw frozen dough, loosen the wrapping and leave dough in the refrigerator for 1–2 hours before slicing.

GERMAN CHOCOLATE BROWNIES WITH CREAM CHEESE

1 box German chocolate cake mix
8-oz. pkg. cream cheese
1 egg
½ c. sugar
½ c. chocolate chips

Prepare cake mix as directed on box. Pour batter in 15½"x10½"x½" pan that has been greased and floured. Combine cream cheese with egg, sugar, and chocolate chips. Drop by spoonful on top of batter, cut through with knife for marble effect. Bake at 350° for 25–30 minutes.

Rosalie Bontrager (Manager of Country Inn)

GRANOLA BARS

2 sticks butter
¼ c. oil
½ c. honey
2 pkg. marshmallows
2 c. chocolate chips
1 c. M&M's® candies
2 pkgs. crushed graham crackers
4½ c. oatmeal
5 c. Rice Krispies® cereal
2 c. coconut
1 c. peanuts, crushed

Mix first 4 ingredients. Heat until marshmallows are just melted. Do not boil. Pour over rest of ingredients and mix well.

Fills 2 18" cookie sheets   Doretta Wingard (Waitress)

MARSHMALLOW BROWNIE DELIGHT

1 c. butter
2 c. sugar
1 t. vanilla
2 eggs, beaten
½ c. cocoa
2 c. flour
¼ t. baking powder
1 c. walnuts, chopped, divided
12 large marshmallows

Frosting:
½ c. brown sugar
2 squares unsweetened chocolate
¼ c. water
3 T. butter
1½ c. powdered sugar

Cream butter and sugar together, add vanilla and eggs. Combine cocoa, flour, and baking powder and add to butter mixture. Beat until smooth and add ¾ c. nuts. Pour into 9"x9"x2" pan and bake 25 minutes at 350°. Then put the marshmallows on top and return to oven for 3 minutes to melt them. Take out and spread marshmallows over the brownies. For the frosting, boil brown sugar, chocolate and water for 3 minutes. Add butter and cool. Then add powdered sugar and beat. If necessary thin with milk. Frost the brownies and put ¼ cup of nuts on top.

Sylvia Smith (Bakery Sales)

MOUND BARS

2 c. graham cracker
    crumbs
½ c. margarine, melted
½ c. sugar
1 pkg. coconut

1 can Eagle® brand sweetened
    condensed milk
12-oz. pkg. chocolate chips,
    melted
2 T. peanut butter

Mix graham cracker crumbs, melted margarine and sugar and spread in 9"x13" pan. Bake at 350° for 10 minutes. Mix coconut and condensed milk and spread over first layer. Bake at 350° for 15 minutes. Spread melted chocolate chips and peanut butter on top while both are still hot. Cut into very small bars.

Sue Miller (Owner)

The recompence of a man's hands
shall be rendered unto him.
Prov. 12:14

Worry is like a rocking chair. It will give you something to do, but it won't get you anywhere.

PEANUT BUTTER CHOCOLATE CHIP GRANOLA BARS

½ c. light corn syrup
⅓-⅔ c. peanut butter
3 c. granola
1 c. Rice Krispies® cereal
1 c. chocolate chips

Heat corn syrup and boil for one minute. Add peanut butter, granola, and then Rice Krispies®. Press into a 9"x13" pan or for a thicker bar a 9"x9"x2" pan. Cool for 10–15 minutes and then press chocolate chips on top.

Makes 32 bars   Mary Pinckert (Waitress)

PUMPKIN PIE SQUARES

1 c. sifted flour
½ c. quick cooking rolled oats
½ c. brown sugar, firmly packed
½ c. butter or margarine
1 lb. can pumpkin
13.5-oz. can evaporated milk
2 eggs
¾ c. sugar
½ t. salt
1 t. ground cinnamon
½ t. ground ginger
¼ t. ground cloves
½ c. pecans, chopped
½ c. brown sugar, firmly packed
2 T. butter or margarine

Combine flour, oats, ½ c. brown sugar, and butter. Mix until crumbly. Press into ungreased 13"x9"x2" pan. Bake for 15 minutes at 350°. Combine pumpkin, evaporated milk, eggs, sugar, salt, cinnamon, ginger, and cloves in bowl and blend well. Pour into crust. Bake for 20 minutes at 350°. Combine pecans, ½ c. brown sugar, and 2 tablespoons of butter. Sprinkle over pumpkin filling. Return to oven and bake 15–20 minutes or until filling is set. Cool in pan on rack and cut in 2" squares.

Makes 2 Dozen   Joyce Miller (Sunshine Farm Manager)

RHUBARB CUSTARD BARS

Crust:
2 c. flour
¼ c. sugar
1 c. cold butter

Top Layer:
6 oz. cream cheese, softened
½ c. sugar
¼ t. vanilla
1 c. whipped cream

Rhubarb Middle:
2 c. sugar
7 T. flour
1 c. cream
3 eggs, beaten
5 c. rhubarb, finely chopped

For crust, combine flour and sugar, and cut in the cold butter. Crumble and put in a 9"x13" pan. Bake at 350° for 10 minutes. Mix together ingredients for the rhubarb middle. Pour over crust and bake 40–45 minutes or until done. Cool. Combine ingredients for top layer, spread on top.

Esther Cross (Accounting)

RICE KRISPIES® CEREAL BARS

¼ c. butter
10 oz. bag marshmallows
6 c. Rice Krispies® cereal

Melt butter in large saucepan over low heat. Add marshmallows and stir constantly until completely melted. Remove from heat. Add Rice Krispies® cereal and stir until well coated. Using buttered spatula or waxed paper, press mixture softly and evenly into buttered 13"x9" pan. Cut into squares when cool.

Makes 2 dozen 2"x2" squares   Norma Lehman (Bakery)

When a man's ways please the LORD,
He makes even his enemies to be
    at peace with him.
Prov. 16:7

RICE KRISPIES® TREATS

¼ c. butter
⅓ c. crunchy peanut butter
8 oz. butterscotch chips

16 oz. marshmallows
6 c. Rice Krispies® cereal
6 oz. chocolate chips

Place marshmallows, butter, and peanut butter in a large microwave-able bowl and microwave on high for 2–2½ minutes or until marshmallows are full and fluffy. Stir mixture until smooth. Stir in Rice Krispies® two cups at a time. Place in a greased 9"x13" pan, smooth and flatten and then set to the side. Mix and microwave chips on high for 30-second intervals until smooth. Spread on treats until evenly covered. Cover and place somewhere cool or cold to let the topping harden. Cut and serve.

Tim Brubaker (Village Shops)

STRAWBERRY BARS

1 box strawberry cake mix,
   or any flavor
2 eggs
⅓ c. oil

8-oz. pkg. cream cheese, softened
1 t. strawberry Nesquik®
⅓ c. sugar

Mix cake mix, one egg, and oil together. Keep out one cup of this mixture and put the rest in 9"x13" cake pan. Bake 15 minutes at 350°. Then mix together cream cheese, strawberry Nestle's Quik®, one egg, and sugar. Put on top of cake, then the reserved cup of cake mixture and bake another 15 minutes. Optional: Use a lemon cake mix and 1 teaspoon of lemon juice instead of strawberry Nestle's Quik®.

Sharon Schlabach (Waitress)

SUGAR CREAM PIE SQUARES

1 box yellow cake mix
1 stick margarine
3 eggs

8-oz. pkg. cream cheese, softened
1 t. vanilla
1 lb. powdered sugar

Mix together cake mix, margarine, and one egg. Pat into a 9"x13" greased pan and set aside. Beat remaining eggs and cream cheese until well-mixed, add vanilla and powdered sugar. Pour this mixture over the first layer and sprinkle with nutmeg. Bake for 30–35 minutes at 350°.

Katie Hochstedler (Bakery)

YUMMY BARS

1 box Club® crackers
¾ c. brown sugar
½ c. white sugar
½ c. milk

½ c. margarine
1 c. graham crackers, crushed
1 c. chocolate chips
⅔ c. peanut butter

In a 9"x13" buttered pan, put a layer of Club® crackers. Boil the following ingredients, brown sugar, white sugar, milk, margarine, and graham crackers, stirring constantly for 5 minutes. Pour over Club® crackers. Melt chocolate chips and peanut butter and then pour over crackers. Cut in squares.

                                          Millie Whetstone (Bakery)

Let all bitterness, wrath, anger, clamor, and evil speaking be put away from you, with all malice. And be kind to one another, tender-hearted, forgiving one another, just as God in Christ also forgave you.

                                          Eph. 4:31–32

BLACK BOTTOM CUPCAKES

8 oz. cream cheese
1 egg
⅓ c. sugar
⅛ t. salt
1 c. chocolate chips
2¼ c. flour
1½ c. sugar

6 T. cocoa
1½ t. baking soda
¾ t. salt
1½ c. water
⅓ c. + scant 3 T. vegetable oil
1½ T. vinegar
1½ t. vanilla

Beat cream cheese, egg, sugar, and salt until well beaten. Add chocolate chips just before putting into pans. In separate bowl, sift together dry ingredients. Add water, oil, vinegar, and vanilla. Fill cupcake papers half full of chocolate batter. Add one tablespoon of cream cheese mixture, with chocolate chips in it, to center of cupcake. Bake at 350° for 20–25 minutes.

Makes 2 dozen   Charlotte Miller (Waitress)
                                          Marilyn Nisley (Bakery)

 For a fluffier omelet, add a pinch of cornstarch before beating.

ORANGE CREAM CUPCAKES

¾ c. shortening
1¼ c. sugar
3 egg yolks, beaten
3 c. flour
¼ t. salt

4 t. baking powder
½ c. orange juice
½ c. water
1 t. vanilla flavoring
2 egg whites, beaten

Cream together the shortening and the sugar. Add the beaten egg yolks and mix well. Add the flour, salt, and the baking powder (which has been sifted together) alternately with the orange juice, water, and vanilla. Then fold in the egg whites. Bake in greased cupcake pans at 350° for 30 minutes.

Makes 3 dozen   Sylvia Smith (Bakery Sales)

SNICKERDOODLE CUPCAKES

½ c. butter
1 c. sugar
2 eggs
1 t. vanilla
2 c. sifted cake flour
2½ t. baking powder
½ t. salt
½ c. milk

Topping:
3 T. sugar
1½ t. cinnamon
¼ c. chopped walnuts

Cream butter and sugar until light and fluffy. Add eggs and vanilla and beat well. Sift flour with baking powder and salt. Add to creamed mixture in thirds, alternately with milk beating until smooth after each addition. Set paper baking cups in medium muffin pans and spoon batter into pan filling about half full. Mix topping and add. Bake at 375° for 20 minutes.

Makes 1 dozen   Geniese Trotter (Bakery Sales)

MOM'S PUMPKIN COOKIES

3 c. sugar
1 c. vegetable oil
2 eggs
1 t. vanilla
1 large can unseasoned pumpkin pie filling
5 c. flour

1 t. salt
2 t. baking powder
2 t. baking soda
2 t. cinnamon
2 t. nutmeg
12 oz. chocolate chips
1 c. chopped walnuts

Combine sugar, vegetable oil, eggs, and vanilla. Sift dry ingredients together. Add pumpkin and dry ingredients alternately to liquid mixture. Mix well with spoon; add chocolate chips and nuts. Drop by teaspoon on greased cookie sheet. Bake at 350° for 10 minutes.

Makes 6 dozen   Diane Butler (Bakery Sales)

My mother never let me do much in the kitchen. As a result, my cooking ability was practically nonexistent when I got married. But I did remember Mother mentioning to her friends that she'd make cakes and pies "from scratch." So on my first trip to the supermarket, I asked a clerk if they had any "scratch." He looked at me rather oddly and said, "You'll have to go to the store at the corner of Colfax and Wadsworth."

That turned out to be a feed store. So I went in and said, "I'd like to buy some scratch." The clerk asked how much I wanted. I suggested a pound or two. "How many chickens do you have?" he asked. "It only comes in 20-lb. bags."

I bought 20 pounds and hurried home. When I opened the bag, I doubted that a beautiful cake could ever come from such rough-looking ingredients.

                           Diane Butler (Bakery Sales)

Pies & Candies

HINTS FOR PIES

A piecrust will be easier to make if all ingredients are cool.

Add a minimum amount of liquid to the pastry, or it will become tough.

Piecrust will not be hard or tough when milk is used in place of the water.

When making piecrust, add a little baking powder to keep the crust light and tender.

To prevent soggy piecrusts, brush the bottom crust with egg white before pouring in fruit filling, or sprinkle with a light coating of flour and sugar.

For a shiny piecrust, brush the top of the pie with a mixture of 1 egg, 1 teaspoon sugar, ¼ teaspoon salt, and 1 teaspoon cooking oil. Bake as usual.

Put a layer of marshmallows in the bottom of a pumpkin pie, then add filling. You will have a nice topping as they come to the surface.

Vanilla adds flavor to fruit pies.

The meringue on pies will be higher if you add a pinch of cream of tartar to the beaten whites.

In making custard-type pies, bake at a high temperature for about ten minutes to prevent a soggy crust. Then finish baking at a low temperature.

APPLE CRUMB PIE

¼ c. sugar
1 T. flour
½ t. cinnamon
dash of salt
6 medium apples, peeled and sliced

Crumb Topping:
¼ c. butter, softened
¾ c. brown sugar
½ c. flour

Preheat oven to 425°. Mix first four ingredients with apples. Press into piecrust. Combine the crumb topping ingredients and sprinkle on top of pie. Bake for 35–40 minutes.

Makes 1 pie   Tiffany Detweiler (Waitress)

BEST-EVER PEANUT BUTTER PIE

9-oz. pie shell, baked
½ c. powdered sugar
½ c. peanut butter
6-oz. box instant vanilla pudding
8-oz. pkg. cream cheese, softened
Cool Whip® (as desired)

Make crumbs using powdered sugar and ¼ c. peanut butter, mixing together until crumbly. Put ¾ of crumbs in pie shell. Make pudding according to box. Add beaten cream cheese and remaining ¼ c. peanut butter. Stir together and put on top of crumbs in pie shell. Top with Cool Whip® and the rest of crumbs.

Makes 1 pie   Mary Stalter (Waitstaff)

Just about the time you think you can make ends meet, somebody moves the ends.

BLACK BOTTOM PIE

½ c. sugar
1 T. cornstarch
2 c. milk, scalded
4 egg yolks, beaten
6 oz. pkg. chocolate chips
1 t. vanilla
9" pie shell, baked
1 envelope unflavored gelatin
¼ c. cold water
4 egg whites
½ c. sugar
optional: sweetened whipped cream, chocolate decorettes

Combine sugar and cornstarch. Slowly add scalded milk to beaten egg yolks. Stir in sugar mixture. Cook until mixture coats a spoon, (160°). To 1 cup of custard, add the chocolate chips. Stir until melted. Add vanilla. Pour in bottom of cooled baked pie shell. Chill. Soften gelatin in cold water and add to remaining hot custard. Stir until dissolved. Chill until slightly thick. Beat egg whites, adding sugar gradually, until mixture stands in stiff peaks. Fold in custard-gelatin mixture. Pour over chocolate layer and chill until set. Garnish with whipped cream and chocolate decorettes.

Makes 1 pie   Becky Parcell (Host/Cashier)

Kindly words and friendly smiles
smooth rough places and shorten miles.

BUTTERSCOTCH PIE

1 c. brown sugar, packed
2 c. milk
⅓ c. flour
½ t. salt
3 egg yolks
½ t. vanilla
2 T. butter
1 pie shell, baked

Cook sugar, milk, flour, salt, and egg yolks until thick and then add vanilla and butter. Cool. Then pour into baked pie shell. Top with a layer of whipped cream.

Makes 1 pie   Marlene Lehman (Busser)

CARAMEL CHIFFON PIE

28 caramels
1¼ c. water
1 envelope unflavored gelatin
½ t. vanilla

1 c. heavy cream, whipped
¾ c. pecans, chopped
9" baked pastry shell

Melt caramels with 1 cup water in double boiler or saucepan over low heat. Stir occasionally until sauce is smooth. Soften gelatin in ¼ c. water. Dissolve in hot caramel sauce. Add vanilla. Chill until slightly thickened. Fold in whipped cream and ½ c. nuts. Pour into pastry shell, sprinkle with remaining nuts. Chill until firm and then garnish with additional whipped cream if desired.

Makes 1 pie   Mary Miller (Waitress)

You visit the earth and water it,
You greatly enrich it;
The river of God is full of water;
You provide their grain,
For so You have prepared it.
                                        Ps. 65:9

CHERRY PIE

9" pie shell, unbaked
2–3 c. canned cherries, undrained
½ c. sugar
¼ t. salt
few drops red food coloring

½ c. water
3 T. clear gelatin
½ t. almond flavoring
1 T. margarine

Combine cherries, sugar, salt, and food coloring in saucepan. Heat until boiling. Add water and clear gelatin and cook until thickened, stirring constantly. Remove from heat. Stir in almond flavoring and margarine. Make a lattice topping from pastry strips. Bake at 350° for 25 minutes or until browned.

Makes 1 pie   Anita Yoder (Daughter of Bob & Sue)

CHOCOLATE CREAM CHEESE PIE

6 oz. milk chocolate chips
8-oz. pkg. cream cheese
¾ c. brown sugar, separated
½ t. salt

1 t. vanilla
2 eggs, separated
16-oz. container Cool Whip®
2 baked pie shells

Melt chocolate chips over hot (not boiling) water. Cool 10 minutes. Blend cream cheese, ½ c. brown sugar, salt, vanilla, and beaten egg yolks. Mix with the melted chocolate. Beat egg whites until stiff, not dry. Slowly beat in ¼ c. brown sugar. Beat until stiff; then add to chocolate mixture; fold in Cool Whip®. Pour into baked pie shells. Top with small chocolate chips or shaved chocolate.

Mary M. Miller (Bakery Production)
Lena Bontrager (Bakery Sales)

COCONUT CUSTARD PIE

1½ c. milk
1 c. heavy cream
1 c. coconut
4 large eggs
¾ c. sugar

1½ t. vanilla
½ t. coconut extract
¼ t. salt
¼ t. nutmeg
9″ pie shell

Place oven rack in lowest position and preheat oven to 350°. In bowl, whisk all ingredients together and pour into unbaked pie shell. Bake 50–60 minutes or until crust is golden and the filling is slightly puffed and just set. Cool.

Serves 6   Ellen Mishler (Administration)

COCONUT PIE

½ c. butter, softened
1 c. sugar
3 T. flour
3 egg yolks

1 c. milk
½ t. vanilla
1 c. coconut
8″ pie shell

Combine butter, sugar, flour, and egg yolks. Add the rest of the ingredients. Pour into pie shell and bake at 375° for 25–30 minutes. Do not overbeat or overbake this pie.

Makes 1 pie   Mary Miller (Waitress)

CONCORD GRAPE PIE

1½ qt. grapes
1½ c. sugar
3 T. quick cooking tapioca

1 t. butter
⅛ t. salt
½ c. pecans, chopped

Slip grape skins from pulp, reserving the skins. Place pulp in saucepan and bring to simmering stage. Remove from heat. Put through sieve to remove the seeds. Add enough of pulp to the skins to make 3½ cups after setting. Combine sugar, tapioca, butter, salt, and pecans and mix well. Add to grape mixture, stirring thoroughly. Pour into pastry lined pie pan. Cover with top pastry shell. Bake at 425° for 15 minutes, reduce heat to 400° and bake for another 30 minutes or until brown.

Makes 1 pie Lena Miller (Meat Room)

CORN FLAKES® CRUMB CRUST

1⅓ c. Corn Flake® crumbs,
 (3 c. Corn Flakes®)

2 T. sugar
¼ c. margarine, melted

Mix together and press into a 9" pie pan. May use as is or bake at 375° for 5–7 minutes. Will hold up better and taste crispy when baked.

Makes 1 piecrust Anita Yoder (Daughter of Bob & Sue)

CREAM CHEESE PECAN PIE

1 unbaked piecrust

1st layer
8 oz. cream cheese, softened
1 egg, beaten
½ c. sugar
½ t. salt
1 t. vanilla

2nd layer
3 eggs, beaten
½ c. brown sugar
1 t. vanilla
¾ t. salt
1 c. corn syrup
1¼ c. pecans, or any nuts

Mix together 1st layer ingredients. Put into unbaked piecrust. Combine 2nd layer ingredients, and then pour over 1st layer in crust. Bake at 400° for 15 minutes then 325° until done.

Fannie Yutzy (Bakery)

Pecan pie was invented in the early 1930s by the wife of a Karo® syrup salesman. In some areas, pecan pie is still called Karo® pie.

CAROL'S BEST PECAN PIE

3 eggs
½ c. sugar
pinch of salt
1 c. Karo® Light Syrup
⅓ c. butter, melted
1 t. vanilla
1 c. pecans, chopped
1 pie shell, unbaked

Cream eggs and sugar together. Add all other ingredients, except pecans, and beat well. Pour mixture into pie shell. Sprinkle pecans on top of mixture in pie shell. Bake at 350° for 50 minutes or until done.

Makes 1 pie   Carol Detweiler (Management)

CREAM PEAR PIE

2–2½ c. pears
2 T. flour
1 c. sugar
½ t. nutmeg
pinch of salt
1½ c. milk and cream, combined

Peel pears, dice or slice and put in unbaked pie shell. Mix the rest of ingredients together and pour over pears. Bake at 400° for 15 minutes and reduce heat to 375° and bake another 30 minutes or until done.

Makes 1 pie   Lena Miller (Meat Room)

PEAR PIE

2 rounded T. flour
½ c. sugar
1 can Carnation® milk
4 large pears, thinly sliced
unbaked pie shell
sugar and cinnamon

Mix pears with other ingredients and pour into unbaked pie shell. Sprinkle sugar and cinnamon on top of pie. Bake at 400° for 10 minutes at 350° until done.

Esther Cross (Accounting)

CREAMY PINEAPPLE PIE

8 oz. cream cheese, softened
1 c. sugar, divided
½ t. salt
2 eggs
1 pie shell

½ c. milk
½ t. vanilla
1 T. cornstarch
15-oz. can pineapple, crushed
¼ c. pecans, chopped

Beat cream cheese, ½ cup sugar, and salt until smooth. Add eggs one at a time, beating well. Blend in milk and vanilla, set aside. In small saucepan, combine cornstarch and remaining sugar. Stir in pineapple. Bring to a boil, stir constantly for 2 minutes and pour into pastry shell. Spoon cream cheese mixture on top and sprinkle with pecans. Bake at 400° for 10 minutes, then reduce to 325° and bake until set. Check after 10 minutes.

Sharon Frye (Waitress)

FRENCH PEACH PIE

1½ c. flour
1½ T. sugar
1 t. salt
2 T. cold milk
½ c. oil

1 c. sugar
4 T. margarine, softened
¾ c. flour
fresh peaches, sliced

Sift flour, sugar, and salt together in a pie pan and pour on milk and oil. Mix and press on sides and bottom of pan. Cut together sugar, margarine, and flour and spread half of this mixture in bottom of pan. Then fill with fresh peaches and sprinkle remainder of sugar mixture on top. Sprinkle with cinnamon and then bake at 350° for 1 hour.

Makes 1 pie   Robyn Pippenger (Hostess/Cashier)

Give us day by day our daily bread.
And forgive us our sins,
For we also forgive everyone who is indebted to us.

Luke 11:3–4

PEACH CRUMB PIE

2 eggs
4 T. flour
2 c. sugar
4 c. peaches, sliced
1 pie shell, unbaked

Crumbs
¾ c. flour
¾ c. oatmeal
⅔ c. brown sugar
½ t. baking soda
dash of salt
1 t. cinnamon
½ c. butter, softened

Beat eggs and then add flour, sugar, and peaches. Pour in unbaked pie shell and cover with crumbs. Bake at 425° for 15 minutes and then 350° for 30 minutes.

Makes 1 pie

Susie Kauffman (Waitress)

GRANDMA'S ICE CREAM PIE

½ stick margarine
8 large marshmallows
¾ bar German chocolate

2 c. Cocoa Krispies® cereal
1 qt. peppermint ice cream,
    softened

Melt together margarine, marshmallows, and German chocolate. Pour this mixture over the Cocoa Krispies®. Press mixture into greased pan, reserve some to sprinkle on top of ice cream. Spread softened ice cream in pan. Sprinkle remaining chocolate mixture on top and then put in freezer.

Makes 1 pie

Mary Oltz (Village Shops)

HERSHEY® BAR PIE

7-oz. Hershey® candy bar
18 large marshmallows
½ c. milk

8 oz. Cool Whip®
8″ or 9″ baked piecrust

In medium saucepan, break Hershey® bar into smaller pieces. Add marshmallows and milk and melt on low heat. Then put in refrigerator to cool for approx. 1 hr. Then add Cool Whip® and mix well. Pour into piecrust and leave in refrigerator overnight or until desired firmness.

Makes 1 pie

Brandie Leonard (Village Shops)

KEY LIME PIE

Crust:
1 pkg. graham crackers
¾ stick of butter
2 T. powdered sugar

Filling:
1 c. real cream
1 can sweetened condensed milk
¼ c. key lime juice
3–4 drops green food coloring

Crush graham crackers then set aside. Melt butter and add cracker crumbs and powdered sugar. Press into pie pan. Whip cream until thick and holds peaks; set aside. Mix condensed milk, lime juice, and coloring, then add whipped cream. Mix well and pour into the cracker pie shell and freeze. Eat frozen. Can be topped with whipped topping.

Makes 1 pie   Judith Kauffman (Kitchen)

 ## KRISPY ICE CREAM PIE

½ c. corn syrup
½ c. peanut butter

3 c. Rice Krispies® cereal
1 qt. vanilla ice cream, softened

Mix corn syrup and peanut butter together. Stir in Rice Krispies® cereal until well coated. Press evenly into a 9" pie pan. Chill in freezer for 5–10 minutes. Spread softened ice cream into crust and then freeze until firm. Remove from freezer 15 minutes before serving. Top with fruit, chocolate chips, chopped peanuts, or chocolate syrup.

Randi Yoder (Administration)

LEMON CAKE PIE

1 c. sugar
3 T. flour
3 T. butter, softened
pinch of salt

2 eggs, reserve whites
1 medium lemon
1½ c. milk
8" pie shell

Mix together sugar, flour, butter, salt, and egg yolks. Beat until it looks creamy, then add the juice and grated rind of lemon. Blend in milk. Beat egg whites until stiff; blend into batter mixture. Pour in unbaked 8" pie shell. Bake at 350° for 40 minutes or until set.

Makes 1 pie   Martha Hochstedler (Bakery)

LEMON PIE

9" pie shell, baked
1¼ c. sugar
6 T. cornstarch
2 c. water
⅔ c. lemon juice
3 egg yolks
1½ t. lemon extract
2 t. vinegar
3 T. butter

Never-Fail Meringue:
1 T. cornstarch
2 T. cold water
½ c. boiling water
3 egg whites
6 T. sugar
1 t. vanilla
pinch of salt

Mix sugar and cornstarch together in the top of a double boiler. Add the two cups of water. Combine egg yolks with lemon juice and beat until well mixed. Add to the rest of the sugar mixture. Cook over boiling water until thick for about 25 minutes. This does away with the starchy taste. Now add the lemon extract, butter, and vinegar and stir thoroughly. Pour mixture into deep 9-inch pie shell and let cool. For meringue, blend cornstarch and cold water in a saucepan. Add boiling water and cook, stirring until clear and thickened. Let stand until completely cold. With beater at high speed, beat egg whites until foamy. Gradually add sugar and beat until stiff but not dry. Turn mixer to low speed and add salt and vanilla. Gradually beat in cold cornstarch mixture. Beat well on high speed. Spread meringue over cooled pie filing and bake at 350° for 10 minutes or until top is browned.

Makes 1 pie   Mary A. Bontrager (Waitress)

A little boy had been locked in his room for misbehaving. Mischievous as he was, he picked the lock and ran into the hallway shouting, "I'm free! I'm free!"

His brother heard it and said, "That's nothing. I'm four."

 Be patient with the faults of others; they have to be patient with yours.

LEMON PIE

1 c. sugar
1 T. butter or margarine
1¼ c. cold water
¼ c. cornstarch
3 T. cornstarch
3 egg yolks
2 T. milk
lemon juice and peel

Topping:
3 egg whites
6 T. sugar
6 t. lemon juice

Combine water, sugar, and butter. Heat until sugar is dissolved. Add cornstarch and blend with cold water. Cook slowly until clear, about 8 minutes. Add lemon juice and peel, and cook 2 minutes. Slowly add egg yolks beaten with milk. Boil and pour in 8" baked crust. To make meringue topping, beat egg whites, sugar, and lemon juice until stiff. Spread on top and bake until lightly browned. Optional: Put whipped cream on top instead of meringue.

Millie Whetstone (Bakery)

SHAKER LEMON PIE

2 large lemons
4 eggs

2 c. sugar

Slice lemons paper thin. Combine with sugar and let stand for 2 hours or preferably overnight. Blend with eggs. Put into 9" unbaked pie shell. Cover with top shell. Cut slits into top shell. Bake at 450° for 15 minutes, reduce to 375° and bake for another 20 minutes.

Makes 1 pie

Lena Miller (Meat Room)

OLD-FASHIONED LEMON PIE

Lemon Filling:
4 c. water
2 c. sugar
3 eggs, beaten
3 T. flour
grated rind and juice of 2 lemons

Sweet Dough:
1 c. sugar
½ c. lard or shortening
1 t. baking soda
½ t. cream of tartar
¼ c. milk
1½ c. flour

For the lemon filling, heat 3 cups of water to boiling. Mix remaining cup of water with sugar, eggs, flour, lemon rind and juice, and add to boiling water, stirring constantly until it reaches the boiling point again. Let cool, then divide among 4 pastry shells. For the sweet dough, mix all ingredients for sweet dough and drop by teaspoonfuls on top of lemon filling. Bake at 350° for 45–60 minutes.

Makes 4 pies   Jim Fisher (Essenhaus Foods Manager)

MIMI'S DOWN HOME CREAM PIE

1 c. sugar
⅓ c. sifted flour
1 t. real butter, soft

½ pint heavy whipping cream
1 pie shell, unbaked
cinnamon

Put in saucepan and heat everything together except cinnamon. Heat until butter is melted. Pour in an unbaked pie shell and then sprinkle on top with cinnamon. Pour all ingredients in gradually. If pie starts to boil over, shake pie pan until it falls back. Bake at 300° for one hour.

Makes 1 pie   Debbie Riley (Waitress)

OLD-FASHIONED CREAM PIE

1 c. white sugar
¾ c. brown sugar
½ c. flour

pinch of salt
1½ c. boiling water
2 c. heavy cream or half and half

Mix dry ingredients together and then add boiling water, then cream. Pour into 9" unbaked pie shell and bake at 350° for 45 minutes or until set.

Martha Hochstedler (Bakery)

MAKE-ITS-OWN-CRUST COCONUT PIE

4 eggs
½ c. flour
2 c. milk
1 t. vanilla

1¾ c. sugar
¼ c. butter, melted
1½ c. coconut
pinch of salt

Combine ingredients in order given. Mix well. Pour into 10" greased pie pan. Bake at 350° for 45 minutes or until golden brown. If baked too long it will be more like a cake. If properly done it will have a delicate crust over top, sides, and bottom. It will be solid enough to cut after it is cooled. The center will be a perfect cream pie.

Mary Schrock (Bakery)

PINEAPPLE PIE

3 eggs
1½ c. white sugar
6 T. bread flour

1½ c. crushed pineapple
½ c. butter, melted

Mix eggs, sugar, and flour together with a fork. Add pineapple and butter; mix together. Pour into 9" unbaked pie shell. Bake 40 minutes at 350° until firm.

Makes 1 pie

Esther Nisley (Bakery)

PUMPKIN CHIFFON PIE

4 oz. cream cheese, softened
1 T. sugar
4-oz. carton frozen whipped topping, thawed
8" graham cracker crust
1 c. milk, cold

2 3.4–oz. boxes instant vanilla pudding
1 c. canned pumpkin
1 t. ground cinnamon
½ t. ground ginger
¼ t. ground cloves

In mixing bowl, beat cream cheese and sugar and then add whipped topping and mix well. Spread into crust. In another bowl, beat milk and pudding mixes on low speed until combined. Beat on high for 2 more minutes. Let stand 3 minutes. Stir in pumpkin and spices and mix well. Spread over cream cheese layer and chill. Garnish with nuts and whipped topping. Can be frozen. Note: Light cream cheese, one box sugar free pudding, and fat-free whipped topping can be used. Makes less sugar and fat.

Clara Mae Miller (Bakery)

PUMPKIN CUSTARD PIE

1½ c. pumpkin
1½ c. sugar
2 T. flour
1 t. vanilla
2 t. pumpkin pie spice

½ t. salt
4 eggs, separated
2 c. milk
2 c. half-and-half
2 9" piecrusts

Preheat oven to 400°. In a large bowl mix first 6 ingredients and egg yolks. Add milk and half and half. Beat egg whites until stiff and fold into pumpkin mixture. Fill both 9" piecrusts and bake for 10 minutes. Reduce heat to 350° until center is set, approximately 30–40 minutes. This pie is best the next day.

Suvilla Gingerich (Waitress)

PUMPKIN PIE

9" piecrust, unbaked
1 c. canned pumpkin
1 egg yolk
⅔ c. sugar
⅛ t. salt
½ t. ground cinnamon

¼ t. ground cloves
1 T. cornstarch
1 t. vanilla
1½ c. milk
1 egg white, stiffly beaten
nutmeg

Combine pumpkin, egg yolk, sugar, salt, cinnamon, cloves, cornstarch, vanilla, and milk together. Mix thoroughly. Fold in egg white. Pour into crust and sprinkle with nutmeg. Bake at 350° for 45 minutes or until center is set.

Makes 1 pie   Anita Yoder (Daughter of Bob & Sue)

RHUBARB CRUMB PIE

1 egg
1 c. sugar
1 t. vanilla
2 c. diced rhubarb
2 T. flour

1 pie shell, unbaked
¾ c. flour
½ c. brown sugar
⅓ c. butter

Mix first 5 ingredients and pour into unbaked pie shell. Combine flour, brown sugar, and butter. Sprinkle on top of pie. Bake at 400° for 10 minutes. Reduce heat to 350° and bake for 30 minutes. Serve warm with ice cream.

Makes 1 pie   Suvilla Gingerich (Waitress)

RHUBARB CRUMB PIE

1½ c. sugar
2 heaping T. flour
1 c. sour cream
1 egg, beaten
¼ t. salt
1 t. vanilla

2 c. rhubarb
unbaked pie shell

Crumbs:
¾ c. flour
½ c. white sugar
⅓ c. butter

Mix first seven ingredients. Put in unbaked pie shell. Mix crumb ingredients together and put on top of pie. Bake at 425° for 10 minutes and then reduce to 375° and bake until done.

Effie Mast (Essenhaus Foods)

"When you give a dinner or a supper, do not ask your friends, your brothers, your relatives, nor your rich neighbors, lest they invite you back, and you be repaid. But when you give a feast, invite the poor, the maimed, the lame, the blind. And you will be blessed, because they cannot repay you; for you shall be repaid at the resurrection of the just."
Luke 14:12–14

RHUBARB PIE

4½ c. rhubarb
2½ c. sugar
5 T. flour

¼ t. salt
3 eggs
1½ T. lemon

Chop rhubarb into desired size. Combine sugar, flour, salt, egg yolks, and lemon juice. Add to rhubarb. Beat egg whites and fold into rhubarb mixture. Bake at 400° for 10 minutes. Reduce temperature to 325° and bake 45 minutes longer.

Makes 1 pie

Ann Mast (Grounds Maintenance)

 One lie brings the next one with it.

STRAWBERRY GLAZED PIE

1 c. sugar
pinch of salt
3 T. clear gelatin, 1 level and 2 heaping
1 c. cold water
1 T. lemon juice
1 T. Karo® syrup
½ box of 13 oz. strawberry gelatin
1 qt. strawberries or less
9" piecrust, baked

Whipped Cream Topping:
1 pint whipping cream
1½ T. sugar
1 t. vanilla

Mix sugar, salt, and clear gelatin together. Add water, lemon juice, and Karo® and bring to a boil. Cook until thick, stirring constantly. Turn burner off and add strawberry gelatin mix. Cool. Add strawberries, leaving some for the top of the pie. Pour into a 9" piecrust. Make sure strawberry gelatin mix is cool before putting strawberries in. This helps the pie crust stay firmer. You can use fewer strawberries so it doesn't make the pie so thick. Put the pie in refrigerator to firm or set up before putting topping on.

Before whipping the cream, put bowl, beaters, spoon, and cream in the freezer for a little bit. The colder the bowl and beaters are, the better it whips to a peak. Beat until peaks form and then put on top of the pie. Cut a few strawberries in half and put on top of whipped cream for color.

Sharon Schlabach (Waitress)

STRAWBERRY PIE

1 c. water
1 c. sugar
3 T. cornstarch
3 T. strawberry Jell-O®
1 qt. strawberries
9" piecrust, baked

Boil water, sugar, and cornstarch. When mixture thickens, remove from heat and add strawberry Jell-O®. When cooled add strawberries. Pour into baked pie shell. Top with whipped cream.

Makes 1 pie

Ann Mast (Grounds Maintenance)

STRAWBERRY RHUBARB JELLO® PIE

3 c. rhubarb, cut up
1 c. sugar
4 T. flour
3-oz. pkg. strawberry Jell-O®
9" unbaked pie shell

Mix together. Let stand 20 minutes. Pour into pie shell. Bake 1 hour at 350°. Cool. Top with whipped cream.

Makes 1 pie   Mary Miller (Waitress)

SWEET POTATO PIE

1 lb. (1⅓ c.) sweet potatoes, cooked and mashed
¼ c. butter
14-oz. can sweetened condensed milk
1 egg, beaten
1 t. cinnamon
1 t. grated orange peel
1 t. vanilla
½ t. nutmeg
¼ t. salt
1 graham cracker crust

Topping:
1 egg
2 T. dark corn syrup
2 T. brown sugar
1 T. butter, melted
½ t. maple flavoring
1 c. pecans, chopped

In large bowl, beat sweet potatoes and butter until smooth. Add sweetened condensed milk, egg, cinnamon, orange peel, vanilla, nutmeg, and salt. Mix well. Pour into crust and bake at 425° for 20 minutes. Meanwhile mix egg, corn syrup, brown sugar, butter, and maple flavoring. Stir in pecans. Spoon topping on pie. Reduce temperature to 350° and bake for 25 more minutes.

Serves 8   Crystal Mays (Waitress)

Happiness is like potato salad: When you share it with others, it's a picnic.

TWO-CRUST BLACKBERRY PIE

1½ c. water
¾ c. sugar
1 qt. blackberries
3 T. cornstarch
½ c. cold water
¼ t. cinnamon
2 T. margarine
½ T. lemon juice
2 10" piecrusts

Heat water, sugar, and blackberries over medium heat. Stir cornstarch into cold water and add to boiling fruit. Remove from heat and add cinnamon, margarine and lemon juice. Fill one pie crust with ingredients and then cover with top crust. If you cover top crust with a tablespoon of milk and then sprinkle with sugar, you'll have a golden brown pie. Bake at 425° for 15 minutes and then 350° for 30 minutes. Serve warm with ice cream.

Makes 1 pie   Joyce Miller (Sunshine Farm Manager)

"Learn to do good;
Seek justice,
Reprove the oppressor;
Defend the fatherless,
Plead for the widow. . . .

If you are willing and obedient,
You shall eat the good of the land. . . .
                                                            Isa. 1:17, 19

VINEGAR PIE

1 c. sugar
½ c. flour
½ t. nutmeg
pinch of salt
1½ T. vinegar
½ c. cold water
1¼ c. hot water
1 t. butter
9" piecrust, baked

Mix sugar, flour, nutmeg, and salt. Add vinegar and cold water. Heat in saucepan until smooth. Then add hot water and butter. Cook until thick, pour into baked pie shell while still hot.

Makes 1 pie   Debbie Riley (Waitress)

Be kindly affectionate to one another with brotherly love, in honor giving preference to one another, not lagging in diligence, ferevent in spirit, serving the Lord; rejoicing in hope, patient in tribulation, continuing steadfastly in prayer; distributing to the needs of the saints, given to hospitality.

Rom. 12:10–13

 SUGAR-FREE APPLE PIE FILLING

13 c. apples
1½ c. water
1½ c. apple juice
1 t. lemon juice
¼ t. cinnamon

⅛ t. nutmeg
1 c. clear gelatin
1 c. water
¼ t. salt
⅛ c. Equal® sweetener

Cook apples, water, apple juice, lemon juice, cinnamon, and nutmeg until boiling. Mix together gelatin, water, and salt and then add to apple mixture. Turn off heat and add Equal® and mix well.

Makes two 9" pies

 MIX-IN-PAN CRUST

1½ c. flour
½ t. salt
½ c. oil

2 T. milk
1 T. sugar

Measure all ingredients into pie pan and toss together with a fork in pan. Press into shape in pan with your hand. Bake at 400° for approximately 10–12 minutes.

Makes 1 pie crust   Anita Yoder (Daughter of Bob & Sue)

SUGAR-FREE BLUEBERRY PIE FILLING

10 c. blueberries
3 c. water
1 t. lemon juice
1¼ c. clear gelatin

1 c. water
½ t. salt
⅛ c. Equal® sweetener

Cook blueberries, water, and lemon juice until boiling. Mix together gelatin, water, and salt and then add to blueberry mixture. Turn off heat and add Equal® and mix well.

Makes two 9" pies

PIECRUST

1¼ c. flour
1 stick butter or margarine

2 T. powdered sugar

Mix together all ingredients and pat into a 10" pie pan. Bake for 10 minutes at 375° or until golden brown.

Makes 1 piecrust   Esther Nisley (Bakery)

SUGAR-FREE CHERRY PIE FILLING

10 c. cherries
3 c. water
1 t. lemon juice
7 drops almond
¼ t. red food coloring

1 c. clear gelatin
1 c. water
¼ t. salt
⅛ c. plus 1½ t. Equal® sweetener

Cook cherries, water, lemon juice, almond, and food coloring until boiling. Mix together gelatin, water, and salt and then add to cherry mixture. Turn off heat and add Equal®. Mix well.

Makes two 9" pies

EASY PIECRUST

1½ c. flour
½ t. salt
½ c. oil

2 T. milk
1 T. sugar

Measure all ingredients into a pie pan. Stir together with a fork. Press into pan and bake 400 for 10–12 minutes.

Makes 1 piecrust   Ann Mast (Grounds Maintenance)

SUGAR-FREE PEACH PIE FILLING

9 c. peaches
3 c. water
1 t. lemon
1⅜ c. clear gelatin

1 c. water
¼ t. salt
⅛ c. Equal® sweetener

Cook peaches, water, and lemon until boiling. Mix together gelatin, water, and salt, then add to peach mixture. Turn off heat and add Equal®. Mix well.

Makes two 9" pies

SUGAR-FREE VANILLA PIE FILLING

2 qts. milk
½ c. eggs
¼ c. egg whites
⅛ c. vanilla
1 t. yellow food coloring

½ c. cornstarch
½ c. clear gelatin
¾ c. evaporated milk
½ t. salt
⅛ c. Equal® sweetener

Heat milk to 160°. Mix together eggs, egg whites, vanilla, food coloring, cornstarch, gelatin, evaporated milk, and salt and then add to milk. Turn off heat and add Equal®. Mix well. Variations: bananas, raisins, or coconut may be added.

Makes two 9" pies

ANGEL CRUNCH

1 lb. white chocolate almond bark
6 c. Crispix® cereal
3 c. Cheerios® cereal
2 c. pretzel sticks

2 c. dry roasted peanuts
1 lb. plain M&M's®, or holiday
    colors for Christmas snack

Melt almond bark in double boiler or microwave. Combine remaining ingredients and pour melted almond bark over them. Stir until well coated. Spread on waxed paper until cool. Break apart and store in airtight container.

Esther Wenger (Corporate Office)

BUCKEYES CANDY

2 c. crunchy peanut butter
¼ lb. butter or margarine,
    softened
3½ c. powdered sugar

3 c. Rice Krispies® cereal, crushed
12-oz. pkg. chocolate chips
⅓ stick paraffin

Mix the first four ingredients thoroughly and then roll into balls. Melt the paraffin with the chocolate chips in a double boiler. Dip balls in chocolate mixture and place on wax paper to cool. Store in refrigerator between layers of wax paper.

Makes 2½ Dozen   Sharon Schlabach (Waitress)

CARAMELS

4 c. sugar
3 c. light Karo® syrup

3 pt. whipping cream
1 T. vanilla

Mix sugar, syrup, and 1 pt. whipping cream and cook to 234° on a candy thermometer. Add second pt. whipping cream and cook to 234°. Add 3rd pt. whipping cream and cook to 240°. Stir constantly. Use wooden spoon to stir. Take off heat, add vanilla and mix well. Pour into greased cookie sheet and let cool. Cut into bite-size pieces and wrap in waxed paper. Cooking time is about one hour.

Angela Miller (Daughter-in-Law of Bob & Sue)

CARTERS CANDY

2 lb. white chocolate
1 c. chunky peanut butter
3 c. Rice Krispies® cereal

2 c. dry roasted peanuts
2 c. miniature marshmallows

Melt white chocolate and peanut butter together over low heat. Mix cereal, peanuts, and marshmallows together in a large bowl. Pour the chocolate mixture over top of other mixture, and mix well. Drop by teaspoonsful onto waxed paper and cool.

Makes 50–60 pieces   Elizabeth Mae Knepp (Essenhaus Foods)

CASHEW BRITTLE

2 c. sugar
1 c. corn syrup
1 c. water
12 oz. cashew nuts, raw

1 t. butter
¼ t. salt
1 t. baking soda (rounded)

Combine sugar, syrup, and water in heavy saucepan. Cook over low heat, stirring until sugar dissolves. Cook until soft ball stage (234°), add cashews and salt and butter. Cook until hard stage (300°). Add baking soda and stir. Pour on lightly buttered cookie sheet. Cool and break into pieces.

Ellen Mishler (Administration)

CHIP KISSES

4 egg whites
¼ t. salt
¼ t. cream of tartar
1½ c. sugar

½ c. broken walnuts
1 t. vanilla
6-oz. pkg. chocolate chips

Beat egg whites until foamy. Add salt and cream of tartar. Continue beating until egg whites are stiff, but not dry. Add sugar 2 tablespoons at a time, beating thoroughly after each addition. Fold in nuts, vanilla, and chocolate chips. Drop from teaspoon onto ungreased heavy paper, like a paper sack, on top of a cookie sheet. I often add different color food colorings to batch. Bake at 300° for 25 minutes. Let cool and enjoy.

Makes 6 dozen   Diane Butler (Bakery Sales)

CHOCOLATE CARAMEL CANDY

1st Layer:
1 c. milk chocolate chips
¼ c. butterscotch chips
¼ c. creamy peanut butter

2nd Layer (Filling):
¼ c. butter
1 c. sugar
¼ c. evaporated milk
1½ c. marshmallow cream
¼ c. creamy peanut butter
1 t. vanilla
1½ c. peanuts, chopped

3rd Layer:
14-oz. pkg. caramels
¼ c. cream
1 c. chocolate chips
¼ c. butterscotch chips
¼ c. creamy peanut butter

Combine ingredients for 1st layer in saucepan and melt over low heat until smooth. Spread into greased cake pan and chill. For 2nd layer melt butter, then add sugar and milk, boil gently 5 minutes and remove from heat. Add the rest of the ingredients for 2nd layer. Pour over 1st layer and chill. Melt caramels and cream together, spread over 2nd layer and chill.

Melt remaining 3rd layer of ingredients together and pour over other layers. Chill at least 4 hours, let set at room temperature for 20 minutes before cutting. Delicious! Tastes like a Snickers® candy bar!

Regina Gingerich (Village Shops)

CHRISTMAS BARK CANDY

10 12-oz. pkgs. vanilla chips or
    milk chocolate chips
2 T. vegetable oil

1¼–1½ c. M&M's® miniature
    baking bits or broken pretzel
    pieces

In a microwave-safe bowl, heat chips and oil at 70% power for one minute. Stir. Microwave 10–20 seconds longer or until chips are melted, stirring occasionally. Cool for 5 minutes and then stir in M&M's® or pretzels. Spread onto a waxed paper lined baking sheet. Chill for 10 minutes. Break into pieces and store in an airtight container at room temperature.

Makes 1 pound

Mary K. Schmucker (Kitchen)

CREAM CHEESE CANDY MINTS

1 lb. powdered sugar   3 oz. softened cream cheese

Mash the cream cheese and then add the powdered sugar gradually until the candy mixture becomes like stiff pie dough. Add desired flavoring and paste color. Roll into small balls and then roll in granulated sugar. Press candy into mold, unmold at once.

Linda Miller (Waitress)

DATE PECAN BALLS

1 c. butter, softened   2 c. flour
¼ c. sugar   2 c. pecans, chopped
2 t. vanilla   1 c. dates, chopped

Cream together butter and sugar, then add vanilla and flour and mix lightly. Add pecans and dates and then mix until well blended. Shape into 1" balls. Bake on cookie sheet at 350° for 20 minutes. Remove from oven and roll in powdered sugar.

Ellen Mishler (Administration)

GRAM'S HOMEMADE CARAMELS

2 c. sugar   ½ c. butter
2 c. Karo® Light Syrup   2 c. evaporated milk
⅛ t. salt   1 t. vanilla

Boil sugar, Karo® syrup, and salt to hard ball, 254°. Add butter, then milk, slowly, so that it doesn't stop boiling. Cook on high, stirring often, to firm ball, 242°–245°. Sticks very easily. Stir constantly. Add vanilla. Quickly pour into a greased shallow pan. If you're making turtles, only cook to 239°.

Mary Stalter (Waitstaff)

 Use cocoa to dust baking tins so muffins and cakes don't have a floury look.

MINTS

12 T. powdered sugar
1 egg white
12 drops red food coloring
4 drops peppermint or cinnamon flavor

Put all ingredients in a bowl and mix well. Might have to add more powdered sugar. Roll in a log and cut thin, then dry. May dip in chocolate after mints are dry.

Susie Kauffman (Waitress)

OHIO BUCKEYE CANDY

3 c. creamy peanut butter
1½ sticks butter, softened
2 lb. powdered sugar
16 oz. dipping chocolate, melted

Mix together first three ingredients. Form into small balls. Using a toothpick, dip balls into the chocolate until almost covered, leaving some of the peanut butter mixture exposed on top. Refrigerate.

Archie Mundy (Material Handling)

Some things you can give away and still keep:

- your word.
- a smile.
- a grateful heart.

PEANUT BUTTER FUDGE

3 c. sugar
½ c. butter
1 c. cream or half and half
1 c. peanut butter, creamy or crunchy
½ c. marshmallow cream

Combine sugar, butter, and cream in a 3-quart pan. Cook over medium heat. After it comes to a boil, let boil 6 minutes stirring constantly. Remove from heat and stir in peanut butter and marshmallow cream. Stir until both dissolve and pour into buttered 9"x13" pan.

April Ridenour (Waitress)

Overripe bananas can be frozen in the peel, then thawed and used for baking without having to mash them.

PEANUT CLUSTERS

½ lb. sweet chocolate
½ c. sweetened condensed milk
1 c. peanuts

Melt chocolate, which has been cut into small pieces. Remove from heat and add milk and peanuts. Stir until mixture thickens. Drop by teaspoonful onto a buttered sheet or plate. Chill thoroughly for several hours.

Sylvia Smith (Bakery Sales)

PEANUT CLUSTERS

12-oz. pkg. chocolate chips
12-oz. pkg. butterscotch chips
½ c. peanut butter

Melt all chips and peanut butter. Drop by spoonful on wax paper and let cool.

Esther Cross (Accounting)

SPECIAL K® CEREAL CANDY

¾ c. Karo® Light Syrup
¾ c. brown sugar
1 T. margarine
1 t. vanilla
1 c. peanut butter
5 c. Special K® cereal
12 oz. chocolate chips

Mix Karo® and brown sugar and bring to a good boil. (Or microwave for 3 minutes.) Remove from heat. Add margarine, vanilla, peanut butter, and cereal. Mix well and press in a buttered 9"x13" pan. Melt chocolate chips and spread on top. When cool cut into bite-size pieces.

Katie Hochstedler (Bakery)

Desserts & Ice Cream

DESSERT HINTS

Add confectioners' sugar to whipping cream before beating. The whipped cream stands up well even if it is not used immediately.

To add a delightful flavor to whipped cream, add a teaspoon of strained honey or maple syrup per half-pint of cream.

Whipping cream retains its shape if when whipping you add ½-1 teaspoon of light corn syrup per half-pint of cream.

Reduce baking temperature 25° to prevent overbrowning when cooking with honey.

To melt chocolate without sticking and burning, grease the pan in which it is to be melted.

A pinch of salt added to very sour fruits while cooking will greatly reduce the amount of sugar needed.

Keep apples, bananas, pears, and other fruits from discoloring when cut up by coating them with orange juice or diluted lemon juice.

ANGEL FOOD CAKE DESSERT

1 angel food cake
2 8-oz. pkgs. cream cheese, softened
2 c. powdered sugar
2 c. whipped cream
1 t. vanilla
1½ qt. strawberries, thickened

Cut angel food cake in bite-size pieces. Cream together cream cheese, powdered sugar, whipped cream, and vanilla. Thicken strawberries using clear gelatin, perma flo, Danish dessert, or a strawberry glaze. After strawberries are cool alternate layers of cake, cream cheese mixture, and strawberries, ending with strawberries on top. Other fruits may be used also.

       Martha Hochstedler (Bakery Production)

APPLE CRISP

8 apples
½ c. sugar
1 t. cinnamon
1 T. flour
½ c. water

Topping:
1 c. flour
1 c. sugar
1 t. baking powder
¼ t. salt
pinch nutmeg
1 t. cinnamon
1 egg
⅓ c. margarine, melted

Peel and slice apples. Put into a 9"x13" pan. Sprinkle sugar, cinnamon, and flour over the apples. Add water and mix thoroughly. Set aside. For the topping, mix all topping ingredients together. Spoon topping on top of apples. Bake uncovered at 325° for 45 minutes.

The largest room in the world is the room for improvement.

APPLE CRISP

4 c. apples, sliced
¼ c. water
1 t. cinnamon
½ t. salt

1 c. sugar
⅓ c. butter, softened
¼ c. flour, sifted

Put sliced apples in a 8" pan and sprinkle water, salt, and cinnamon on top of the apples. Work together sugar, butter, and flour until crumbly. Spread crumb mixture over apples. Bake uncovered for 30–40 minutes at 350°. Serve warm with ice cream.

Serves 10–12   Sharon Schlabach (Waitress)

[God's people] will neither hunger nor thirst,
> nor will the desert heat or the sun beat upon them.

He who has compassion on them will guide them
> and lead them beside springs of water.

>   Isa. 49:10

APPLE OR BLUEBERRY SQUARES

½ c. light brown sugar
½ c. white sugar
¼ c. butter, melted
1 egg
1 t. vanilla
1 c. flour

1 t. baking powder
¼ t. cinnamon
¼ t. salt
½ c. walnuts or pecans, chopped
½ c. pared apples, chopped or fresh, or frozen blueberries

Cream together sugars with butter and egg, stir in vanilla. Combine flour, baking powder, cinnamon, salt, nuts, and fruit. Stir mixtures together until moistened. Spread into 8" square greased pan. Sprinkle with 2 tablespoons of cinnamon sugar: ¼ teaspoon cinnamon and 2 tablespoons sugar. Bake at 350° for 30 minutes until light brown. This recipe doubles nicely.

Serves 9   Mary Pinckert (Waitress)

 Even if you're on the right track, you'll get run over if you just sit there.

FAT-FREE SUGAR-FREE APPLE CRISP

8–10 baking apples
2 c. water
1 c. Splenda®
¼ c. cornstarch
½ c. water
1 t. cinnamon

Topping:
¾ c. flour
¾ c. quick oatmeal
¾ c. Splenda®
1 t. cinnamon
¼ c. Parkay® butter spray

Peel apples and slice into 8"x13" pan. Sprinkle with cinnamon. Place water in saucepan to heat. Mix cornstarch into ½ cup of cold water. Pour into hot water stirring while mixing together. Cook until thick. Add one cup Splenda® to hot mixture; then pour over apples in pan. Mix together. For the topping, mix together ingredients until crumbs form. Place on top of apples. Bake for 35–40 minutes at 350°. Eat warm with fat free ice cream or cold with lite Cool Whip®.

Serves 6–8   Ryan Zimmerman (Administration)

CREAMY APPLE SQUARES

yellow cake mix with pudding
½ c. butter, softened
3–4 apples
1 egg

1 c. sour cream
½ t. cinnamon
¼ c. brown sugar

Mix cake mix and butter together, saving ⅔ cup to put on top. Then press the rest in a 13"x9"x2" pan. Dice the apples and put on top of cake mixture. Beat egg and sour cream together and pour over apples. Take the ⅔ cup cake mixture and mix cinnamon and brown sugar together and sprinkle on top. Bake at 350° for 25–30 minutes. Serve warm with ice cream.

Darlene Schmucker (Bakery)

QUICK APPLE CRISP

5 Granny Smith apples
9-oz. pkg. yellow cake mix
2 T. sugar
1 T. ground cinnamon

¼ c. butter or margarine, melted
½ c. nuts, chopped
vanilla ice cream or frozen
   whipped topping, optional

Preheat over to 350°. Peel, core, and slice apples. Cut apples in half crosswise. Place apples in pan and then combine remaining ingredients, except ice cream. Mix until crumbly. Sprinkle mixture over apples and bake for 35–40 minutes or until apples are tender. Serve with ice cream or whipped topping.

Serves 10   Rachel Yoder (Waitress)

SOUR CREAM APPLE SQUARES

2 c. flour
2 c. brown sugar, packed
½ c. butter
1 c. nuts, chopped
1½ t. cinnamon
1 t. baking soda

½ t. salt
1 c. sour cream
1 t. vanilla
1 egg
2 c. apples, peeled and finely
   chopped

Preheat oven to 350°. In large bowl, combine flour, brown sugar, and butter. Beat at low speed until crumbly and stir in nuts. Press 2¾ cups of crumbs in bottom of ungreased 9"x13" pan. To the remaining crumbs, add cinnamon, baking soda, salt, sour cream, vanilla, and beaten egg. Mix well and then stir in apples. Spoon this over the mixture in the pan. Bake at 350° for 30–40 minutes or until toothpick inserted in center comes out clean. Cool. Cut in squares and serve with ice cream or whipped cream.

Serves 12   Ellen Mishler (Administration)

 Life is too short to quarrel. Hearts are too precious to break.

CRANBERRY APPLE CRISP

Filling:
5 medium apples, peeled, cored, and sliced
16-oz. can whole-berry cranberry sauce
¼ c. sugar
2 T. flour

Topping:
¼ c. nuts, chopped
1 c. rolled oats
⅓ c. flour
1 t. cinnamon
¼ c. margarine, melted
⅓ c. brown sugar, packed

Preheat oven to 375°. Cut apples crisscross in half and place in 9"x13" pan. Combine cranberry sauce, sugar, and flour, mix well. Pour mixture over apples, toss to coat evenly. For topping, combine nuts, oats, brown sugar, flour, and cinnamon. Melt margarine and add; mix well. Sprinkle topping over fruit mixture and bake for 35–40 minutes or until fruit is tender. Serve warm. Good with ice cream.

Serves 12   Doretta Wingard (Waitress)

[Jesus said,] "I am the living bread that came down from heaven. If anyone eats of this bread, he will live forever. This bread is my flesh, which I give for the life of the world."

John 6:51

BAKED RICE PUDDING

8 eggs
4 c. whole milk
1⅓ c. sugar
1 t. salt
2 t. vanilla

2 T. cornstarch
4 c. rice, cooked
1 t. cinnamon
½ t. nutmeg

Beat eggs in a large ovenproof bowl or casserole. Add all other ingredients and mix well. Place the bowl in a pan of 1" water on the center rack in the oven. Bake at 325° for 1 hour and 45 minutes to 2 hours. Stir every 15 minutes the first hour and a half. Sprinkle the top with cinnamon and nutmeg and finish baking. Serve warm or cold.

Serves 8–10   Verna Lickfeldt (Restaurant Administration)

Since an overseer is entrusted with God's work, he must be blameless. ... He must be hospitable, one who lives what is good, who is self-controlled, upright, holy and disciplined.

Tit. 1:7–8

BANANA SQUARES

1½ c. white sugar
⅔ c. shortening
2 eggs, beaten
1 c. mashed bananas
½ t. vanilla flavoring
1 t. baking soda

1½ c. flour
¼ c. sour milk (add 1 T. white vinegar to milk)
½ c. walnuts, chopped
Cool Whip®
sliced bananas, optional

Mix together sugar and shortening. Mix in eggs, bananas, vanilla, and baking soda. Mix well. Add flour to creamed mixture alternately with sour milk, beating well after each addition. Fold in nuts if desired. Pour into 9"x13"x2" baking pan and bake at 350° for 45–50 minutes. Cool. If desired, garnish with a dollop of Cool Whip® and a few banana slices.

Serves 12–16   Norma Lehman (Bakery)

BLACKBERRY COBBLER

3 c. berries
3 T. clear gelatin
1 c. water
¾ c. butter
1 T. sugar

½ t. salt
1½ t. baking powder
1 c. flour
½ c. milk

Mix gelatin, water, and sugar in pan and bring to a boil. Remove and stir in berries. Put into a 2-quart dish. Mix butter, sugar, salt, baking powder, flour, and milk. Drop mixture on berries by tablespoon. Bake at 400° for 30 minutes.

Cletus Miller (Grounds Maintenance)

BLACKBERRY DELIGHT

1¼ c. flour
1 stick margarine
½ c. nuts
1 pkg. whipped topping mix, whipped
8 oz. pkg. cream cheese

Blackberry Filling:
1½ c. water
¾ c. sugar
2 T. cornstarch
3 T. blackberry gelatin
1 t. lemon juice
1 qt. blackberries

Mix flour, margarine, and nuts together and spread in 9"x12" pan. Bake at 375° for 20 minutes. For the filling, boil together water, sugar, and cornstarch for one minute. Remove from heat and add blackberry gelatin and lemon juice. Cool slightly and add blackberries. Pour into pan.

Mix whipped topping and cream cheese together and then spread on top of blackberry filling. Garnish with a few large berries. May be made day before serving.

Serves 18   Joyce Miller (Sunshine Farm Manager)

BLACKBERRY PINWHEEL COBBLER

1 c. sugar
2 c. water
½ c. butter or margarine
½ c. shortening

1½ c. self-rising flour
⅓ c. milk
3 c. fresh blackberries
1 t. ground cinnamon

Combine sugar and water in a saucepan and stir well. Cook over medium heat, stirring constantly, until sugar dissolves. Set aside. Place butter in a 13"x9"x2" baking dish in a 350° oven for 3 minutes or until butter melts. Set aside. Cut shortening into flour until mixture resembles coarse meal; add milk, stirring just until dry ingredients are moistened.

Turn dough out onto a lightly floured surface and knead lightly 4 or 5 times. Roll dough into a 12"x9" rectangle. Spread blackberries over dough; sprinkle with cinnamon. Roll up jelly-roll fashion, beginning with long side. Cut dough into 12 1" slices; place slices, cut side down, in butter. Pour sugar syrup around slices; bake at 350° for 55–60 minutes or until golden.

Makes 12 servings   Joyce Miller (Sunshine Farm Manager)

BLUEBERRY BUCKLE

¾ c. sugar
⅓ c. oleo
2 eggs
½ t. vanilla
1½ c. flour
2 t. baking powder
½ t. salt
½ t. cinnamon
¼ t. nutmeg
¼ t. cloves
½ c. milk
2 c. blueberries, fresh

Crumbs for top:
½ c. brown sugar
½ c. flour
3 T. margarine
½ t. cinnamon

Cream sugar and margarine together and then add eggs and vanilla and beat until fluffy. Sift dry ingredients together. Mix into batter, alternate with milk. Fold in blueberries. Spread batter in a greased 8"x12" pan. Mix ingredients together for crumbs on top. Sprinkle on top of batter and bake at 350° for 35 minutes.

Serve with whipped cream or ice cream.

Esther Nisley (Bakery)

BUTTERSCOTCH PECAN DESSERT

½ c. butter or margarine, cold
1 c. all-purpose flour
8-oz. pkg. cream cheese, softened
1 c. powdered sugar

8 oz. frozen whipped topping
3½ c. milk
2 pkg. instant butterscotch or vanilla pudding mix
¾ c. pecans

In a bowl, cut the butter into the flour until crumbly. Stir in ½ cup pecans. Press into an ungreased 13"x9"x2" baking pan. Bake at 350° for 20 minutes or until lightly browned, cool. In a mixing bowl, beat cream cheese and sugar until fluffy. Fold in one cup whipped topping and spread over crust. Combine milk and pudding mix until smooth. Pour over cream-cheese layer.

Refrigerate for 15–20 minutes or until set. Top with remaining whipped topping and pecans.

Serves 16–20

Mary K. Schmucker (Kitchen)

BUTTERSCOTCH PUDDING

1½ c. brown sugar
1 T. butter
1 pt. water
1 qt. milk
2 T. flour

2 eggs
2 boxes butterscotch pudding,
   not instant
milk, small amount
2 c. mini marshmallows

Cook brown sugar, butter, and water together for a few minutes and then add milk, do not let it boil. In a separate bowl mix together pudding mixes, flour, and eggs. Mix well and add enough milk until it can stir well. Stir into other mixture. Bring to a boil, then add marshmallows, stir until melted. Cool and serve with whipped cream on top.

Luella Yoder (Kitchen)

CHERRY CHIFFON DESSERT

21-oz. can cherry pie filling,
   chilled
15 oz. can pineapple chunks,
   chilled and well drained

14-oz. can Eagle® brand
   sweetened condensed milk
8 oz. whipped topping
1 c. miniature marshmallows

In large bowl combine all ingredients and mix well. Then spoon into individual serving bowls or a large serving bowl and chill for 30 minutes. You can substitute crushed pineapple for the chunk style.

Sue Meeks (Kitchen)

CHOCOLATE CHIP CHEESECAKE

1 c. chocolate cookie crumbs
2 T. butter, melted
16 oz. cream cheese, softened
1 c. white sugar

2 c. sour cream
3 eggs
1 T. vanilla
1½ c. mini chocolate chips

For the crust: combine crushed cookie crumbs with the melted butter. Press into bottom of cheesecake pan. Mix cream cheese, sugar, sour cream, eggs, and vanilla. Stir until smooth. Fold in the mini chocolate chips. Pour into pan on top of cookie crust. Bake at 350° for approximately 40 minutes and turn off oven. Leave door shut and let sit in oven for 1 hour. Remove and chill. May add whipped topping with more cookie crumbs if desired.

Jill Miller (Daughter-in-law of Bob & Sue)

CHOCOLATE CHIP COOKIE DOUGH CHEESECAKE

Part 1:

2 pack Chips Ahoy® cookies,
    crushed
⅓ c. melted butter

¼ c. sugar
¼ c. brown sugar

Part 2:

¼ c. sugar
¼ c. melted butter
1 T. water

1 t. vanilla
½ c. flour
1½ c. chocolate chips

Part 3:

2 8-oz. pkgs. cream cheese,
    softened
1 c. sugar

3 eggs
1 c. sour cream
½ t. vanilla

Mix together crushed cookies, butter, and sugar. Press into spring form pan. Mix together Part 2, sugar, butter, water, and vanilla. Mix well and add flour and chocolate chips. Press into pan on top of cookie crumb mix. In another bowl, mix together cream cheese, sugar, and eggs from Part 3. Mix well and then add sour cream and vanilla. Pour over everything else in pan. Bake at 350° for 55–60 minutes or until it starts to turn golden brown on top. Garnish with chocolate chips or shaved chocolate.

Serves 12–16

Louie Mast (Waitress)

NEW YORK CHEESECAKE

1 c. graham cracker crumbs
1 c. plus 3 T. sugar, divided
3 T. butter, melted
5 8-oz. pkg. cream cheese,
    softened

3 T. flour
1 T. vanilla
3 eggs
1 c. sour cream
21-oz. can cherry pie filling

Mix graham cracker crumbs, 3 tablespoons sugar, and butter. Press into bottom of 9″ spring form pan. Bake at 350° for 10 minutes. Beat cream cheese, 1 cup of sugar, flour, and vanilla until well blended. Add eggs, one at a time, mixing just until blended. Blend in sour cream. Then pour over crust and bake at 350° for 65 minutes or until center is almost set. Cool before removing from pan. Refrigerate for 4 hours or overnight. Top with pie filling.

Sharon Frye (Waitress)

NO-BAKE CHERRY CHEESECAKE

Crust:
16 graham crackers, crushed
½ c. sugar
⅓ c. butter, melted

Filling:
16 oz. cream cheese, softened
1 c. powdered sugar
14 oz. sweetened condensed milk
⅓ c. lemon juice
1 t. vanilla
1 can cherry pie filling
8 oz. whipped topping

For the crust, mix all ingredients and then pat into a 9"x13" pan. For the filling, mix together cream cheese, powdered sugar, condensed milk, lemon juice, and vanilla. Blend whipped topping into cream cheese mixture and spread on crust. Chill and top with pie filling.

Sharon Frye (Waitress)

PEACHES 'N' CREAM CHEESECAKE

¾ c. Pillsbury® all-purpose flour
1 t. baking powder
½ t. salt
3¼ oz. pkg. dry vanilla pudding mix, not instant
3 T. margarine or butter
1 egg
½ c. milk

15-oz. can sliced peaches or pineapple chunks, drained well (reserve juice)
8-oz. pkg. cream cheese, softened
½ c. sugar
1 T. sugar
½ t. cinnamon

Combine first 7 ingredients in large mixer bowl. Beat 2 minutes at medium speed. Pour into greased 9" deep dish or 10" pie pan. Place fruit over batter. Combine cheese, sugar, and juice in mixing bowl. Beat 2 minutes at medium speed. Spoon to within 1" of edge of batter. Combine sugar and cinnamon and sprinkle over cream cheese filling. Bake at 350° for 30–35 minutes or until crust is golden brown. This is very good with ice cream!

Serves 6–8

Sue Miller (Owner)

The best thing you can spend on your children is TIME.

"Then the righteous will answer him, 'Lord, when did we see you hungry and feed you . . . ?'

"The King will reply, 'I tell you the truth, whatever you did for one of the least of these brothers of mine, you did for me.'"

Matt. 25:37, 40

TURTLE PECAN CHEESECAKE

2 c. vanilla wafers, crushed
½ stick butter, melted
2½ 8-oz. pkgs. cream cheese, softened
1 c. sugar
1½ T. flour
¼ t. salt
1 t. vanilla
3 eggs
2 T. whipping cream
1 c. pecans, chopped

Caramel Topping:
½ of a 14-oz. pkg. caramels
⅓ c. whipping cream

Chocolate Topping:
4-oz. pkg. German sweet chocolate
1 t. butter
2 T. whipping cream

Preheat oven to 450°. Combine cookie crumbs and butter and press into bottom of 9" spring form pan. Beat cream cheese in large bowl until creamy. Add sugar, flour, salt, and vanilla. Mix well. Add eggs one at a time, beating well after each addition. Blend in whipping cream. Pour over crust. Bake for 10 minutes. Reduce oven temperature to 200° and continue baking 35–40 minutes or until set. Loosen cake from pan. Cool before removing rim of pan. Drizzle with carmel and chocolate toppings. Caramel topping: Combine caramels and whipping cream in small saucepan and stir over low heat until smooth. Chocolate topping: Combine German sweet chocolate, butter, and whipping cream in small saucepan and stir over low heat until smooth. Refrigerate and then sprinkle with pecans before serving. Hint: place a pan half filled with water on lower baking rack while baking cheesecake to prevent from splitting.

Makes 1 cheesecake   Karen Arrington (Bakery Sales)

CHOCOLATE ÉCLAIR

2 boxes vanilla pudding
3 c. milk
8 oz. pkg. cream cheese, softened
1 c. whipped topping
graham crackers

Frosting:
3 T. cocoa
3 T. milk
1½ c. powdered sugar
3 T. vegetable oil
2 T. Karo® Light Syrup
3 T. butter
1 t. vanilla

Cook pudding mix and milk together and then cool. Mix cream cheese and whipped topping and then add it to the pudding. Line dish with whole graham crackers, putting half of pudding mixture on crackers. Line with crackers again and put the rest of the pudding on top. Top with crackers and then with frosting. For frosting, mix all ingredients together until smooth and to right consistency.

Rachel Miller (Bakery)

EASY ÉCLAIR DESSERT

2½ c. low-fat graham cracker crumbs
3 c. skim milk
6 oz. fat-free vanilla pudding mix

12 oz. Cool Whip® Free, thawed
16 oz. reduced-fat milk
chocolate frosting

Arrange 1½ cups of the graham cracker crumbs on bottom of 13"x9" pan. In a mixing bowl, combine milk and vanilla pudding mixes. Beat with a wire whisk for 2 minutes. Gently stir in whipped topping. Spread pudding mixture over graham cracker crumbs. Place remaining graham cracker crumbs over pudding. Remove top and foil from frosting container. Microwave frosting in container on high for 1 minute or until it is easy to pour. Spread evenly over cracker crumbs. Refrigerate 4 hours or overnight.

Serves 12

Sue Meeks (Kitchen)

It doesn't matter what size of clothes you wear, as long as they fit.

CHOCOLATE LUSH

1 c. flour
1 stick butter, softened
8 oz. cream cheese, softened
1 c. powdered sugar

1 c. Cool Whip®
2 pkgs. instant chocolate pudding,
3 c. milk
pecans, chopped

Mix flour and butter and press into 9"x13" pan and then bake 15 minutes at 350° or until lightly browned. Then combine cream cheese, powdered sugar, and 1 cup of Cool Whip®. Pour on top of baked mixture. Mix pudding and milk together and then pour on top of cream cheese mixture. Top with the remaining Cool Whip® and sprinkle with pecans.

Pam Frey (Bakery)

CREAMY CHOCOLATE CHIP NUT ROLL

3 eggs
½ c. sugar
⅓ c. water
1 t. vanilla
1 c. flour
1 t. baking powder
¼ t. salt
1 c. mini chocolate chips
1 c. mini butterscotch chips

1 c. peanut butter
¾ c. buttered pecans, chopped

Filling:
8 oz. cream cheese, softened
8 oz. sour cream
8 oz. Cool Whip®
1½ c. powdered sugar
1 t. lemon juice

Preheat oven to 375°. Line 15½"x10½" jelly roll pan with waxed paper and grease. Beat eggs for about 5 minutes until thick and lemon colored. Pour into a mixing bowl and gradually add sugar. Blend in water and vanilla on low. Add flour, baking powder, and salt gradually, beat until smooth. Pour into pan, spreading into corners. Sprinkle with ½ c. each chocolate and butterscotch chips. Bake 12–15 minutes or until cake tester comes out clean. Loosen from edges of pan and invert to a towel sprinkled with powdered sugar. Remove waxed paper and roll the towel up. When almost cool, unroll towel and spread 1 c. peanut butter onto roll. For the filling, combine cream cheese, sour cream, and Cool Whip®. Gradually add powdered sugar. Mix in lemon juice and beat until fluffy. Divide filling in half and spread half on top of peanut butter. Sprinkle with ⅓ cup buttered pecans. Roll up the roll. Spread the rest of the filling on the roll. Sprinkle with remaining chocolate chips, butterscotch chips, and pecans.

Serves 8–12

Norine Yoder (Restaurant Gifts)

CHOCOLATE PUDDING

2 t. butter
3 c. milk
1 egg, beaten
1 c. sugar

3 T. cornstarch
1½ T. cocoa
1 t. vanilla

Brown 1 teaspoon of butter in sauce pan and then add the milk; heat. Meanwhile stir together egg, sugar, cornstarch, and cocoa. Mix all together and mix in the hot milk. Bring pudding to a boil and boil until thickened. Then add vanilla and the remaining butter. Cool.

Ellen Mishler (Administration)

CINNAMON CREAM CHEESE SQUARES

2 pkgs. crescent rolls
2 8-oz. pkg. cream cheese, softened
1 c. sugar
1 egg

1 t. vanilla
½ t. cinnamon, mixed with ¼ c. sugar
½ c. sliced almonds

Spread 1 package of crescent rolls in 9"x13" pan. Beat cream cheese, 1 cup sugar, and egg. Then add vanilla. Spread this mixture over crust. Roll out second crescent roll package on plastic wrap. Lift off of counter and place over cream cheese layer. Sprinkle the cinnamon and sugar on top, along with the almonds. Bake at 350° for 30–35 minutes.

Serves 10

Mary Stalter (Waitress)

"Therefore you shall keep the commandments of the LORD your God, to walk in His ways and to fear Him. For the LORD your God is bringing you into a good land, . . . a land in which you will eat bread without scarcity, in which you will lack nothing. . . ."

Deut. 8:6–7, 9

COCONUT CRUNCH

½ c. butter, melted
1 c. flour
1¼ c. coconut
1 c. almonds, slivered
¼ c. brown sugar, packed

1 pkg. coconut pudding
1 pkg. vanilla pudding
4 c. milk
2 c. whipped topping

In a 9"x13" pan, combine first 5 ingredients and press into an even layer. Bake at 350° for 25–30 minutes stirring every 10 minutes to form coarse crumbs. Cool and divide in half. Press half into same pan. Combine puddings and cook according to directions on box. Cool and add whipped topping. Spoon over crust and then top with remaining crumb mixture. Garnish with strawberries if desired. You can use instant pudding but it will not keep as long.

Serves 10–12   Betty Miller (Waitress)

CREAMY ORANGE FLUFF

6-oz. pkg. orange gelatin
2½ c. boiling water
2 11-oz. cans mandarin oranges, drained
8 oz. can crushed pineapple, undrained
6 oz. can frozen orange juice concentrate, thawed

Topping:
8-oz. pkg. cream cheese, softened
1 c. cold milk
3.4-oz. pkg. instant vanilla pudding

In a bowl, dissolve gelatin in boiling water. Stir in oranges, pineapple, and orange juice concentrate. Coat a 13"x9" dish with nonstick cooking spray and then add gelatin mixture. Refrigerate until firm. In a mixing bowl, beat cream cheese until light. Gradually add milk and pudding mix. Beat until smooth. Spread over orange layer. Chill until firm.

Serves 12–16   Jeanie Mast (Bakery Sales)

What we own is not as important as
Who owns us.

CREAMY RICE PUDDING

½ c. rice, uncooked
½ c. sugar
½ t. salt

½ c. raisins
4 c. milk, scalded
⅓ t. cinnamon or nutmeg

Wash rice. Mix all ingredients together in a 2-quart baking dish. Bake in a slow oven at 300° until rice is tender and milk is creamy, about 2 hours. Stir three or four times during the first hour. Serve warm or cold.

Serves 4–6   April Ridenour (Waitress)

Amish Expressions

"The cookies are all." (There are no more cookies.)

"I need to red up the house." (I need to clean house.)

DATE PUDDING

2 t. baking soda
2 c. boiling water
2 c. pitted chopped dates
1 c. butter
1 c. sugar
2 eggs, beaten
3½ c. flour
2 t. baking powder
½ t. salt
2 t. vanilla

1 c. nuts, chopped
1 c. candied cherries, chopped

Butter Sauce:
½ c. butter
2 T. flour
1 c. sugar
3 c. milk
1 t. vanilla

Combine baking soda, water, and dates. Cool. Cream together butter and sugar. Add eggs and mix well. Add date mixture, flour, baking powder, salt, vanilla, nuts and cherries. Pour into greased 9"x13" pan and bake at 325° for 1 hour or until done. For the butter sauce, melt butter over low heat. Combine flour and sugar and then add to butter. Cook slowly and keep stirring, pour in milk and bring to a boil. Remove from heat and add vanilla. Cool. Layer date pudding, sauce, and whipped cream. You can add sliced bananas if you wish.

Arlene Miller (Waitress)

DEATH BY CHOCOLATE

21-oz. pkg. brownie mix
1 t. sugar mixed with
    ¼ c. black coffee
2 2.8-oz. pkgs. instant chocolate mousse or 4-serving pkg. instant chocolate pudding
8 1.4-oz. Heath® toffee bars, coarsely crushed
12-oz. container frozen whipped topping, thawed

Prepare brownie batter according to package directions. Preheat oven and bake brownie batter in a 9"x13" pan. Allow to cool completely. Use a fork to prick holes in the top of the cooled brownies. Drizzle with coffee. Break up the brownies into small pieces; place half in bottom of a large glass serving bowl. Cover with half of the mousse; then ⅓ of the crushed candy and half of the whipped topping. Repeat layers. Top with remaining crushed candy. Cover and chill at least 2 hours before serving.

Makes 24 servings   Susan Yoder (Bakery)

DOUBLE BERRY DESSERT

1 qt. strawberries, fresh
8-oz. carton strawberry-flavored yogurt
¼ c. sugar
3 drops red food coloring

Wash and hull strawberries and then spoon them into sherbet dishes. Combine remaining ingredients and drizzle over the strawberries.

Serves 6   Mary Miller (Dishwasher)

FROZEN FRUIT DESSERT

8 oz. cream cheese
1 c. sugar
10 oz. box strawberries
1½ c. crushed pineapple, undrained
2–3 sliced bananas
8 oz. Cool Whip®

Cream sugar and cream cheese thoroughly together and then fold in remaining ingredients. Place in 9"x13" pan and then freeze. Remove from freezer 15–20 minutes before serving.

Sharon Frye (Waitress)

Before trying to keep up with your neighbors, you should find out where they are going.

FROZEN STRAWBERRY DESSERT

Crust:
1 c. flour
½ c. nuts, chopped
½ c. margarine, at room temperature
¼ c. sugar

Filling:
8-oz. pkg. cream cheese, softened
¾ c. sugar
20-oz. can crushed pineapple, drained
1 pt. or 10 oz. frozen strawberries, slightly thawed and chopped
1 large container whipped topping

Blend together crust ingredients. Press into a baking pan and bake at 300° for 5–8 minutes. Let cool a little then crumble crust. Put half of crumbs in bottom of 9"x9" baking pan. Combine filling ingredients and beat until smooth. Pour over crumbs in baking pan. Sprinkle the remaining crumbs on top. Cover and freeze. Let thaw slightly before serving.

Serves 10–12   Lorene Miller (Busser)

GRAPE DESSERT

5 lb. seedless grapes
8 oz. cream cheese
8 oz. sour cream
8 oz. Cool Whip®
1½ c. powdered sugar
1 t. lemon juice

Wash and drain grapes. While grapes are draining, mix together softened cream cheese, sour cream, and Cool Whip®. Mix in powdered sugar and lemon juice. Cream until light and fluffy. Add drained grapes and mix.

Serves 20–22   Norine Yoder (Village Shops)

HOT FUDGE PUDDING

1 c. flour
⅔ c. sugar
2 T. baking powder
½ t. salt
1 t. cinnamon
½ c. unsweetened cocoa

½ c. milk
2 T. margarine, melted
1 t. vanilla
1 c. brown sugar
1½ c. boiling water

Preheat oven to 350° and grease 8"x8" baking dish. Combine flour, sugar, baking powder, salt, cinnamon, and half of the cocoa. Mix in milk, butter, and vanilla. Spread batter into greased baking dish. Mix together brown sugar and the rest of the cocoa and then sprinkle over batter. Slowly pour water over mixture in baking dish. Do not stir. Bake 30 minutes and serve warm with ice cream.

Serves 8   Mary Lewallen (Bakery Sales)

 ## ICE CREAM SANDWICH DESSERT

19 ice cream sandwiches
12-oz. carton whipped topping, thawed

11¾-oz. jar hot fudge ice cream topping
1 c. salted peanuts
1 c. chocolate chips

Cut one ice cream sandwich in half, place one whole and one half sandwich on short side of 13"x9" pan. Arrange 8 sandwiches in opposite direction. Spread with half of whipped topping. Spoon fudge topping on by teaspoonfuls on top of whipped topping. Sprinkle with ½ cup peanuts and chocolate chips. Repeat layers. Cover and freeze. Remove from freezer 20 minutes before serving. Cut in squares.

Serves 12   Anita Yoder (Daughter of Bob & Sue)

 If you blame others for your failures, do you credit them for your success?

 JIFFY RHUBARB DESSERT

4 c. rhubarb, cut up
1 c. sugar
3-oz. pkg. strawberry or
   raspberry Jell-O®

2 c. yellow or white cake mix
1 c. cold water
5 T. margarine, melted

Grease a 7"x10" pan and place rhubarb in pan. Sprinkle sugar, then dry Jell-O®, followed by two cups dry cake mix over rhubarb. Pour water over all. Drizzle margarine over top. Bake at 350° for 1 hour. Serve with ice cream or your favorite topping.

Serves 4–6   Leon Nafziger (Grounds Maintenance)

 A bad habit is like a soft chair: Easy to get into, but hard to get out of.

LAYERED BANANA PUDDING

⅓ c. flour
⅔ c. brown sugar
2 c. milk
2 egg yolks, beaten
2 T. butter

1 t. vanilla flavoring
8 oz. Cool Whip®
4 to 6 firm bananas, sliced
chopped nuts, optional

In a medium saucepan, combine the flour and brown sugar, stir in milk. Cook and stir over medium heat until thickened and bubbly. Cook and stir 1 minute more. Remove from heat. Gradually stir about one cup hot mixture into egg yolks. Return all to the saucepan. Bring to a gentle boil and cook and stir for 2 minutes. Remove from the heat and stir in butter and vanilla. Cool to room temperature, stirring occasionally. Fold in Cool Whip®. Layer a third of the pudding in a 2-quart glass bowl and top with half of the bananas. Repeat layers ending with pudding on top. Sprinkle with nuts if desired. Cover and chill at least 1 hour before serving.

Serves 8   Norma Lehman (Bakery)

The simplest toy a young child can operate is called a grandparent.

LAZY MAN'S COBBLER

1 stick margarine
4 c. blackberries
1 c. sugar
1½ c. water
1 c. self-rising flour

1 c. sugar
1 c. milk
1 t. vanilla
1 t. cinnamon

Melt margarine in 9"x12" pan. Bring blackberries, sugar, and water to a boil and pour over oleo. Sift together flour and sugar and then add milk and vanilla. Mix well. Pour mixture over hot berries. Sprinkle cinnamon over top and bake at 450° for 20 minutes. May be eaten hot with milk.

Serves 8　　　　　　　　　　　　Joyce Miller (Sunshine Farm Manager)

LEMON FLUFF

6-oz. box lemon Jell-O®
3 c. boiling water

6 oz. frozen lemonade
8 oz. Cool Whip®

Dissolve Jell-O® in boiling water. Add lemonade. Chill till partially set and beat until fluffy. Stir in Cool Whip® and then put into mold and chill.

　　　　　　　　　　　　　　　　　　　　Norma Velleman (Bakery Sales)

LIME MINT DESSERT

1 box butter mints
1½ c. boiling water
1 small box lime Jell-O®

10 oz. crushed pineapple, undrained
8-oz. tub Cool Whip®

Melt mints and Jell-O® in boiling water and then add pineapple and refrigerate until completely cold. Add Cool Whip® and mix well; return to refrigerator. Can be frozen and cut into squares.

Serves 12　　　　　　　　　　　　　　　　　　Fran Blough (Waitress)

MRS. BOWDEN'S DESSERT

graham cracker crust
3 bananas
2 pkgs. whipped topping mix
2 8-oz. pkgs. cream cheese, softened
1 c. powdered sugar

Blackberry Filling:
1½ c. water
¾ c. sugar
2 T. cornstarch
3 T. blackberry gelatin mix
1 t. lemon juice
1 qt. blackberries

Bake graham cracker crust in 9"x12" pan. Slice 3 bananas over cooled crust. Whip the packages of whipped topping mix. In separate bowl, combine cream cheese and powdered sugar. Combine mixture with whipped topping and pour over bananas. Chill several hours in refrigerator. For the filling, boil water, sugar, and cornstarch for one minute. Remove from heat and add blackberry gelatin and lemon juice. Cool slightly and add blackberries. Carefully pour 1 quart of blackberry filling over cream mixture.

Serves 12   Joyce Miller (Sunshine Farm Manager)

OREO® COOKIE DESSERT

½ gallon vanilla ice cream
8-oz. container whipped topping

8 oz. Oreo® cookies

Soften ice cream, thaw whipped topping, and crush Oreo® cookies. Mix together ice cream and whipped topping. When well blended add crushed Oreo® cookie crumbs and stir until blended. Press into an 8"x11" pan and refreeze. Serve when firm again.

Serves 8–10   Michele Shetler (Sunshine Farm)
                               Elizabeth Miller (Kitchen)

 Early morning rain is like an old woman's dance—neither will last long.

OREO® FUDGE COOKIE DESSERT

1 lb. Oreo® cookies
½ stick margarine
1 qt. ice cream, softened
1 jar chocolate fudge topping

Crush Oreo® cookies and mix with melted margarine. Press half of crumb mixture in bottom of 9"x13" baking dish. Spread ice cream on top of crumbs. Spread chocolate fudge topping on top of ice cream and then sprinkle remaining crumbs on top of fudge topping. Freeze.

Serves 12   Mary Lewallen (Bakery Sales)

OREO® PUDDING DESSERT

1 pkg. Oreo® cookies
8 oz. Cool Whip®
2 small pkgs. instant vanilla pudding mix

Crush cookies and put in a 9"x13" pan, saving one cup to sprinkle on top. Mix pudding according to directions on box. Fold in Cool Whip®. Pour over cookie crumbs and sprinkle with remaining crumbs. Refrigerate.

Katie Hochstedler (Bakery)

Kindly words and friendly smiles smooth rough places and shorten miles.

PEANUT BUTTER MOUSSE DESSERT

2 c. Oreo® cookies
1 c. whipping cream
8-oz. pkg. cream cheese, softened
1 c. peanut butter
1 c. powdered sugar
1 t. vanilla
6 oz. chocolate chips
2 T. milk

Put crushed cookies in bottom of dish. Beat whipping cream and set aside. Mix together cream cheese and peanut butter. Add powdered sugar and vanilla. Mix well and then fold in whipped cream. Pour over cookie crumbs and refrigerate. Melt chocolate chips with milk, stir until smooth and spread over filling.

Katie Hochstedler (Bakery)

PECAN PIE SQUARES

3 c. flour	1½ c. sugar
⅓ c. sugar	1½ c. Karo® syrup
¾ c. butter, softened	3 T. butter, melted
¾ t. salt	1½ t. vanilla
4 eggs, beaten	2½ c. pecans, chopped

Combine first four ingredients in large bowl until crumbly. Press into a greased jelly roll pan. Bake at 350° for 20 minutes or until lightly golden. Combine eggs, sugar, Karo® syrup, melted butter, and vanilla, blend well. Stir in pecans. Pour mixture over baked crust and bake until filling is set, about 25 minutes. Do not overbake! Cool and cut into squares.

Sharon McSorley (Management)

PINEAPPLE RINGS

can of pineapple rings	whipped topping
evaporated milk	

Place unopened can of evaporated milk in a pan, cover with water. Boil for 3 hours; let it cool. Put pineapple rings on a tray. Take both ends off evaporated milk can and push the carmelized milk through. Slice on pineapple. Then put whipped topping on top.

Serves 10   Lena Bontrager (Bakery Sales)

PUMPKIN CRUNCH

15 oz. can pumpkin	½ t. salt
12 oz. can evaporated milk	1 box yellow cake mix
3 large eggs	½ c. pecans, chopped
1½ c. sugar	1 c. butter, melted
1 t. cinnamon	whipped topping

Preheat oven to 350°. Grease bottom of 13"x9" pan. Combine pumpkin, milk, eggs, sugar, cinnamon, and salt in a large bowl. Pour into pan. Sprinkle dry cake mix evenly over pumpkin mixture. Top with pecans. Drizzle melted butter over pecans. Bake for 50–55 minutes or until golden brown. Cool and then top with whipped topping when served.

Sharon Frye (Waitress)

PUMPKIN PIE DESSERT

Crust:
1 yellow cake mix, reserve 1 cup for topping
1 egg
1 T. flour
2 c. margarine

Topping:
1 c. cake mix
½ c. sugar
1 t. cinnamon
2 T. margarine

Filling:
1 lb. 13 oz. canned pumpkin
2½ t. pumpkin pie spice
2 eggs
½ c. brown sugar
⅔ c. milk

Stir crust ingredients together and line bottom of 9"x13" greased metal cake pan. Mix filling ingredients together and pour over crust. Crumble topping ingredients and place on top of filling. Bake at 350° for 45 minutes.

Kathy Miller (Daughter-in-Law of Bob & Sue)
Esther Cross (Accounting)

RED RASPBERRY DESSERT

2 3-oz. boxes red raspberry Jell-O®
2 3-oz. boxes vanilla pudding, not instant
4 c. water
2 6–8 oz. boxes frozen red raspberries

Bring all ingredients to a rolling boil. Let set for 24 hours. Serve over slices of angel food cake and top with whipped cream.

Serves 12–15   Ellen Mishler (Administration)

My soul, wait silently for God alone,
For my expectation is from Him.
He is my only rock and my salvation;
He is my defense;
I shall not be moved.
Ps. 62:6

STRAWBERRY ANGEL FOOD CAKE

1 angel food cake
3 c. whipped topping
6-oz. container strawberry yogurt
2½ c. strawberries cut into fourths
2 drops red food coloring

Cut angel food cake into 3 equal layers. Mix together whipped topping, strawberry yogurt, 1½ cups strawberries, and red food coloring. Mix well and then spread ⅓ of mixture between each layer and on top of the cake. Top with 1 cup of strawberries cut into fourths. Before serving sprinkle with powdered sugar.

Serves 15   Joyce Miller (Sunshine Farm Manager)

 ## STRAWBERRY PINEAPPLE DELIGHT

1 small tub Cool Whip®
8 oz. container cottage cheese
1 small pkg. strawberry Jell-O®
8-oz. can pineapple, crushed
1 c. walnuts, chopped

Mix all ingredients together and then chill in refrigerator.

Sharon McSorley (Management)

STRAWBERRY PIZZA

2 c. flour
2 sticks butter
1 c. pecans, chopped
8 oz. cream cheese, softened
3 c. powdered sugar
12 oz. whipped topping
1 c. sugar
1 c. water
3 T. cornstarch
3 oz. strawberry gelatin
2 pints fresh strawberries

Mix flour, butter, and pecans together and press into 9"x12" pan. Bake at 350° until light brown, about 20 minutes. Cool. Blend cream cheese and powdered sugar until smooth. Fold in whipped topping. Place this mixture on crust and bring up sides so next mixture won't run. Mix sugar, water, and cornstarch together and boil one minute, stirring constantly. Add strawberry gelatin and mix well. Cool and then add strawberries. Put on top of cream cheese mixture. Serve.

Serves 12   Joyce Miller (Sunshine Farm Manager)

STRAWBERRY SHORTCAKE

2 c. self-rising flour
2 T. sugar
⅓ c. shortening

1 egg
milk

Cut flour, sugar, and shortening together until fine. Slightly beat one egg in a measuring cup, add enough milk to make 1 cup. Combine all ingredients until just blended. Spread dough in 7"x12" baking pan and dot with butter. Bake at 450° for 12–15 minutes. Serve warm with strawberries.

Serves 8   Joyce Miller (Sunshine Farm Manager)

STRAWBERRY TRIFLE

yellow cake mix
4 c. sweetened strawberries, sliced

1 large box French vanilla pudding
1 pkg. whipped topping mix

Bake cake mix as directed on box. Break into bite-size pieces in 9"x13"pan. Sprinkle sweetened strawberries on cake. Mix pudding mix as directed on box and add whipped topping mix. Spread on top of strawberries. Attractive when layered in large glass bowl. May be made the day before.

Serves 15   Joyce Miller (Sunshine Farm Manager)

STRIPED DELIGHT

1½ c. graham cracker crumbs
¼ c. sugar
⅓ c. butter, melted
8 oz. cream cheese, softened
¼ c. sugar

2 T. milk
1½ c. whipped topping
2 4-oz. chocolate instant pudding
3½ c. milk
1½ c. whipped topping

Combine graham cracker crumbs, ¼ cup of sugar, and melted butter. Press firmly into bottom of 9"x13" pan. Chill 15 minutes. Beat cream cheese, ¼ cup sugar, and milk until smooth. Fold in 1½ cup whipped topping. Spread over crust. Prepare pudding as directed, using the milk. Pour over cream cheese layer. Chill several hours or overnight. Spread remaining whipped topping over pudding before serving.

Serves 15   Esther Wenger (Corporate Office)

TAPIOCA PUDDING

3¾ c. water
½ t. salt
¾ c. tapioca pearls
1 c. light brown sugar
1 egg
½ c. whole milk
¼ c. sugar

¾ t. dark vanilla
2 T. butter

Day 2:
⅓ c. Cool Whip®
¼ c. bittersweet chocolate

Spray a kettle with Crisco® pan spray. Bring water and salt to a boil. Add tapioca and simmer until the tapioca is clear in color. Add brown sugar and mix well. Beat together eggs, milk, white sugar, and vanilla. Add egg mixture to the tapioca and cook until it begins to boil. Turn the heat off. Melt butter and mix into tapioca. Refrigerate overnight.

On the second day, pour tapioca into large bowl and add Cool Whip®. Mix thoroughly. Add chocolate shavings and mix thoroughly.

TOFFEE MOCHA CREAM TORTE

1 c. butter, softened
2 c. sugar
2 eggs
1½ t. vanilla
2⅔ c. flour
¾ c. baking cocoa
2 t. baking soda
¼ t. salt
1 c. buttermilk

2 t. instant coffee granules
1 c. boiling water

Topping:
½ t. instant coffee
1 t. hot water
2 c. whipping cream, not whipped
3 T. light brown sugar
6 Heath® candy bars, crushed

In mixing bowl, cream butter and sugar, then add eggs and vanilla. Combine flour, cocoa, baking soda, and salt. Add to creamed mixture alternately with buttermilk. Dissolve coffee in hot water and add to batter. Beat for 2 minutes. Pour into 3 greased and floured 9" round pans and bake at 350° for 16–20 minutes. Cool for 10 minutes before removing from pans to wire racks to cool completely. For topping, dissolve coffee in water and cool. Add cream and sugar, beat until stiff peaks form. Place bottom layer on plate with ⅓ of topping. Sprinkle with ½ cup crushed candy. Repeat layers twice and store in refrigerator.

Serves 12–16   Ruby Bontrager (Bakery)

TWINKIE® STYLE DESSERT

Cake:
1 box yellow or chocolate cake mix
¾ c. oil
¾ c. water
1 small box instant vanilla pudding
4 eggs

Filling:
2 c. powdered sugar
1 t. vanilla
1 c. marshmallow cream
½ c. Crisco®
3 T. milk

Mix all cake ingredients together in mixing bowl. Pour into 2 large cookie sheets to bake. Bake at 350° until a toothpick comes out clean. Flip one cake onto a board, spread with filling and put other cake on top. Mix together filling ingredients. If batter is too stiff, add more milk until desired consistency.

Treva Yoder (Millers' Housekeeper)

 FUDGESICLE® STYLE DESSERT

8 oz. pkg. instant chocolate pudding
2½ c. milk
wooden sticks or plastic spoons

Mix first two ingredients and then pour into small paper cups. Add stick or spoon in middle and freeze. Makes a wonderful cool treat. Enjoy. May use other flavors of pudding.

Serves 10–12

Diane Butler (Bakery Sales)

 ICE CREAM CRUNCH

2 c. Corn Chex® or Rice Chex®, crushed
⅓ stick butter
⅓ c. peanuts, chopped
½ c. brown sugar

Bake crushed Chex® for 10 minutes at 350°. Cool. Combine cooled Chex® and brown sugar. Add melted butter then peanuts, mixing well. Place a scoop of vanilla ice cream in crunch mixture and roll to coat. Eat right away or place rolled balls on cookie sheet lined with waxed paper and freeze. Good with chocolate topping.

Kathy Miller (Daughter-in-Law of Bob & Sue)

ICE CREAM SUNDAE DESSERT

2 c. or 12 oz. semi-sweet
 chocolate chips
12-oz. can evaporated milk
½ t. salt

12-oz. pkg. vanilla wafers, crushed
½ c. butter or margarine, melted
2 qt. vanilla ice cream or flavor
 of your choice, softened

In a saucepan over medium heat, melt chocolate chips with milk and salt. Cook and stir until thickened. Remove from heat, set aside. Combine the wafer crumbs and butter; set aside 1 cup. Press remaining crumbs into a greased 9"x13" pan and chill 10 to 15 minutes. Pour chocolate over crumbs. Cover and freeze for 20–25 minutes or until firm. Spread ice cream over chocolate and then sprinkle with reserved crumbs. Freeze at least 2 hours before serving.

Serves 12–16   Martha Coblentz (Bakery)

MINT ICE CREAM DESSERT

26 Oreo® cookies, crushed in
 blender
¼ c. butter, melted

½ gal. mint chocolate chip ice cream
1 jar Hershey's® hot fudge
Cool Whip®

Mix cookie crumbs and butter. Pat in 9"x13" pan and freeze. Soften ice cream just enough to spread on frozen cookie mixture. Freeze. Top with hot fudge, warmed just a bit in the microwave. Freeze. Top with Cool Whip® and freeze once again.

Charlotte Miller (Waitress)

PEACH SLUSH

4 c. water
4 c. sugar
½ c. Perma-Flo® modified starch,
 mixed with 2 c. water

20-oz. can crushed pineapple
1 pint frozen orange juice
 concentrate
6–8 c. peaches, finely chopped

Combine water and sugar in saucepan and bring to a boil. Add Perma-Flo® and boil for 2 more minutes. Let cool and then add pineapple, frozen orange juice, and peaches. Mix well. Freeze. Thaw about 30 minutes or more before serving. Other fruits may be added.

Luella Yoder (Kitchen)

 WATERMELON LOOK SHERBET MOLD

1 qt. green sherbet
1½ qt. raspberry sherbet
6-oz. pkg. chocolate chips

Put green sherbet in large bowl, leave a hole in the middle, freeze. Mix chocolate chips and raspberry sherbet. Put in middle of green sherbet. Freeze for one hour. Invert onto plate. Slices will look like watermelon.

Serves 6–8   Diane Butler (Bakery Sales)

FRIED ICE CREAM

½ c. butter
1 c. sugar
2½ c. Corn Flakes® cereal, slightly crushed
½ c. nuts, chopped
½ c. coconut, optional
2 qt. vanilla ice cream, softened
honey, optional

Melt butter in skillet. Add sugar, Corn Flakes®, nuts, and coconut, if desired. Heat until lightly browned. Spread half of mixture in 9"x13" pan. Spoon ice cream on top. Top with remaining crumbs. Freeze. Drizzle with honey if desired.

Serves 15   Jan Bontrager (Waitress)

FRIED ICE CREAM

1 qt. vanilla ice cream
¼ c. whipping cream
2 t. vanilla extract
2 c. flaked coconut
2 c. Corn Flakes®, finely crushed
½ t. ground cinnamon

Using an ice cream scoop, place 8 scoops of ice cream, shaped into balls, on a baking sheet, cover and freeze for 2 hours or until firm. In a bowl, combine whipping cream and vanilla. In another bowl, combine coconut, Corn Flakes®, and cinnamon. Dip ice cream balls into cream, then coconut mixture. Place back on cookie sheet and freeze again for 3 hours. Heat oil to 375°. Fry ice cream until golden brown for about 30 seconds. Drain on paper towels and serve immediately with chocolate or caramel topping and lots of whipped cream.

Serves 8   Mary Stalter (Waitress)

Count your age by friends, not years.
Count your life by smiles, not tears.

HOMEMADE PUMPKIN ICE CREAM

6 eggs
2 c. sugar
1 can evaporated milk
1 can sweetened condensed milk
2 t. vanilla
3 oz. pkg. instant vanilla pudding
2 15-oz. cans pumpkin
½ t. pumpkin pie spice
4 t. cinnamon
½ t. salt

Add enough milk to fill 1½-gallon freezer.

Serves 15   Mary Stalter (Waitress)

ICE CREAM

1 qt. cream
1 qt. milk
6 eggs
2 small boxes any flavor instant pudding mix
2 c. sugar
pinch of salt

Combine all ingredients above. Put in can and then fill can with milk until ¾ full. Freeze.

Linda Miller (Waitress)

VANILLA ICE CREAM

5 eggs
4 c. sugar
pinch of salt
1 t. baking powder, optional
3 qt. half-and-half cream
1½ T. vanilla
whole milk

Beat eggs until very stiff, approximately 15–20 minutes on high speed. Slowly add sugar, salt, and baking powder and then add half and half and vanilla. Continue to beating until thoroughly mixed. Pour into 1½-gallon freezer can and fill until about 2–2½" from top of can with whole milk. Freeze according to your freezer instructions. This makes a very rich and smooth ice cream. It's our family's favorite.

Makes 1½ gallons   Leon Nafziger (Grounds Maintenance)

BUTTER CRISP ICE CREAM TOPPING

½ c. Corn Flakes®, finely crushed ½ c. pecans, chopped
¼ c. brown sugar 2 T. butter, melted

Combine first 3 ingredients and then blend in butter. Mix well, spread on cookie sheet, and bake. Stir frequently, then serve on ice cream.

Sue Miller (Owner)

FUDGE SAUCE FOR ICE CREAM

1 can condensed milk hot water to thin
2 squares semi-sweet chocolate

Melt chocolate and condensed milk in microwave. Stir often so it doesn't burn. As it thickens, add hot water and microwave to make it the consistency that you want it as it cools. This is my favorite fudge sauce. Optional: Add 2 tablespoons peanut butter and 1 cup chopped salted peanuts to the fudge sauce after it is cooked.

Millie Whetstone (Bakery)

STRAWBERRY TOPPING FOR ICE CREAM

1 c. cold water 4 c. crushed strawberries
1 box Sure-Jell® or ⅓ c. fruit 5 c. sugar
   pectin

Boil cold water and Sure-Jell® for 1 minute. Stir together strawberries and sugar. When sugar is dissolved stir into other mixture and stir for 2 minutes. Also makes good shakes.

Lorene Mast (Kitchen)

Now may He who supplies seed to the sower, and bread for food, supply and multiply the seed you have sown and increase the fruits of your righteousness.

2 Cor. 9:10

Snacks, Dips, Appetizers & Beverages

MICROWAVE HINTS

Whipped topping, small carton: Heat 1 minute on LOW. Center should still be slightly firm but will blend in. Don't overheat!

To toast coconut: Spread ½ cup in pie plate; cook 3–4 minutes, stirring every 30 seconds after 2 minutes. Watch closely, as it browns quickly once it starts turning brown.

When warming rolls, place cup of water in a corner of the microwave.

Cook meat loaf in a ring. Place custard cup upside down in center and grease will come up into glass.

For raising bread dough: Put dough in proper container, cover with plastic wrap and damp cloth. Heat on lowest power for 2–3 minutes. May repeat. Leave bread in microwave to rise.

Soften hard ice cream in a few seconds. This will make it easier for you to serve.

For better barbecues, microwave-cook chicken pieces until partially done, then finish on grill. They'll be moist and have charcoal flavor.

Quick-cook chicken parts you need for salads, sandwiches, main dishes; cook in covered casserole.

Toast almonds in a glass dish with butter, heating them until nuts are lightly browned. Stir occasionally.

Dry herbs the fast way in the microwave. Place a few sprigs or ½ cup leaves between paper towels and heat for about 2 minutes, until dry and crumbly. Exact timing depends on the herb.

Warm cheese before serving—it's better at room temperature. One ounce will take about 15 seconds; then allow to stand one minute.

Soften too-dry dried fruit by sprinkling with ½–1 teaspoon of water. Cover; heat for 15–30 seconds.

To soften hard brown sugar, place in a glass dish, add a slice of white bread or apple wedge, and cover. A cup takes 30–45 seconds.

AFTER-SCHOOL TREATS

12 oz. semi-sweet chocolate chips
¼ c. butter flavored shortening
5 c. Rice Krispies®

1 pkg. Milk Duds® candies
1 T. water

In a large microwave-safe bowl, combine chocolate chips and shortening. Cover and microwave on high until chocolate is melted, about 2 minutes. Stir until well blended. Stir in cereal until well-coated. In another microwave safe bowl combine Milk Duds® and water. Cover and microwave on high for one minute or until mixture is pourable. Mix well. Stir into cereal mixture. Spread into a buttered 13"x9"x2" pan cover and refrigerate for 30 minutes or until firm. Cut into bars.

Makes 2 dozen

Mary K. Schmucker (Kitchen)

AUNT ANNIE'S STYLE SOFT PRETZELS

1¼ c. water
1 t. yeast
¼ c. brown sugar
4 c. flour, best if you use wheat

2 c. water
2 T. baking soda
pretzel salt, if you desire

Dissolve yeast and brown sugar in water. Add flour. Knead. Let dough rise 20 minutes. Shape into pretzels. Dip in 2 cups water and 2 tablespoons baking soda. Sprinkle with pretzel salt. Bake at 500° for 6–8 minutes. Dip in melted butter. Serve with cheese, pizza sauce, or mustard.

Serves 8

Mary Stalter (Waitress)

CARAMEL CORN WITH CASHEWS

10 c. popped corn
   (¾ c. unpopped corn)
1 c. brown sugar
¾ c. butter, no substitutes

¼ c. Karo® Light Syrup
¼ t. baking soda
1 c. cashews

Boil brown sugar, butter, light Karo®, and baking soda. Pour over popped corn and cashews and stir. Bake at 200° for 15 to 20 minutes.

Susie Kauffman (Waitress)

CASHEW CRUNCH

1 c. butter
1 c. sugar
1 c. raw cashews

Combine all ingredients in a stainless steel saucepan. Cook mixture till it's a good caramel color and the cashews are golden. Stir all the time, not fast. Will only take 5–6 minutes. Place on a cookie sheet.

Linda Miller (Waitress)

CHEDDAR MIX

8 c. Wheat Chex®
3 c. Corn Chex®
16 oz. pretzels
16 oz. honey-roasted peanuts
1 c. vegetable oil
1 c. cheddar powder

Combine cereal, peanuts, and pretzels. Mix oil and cheddar powder. Pour over other ingredients and stir to coat. Bake at 250° for 30 minutes, stirring every 10 minutes. Cool and enjoy!

Loranna Hochstetler (Kitchen)

Pies should be baked in non-shiny pans to enhance the browning. Glass baking dishes also work well.

CHEERIO® CLUSTERS

1 c. sugar
1 c. corn syrup
1 c. peanut butter
1 T. butter
7 c. Cheerios® cereal

Mix sugar and corn syrup and bring to a boil. Then remove from heat and add peanut butter. Last mix the Cheerios® in and then spoon out clusters onto wax paper to whatever size desired.

Jill Miller (Daughter-in-Law of Bob & Sue)

CHOCOLATE COVERED CHIPS

24 oz. white chocolate
confectionery coating
14 oz. thick ripple-cut potato
chips

24 oz. milk chocolate or dark
chocolate confectionery
coating

Melt white coating in a double boiler over simmering water or in a micro-wave-safe bowl. Dip chips halfway in coating; shake off excess. Place on waxed paper-lined baking sheets to harden. When hardened, melt milk or dark chocolate coating and dip other half of chips. Allow to harden.

Makes 4 lbs.   Anna Mary Yoder (Waitress)

CINNAMON POPCORN

3 qt. popped corn
⅓ c. butter
¼ c. sugar

¾ t. cinnamon
¼ t. salt

Place popped corn in large baking pan and set aside. In small saucepan combine remaining ingredients and cook over low heat until butter is melted and sugar dissolved. Remove from heat. Add to popped corn and toss lightly to mix well. Bake at 300° for 15 minutes or until hot and crisp.

Matt Blosser (Waiter)

ELEPHANT EARS

2 c. milk
5 T. sugar
5 T. shortening
1 T. salt

2 pkgs. yeast
2 c. warm water
6 c. flour
2 qt. oil for frying

Scald milk. Add sugar, shortening, and salt. Cool. Sprinkle yeast into warm water. Add milk mixture and 2 cups flour. Beat until smooth. Stir in enough flour to make dough stiff. Turn onto floured board and knead until smooth and elastic, 8–10 minutes. Place in greased bowl. Cover and let rise until doubled, 1 hour. Divide into 6–8 balls. Roll to form elephant ears. Deep fry one at a time at 375° for 3–5 minutes per side and then coat with cinnamon and sugar. Serve hot.

Makes 6–8   Christina Yoder (Busser)

FINGER JELL-O®

4 envelopes Knox® gelatin
3 3-oz. pkgs. Jell-O®, any flavor you wish
4 c. boiling water
½ c. cold water to dissolve gelatin

Mix Jell-O® and hot water and stir. Then mix gelatin and cold water together, stirring well. Then pour into hot mixture and stir. Pour into 9"x13" pan. Let chill and set before you cut it.

Anita Wanamaker (Kitchen)

2-LAYER FINGER JELL-O®

3 pkgs. Knox® gelatin
3 small boxes Jell-O®, any flavor
½ pt. whipping cream

Dissolve 3 packages of gelatin in ½ cup of cold water. Mix 2½ cups boiling water with the 3 packages of Jell-O®, then combine with the gelatin. Mix well until all ingredients are dissolved, then add ½ pint of whipping cream. Stir well. Put in a 9"x13" pan and cool in refrigerator immediately. As this cools it will separate into two layers, one dark and one light.

Jody Yoder (Waitress)

FRIED PECANS

½ c. butter
1 t. salt
1 t. Accent® seasoning
1 t. garlic powder
2 qt. pecan halves

Melt butter, then add seasonings and mix well. Then add pecans. Bake at 250° until good and crisp, stirring every 15 minutes. Delicious just to munch on at snack time.

Christina Yoder (Busser)

My son, eat honey because it is good,
And the honeycomb which is sweet to your taste. . . .

Prov. 24:13

SPICED PECANS

1 egg white
1 t. cold water
1 lb. pecan halves

½ c. sugar
1 t. salt
½ t. cinnamon

Beat egg whites slightly, add water, beat until frothy, but not stiff. Fold in pecans. Combine sugar, salt, and cinnamon and mix well. Spread on 9"x12" buttered pan. Bake at 250° for 1 hour.

Sue Miller (Owner)

HOLIDAY CHOCOLATE PRETZEL RINGS

48–50 pretzel rings or mini twists
8-oz. pkg. milk chocolate kisses

¼ c. M&M's® candies, seasonal colors

Place pretzels on greased baking sheets. Place a kiss in the center of each pretzel and bake at 275° for 2–3 minutes or until chocolate is softened. Remove from oven, place 1 M&M® on each pretzel and press down slightly. Refrigerate 5–10 minutes or until chocolate is firm. Store at room temperature.

Makes 4 dozen   Conrad Yoder (Grandson of Bob & Sue)

NUTTY CRACKERS

1 stick butter
1 stick margarine
6 T. sugar

1 pkg. Club® Crackers
½ c. pecan pieces

Line a jelly roll pan with foil. Lay the cracker in a single layer over the bottom of the foil lined pan. Bring the butter, margarine, and sugar to a boil for 2 minutes. Pour over the crackers and sprinkle on the nuts. Bake 10 minutes in a 350° oven. Immediately transfer to a brown paper bag to drain and cool. The foil and brown paper bag are extremely important; do not substitute.

Alice Moy (Administration)

PARTY MIX

½ c. butter
3 T. Worcestershire sauce
2 t. Lawry's® seasoning salt
½ t. garlic powder
2 c. pretzel sticks
14 c. cereal: Crispix®, Oat Squares®, and Kix® (any proportion is okay)
4 c. cashews, pecans, or mixed nuts

Add first 4 ingredients and put in microwavable bowl. Heat until butter is melted. Stir. Put cereal, pretzels, and nuts into stainless bowl. Pour butter mixture over everything and coat well. Bake on a cookie sheet for 45 minutes at 275°, stirring every 15 minutes. Wonderful for snack time. You may also add corn chips or Bugles® if you like.

Melissa Miller (Waitress)

 If happiness could be bought, we'd be unhappy about the price.

POPCORN BALLS

2 gal. popped popcorn
1 c. corn syrup
1 T. vinegar
1 T. butter

Combine corn syrup, vinegar and butter and boil until brittle ball forms in cold water. To test for brittle ball, put a couple drops in cup of cold water. If it forms a small hard ball, it's ready to pour over popped corn; stir. Butter hands and form into balls.

Makes 2–3 dozen

Mary Lewallen (Bakery Sales)

PUPPY CHOW® STYLE CANDY

10–11 c. Rice Chex® cereal
12 oz. chocolate chip or butterscotch chips
1 stick butter
½ c. peanut butter
2 c. powdered sugar

Melt chips and butter and then add peanut butter and powdered sugar. Pour over cereal and stir. Store in an airtight container.

Wanda Mullett (Waitress)

Lemons that are heated before squeezing will give almost twice the quantity of juice.

RACHEL'S RANCH PARTY MIX

1 box Cheerios® cereal
1 box Corn Chex® cereal
1 box Rice Chex® cereal
1 box Honeycomb® cereal
1 bag pretzels
1 or 2 pkgs. ranch dressing mix, dry
¼ c. vegetable or corn oil

Pour all ingredients in trash bag. Shake till all is mixed. Serve. You can add peanuts, nuts or whatever you wish.

Rachel Yoder (Waitress)

SEASONED PRETZELS

24-oz. bag pretzels
¼ t. garlic salt
½ t. dill seed
½ t. lemon pepper
1 pkg. ranch dressing mix

Mix together in a big bowl. Let it set out and stir occasionally until dry.

Jody Yoder (Waitress)

MUSTARD PRETZELS

1 pkg. or 4 T. Hidden Valley® salad dressing dry mix
1½ c. salad oil
1 t. garlic
1½ t. dill, weed or seed
¾ t. lemon pepper
3 T. dry mustard
pretzels

Mix all ingredients (except pretzels) together in a large bowl; add pretzels. Toss until all are covered. Put on cookie sheets. Bake at 200° or 250° until they are dry. You can also add accent salt if desired.

Marilyn Nisley (Bakery)

TRAIL MIX

2 lb. dry roasted peanuts
2 lb. cashews
1 lb. raisins

1 lb. M&M's®
½ lb. flaked coconut

Combine all ingredients in a large bowl. Store in an airtight container. This is a super snack. This mix is a tasty treat anytime.

Makes 6 quarts   Mary K. Schmucker (Cook)

WHITE CHOCOLATE PARTY MIX

5 c. Cheerios® cereal
5 c. Corn Chex® cereal
2 c. salted peanuts
1 lb. M&M's® cereal

2 12-oz. pkgs. vanilla baking
   chips or white chocolate bark
3 T. vegetable oil

In a large bowl combine the first four ingredients, set aside. In a microwave safe bowl, heat chips and oil on medium high for two minutes, stirring once. Microwave on high for 10 seconds. Stir until smooth. Pour over cereal mixtures and mix well. Spread onto 3 waxed paper-lined baking sheets and let cool. Break apart and store in an airtight container.

Makes 5 quarts   Ellen Mishler (Administration)

WHITE TRASH

6 c. Crispix® cereal
4 c. small pretzels
2 c. dry roasted peanuts

½ lb. M&M's® candies
1¼ lb. white chocolate
a few sprinkles of paraffin

Mix all ingredients together in a bowl, except paraffin and white chocolate. Melt together the white chocolate and paraffin; pour over snacks. Put on cookie sheet to cool. Break in pieces and store in an airtight container.

                                              Wanda Mullet (Waitress)

 The meek shall eat and be satisfied.
Ps. 22:26

WHITE TRASH

1 lb. white chocolate
4 c. Crispix® cereal
4 c. pretzels
1 c. peanuts
1 lb. M&M's® candies, optional

Mix Crispix®, pretzels, peanuts, and M&M's® together. Then melt white chocolate and mix well. Let dry.

Susie Kauffman (Waitress)

APPLE DIP

8 oz. cream cheese, softened
½ c. apple butter
½ c. brown sugar
½ t. vanilla
½ c. peanuts, chopped

Mix together all ingredients. Then serve and dip apples in it. May also be used with other fruit. Variation: Add 1 c. marshmallow creme.

Sylvia Smith (Bakery Sales)
Mary Miller (Bakery Production)
Kathy Miller (Daughter-in-Law of Bob & Sue)

APPLE CARAMEL DIP

1 can Eagle Brand® milk
1 stick butter
1 c. brown sugar
½ c. white Karo® syrup

Cook in a double boiler until smooth and creamy. Cool and then serve.

Charlotte Miller (Waitress)

 FRUIT DIP

13-oz. jar marshmallow cream
8-oz. pkg. cream cheese
8-oz. tub whipped topping

Combine all ingredients and mix well. Serve with fresh fruit.

Kathy Miller (Daughter-in-Law of Bob & Sue)

FRUIT DIP

2 c. pineapple juice
2 T. clear gelatin
½ c. sugar

8-oz. pkg. cream cheese, softened
9 oz. Cool Whip®

Cook pineapple juice, gelatin, and sugar until thick. When cool, add cream cheese and Cool Whip®. Mix together until creamy. Serve with sliced apples, bananas, grapes, kiwi, and strawberries.

Norma Lehman (Bakery)
Elizabeth Miller (Kitchen)

SUGAR-FREE FRUIT DIP

1 c. low-fat cottage cheese
4 t. vanilla

8 packets of Equal® sweetener

Put all ingredients into a blender and blend until smooth.

Sylvia Smith (Bakery Sales)

YUMMY FRUIT DIP

8 oz. cream cheese, softened
8 oz. sour cream
⅔ c. cream of coconut,
    Coco Lopez®

¾ c. brown sugar
1 t. vanilla
12-oz. tub Cool Whip®

Mix ingredients together until smooth. Fold in Cool Whip® last. Refrigerate or freeze up to 6 months. This makes plenty of dip!

Jill Miller (Daughter-in-Law of Bob & Sue)

JODI'S DIP

1 pkg. ranch powdered dip
16 oz. sour cream

1 c. shredded cheddar cheese
¼–½ c. bacon bits

Add all ingredients in bowl and stir together. Refrigerate a couple hours before using. This makes for a better flavor! Good with pretzels, baby carrots, or celery.

Serves 8–10

Judith Kauffman (Cook)

B.L.T. DIP WITH PITA BREAD

1 tomato
6 bacon slices, cooked crisp
½ c. celery
2 T. onion
8 oz. cream cheese, softened
1 t. sugar
½ c. ranch dressing
4 pita bread rounds

Dice tomatoes, chop bacon, celery, and onion. Combine all ingredients except pita bread. Slice open pita breads and cut each half into 6 wedges. Lay flat on baking stone and bake 8 minutes at 400°. Serve alongside dip.

Serves 12   Doretta Wingard (Waitress)

CHIP DIP

2 lb. hamburger
1 pkg. taco seasoning
1 can cream of mushroom soup
1 can refried beans
1 sm. container sour cream
1 sm. jar salsa
1 pkg. grated cheddar cheese

Brown hamburger in skillet, drain, and put meat in Crock-Pot®. Add seasoning, cream of mushroom soup, refried beans, sour cream, and salsa. Stir well. Last add the package of cheese and continue heating until cheese melts. Serve with cheese-flavored chips.

Rachel Yoder (Waitress)

Amish Expression
"It wonders me."
(It makes me wonder.)

DAIRY DELICIOUS DIP

8 oz. cream cheese, softened
½ c. sour cream
¼ c. white sugar
¼ c. brown sugar
2 T. maple syrup

Mix cream cheese, sour cream, sugars, and syrup. Beat until smooth. Chill and serve with fresh fruit.

Makes 2 cups   Norma Lehman (Bakery)

EASY NACHO DIP

1 lb. ground beef or ground turkey
½ pkg. taco seasoning mix
1 lg. can Cheez Whiz®
1 can cream of mushroom soup

1 bottle mild salsa
1 can refried beans
sour cream
shredded cheese

Brown meat, drain and add taco seasoning mix. Put in slow cooker and add Cheese Whiz®, cream of mushroom soup, salsa, and beans. Heat and simmer until ready to serve. Garnish with shredded cheese on top and spoon sour cream on top of cheese. Serve with nacho chips.

Anita Yoder (Daughter of Bob & Sue)

FRESH SALSA

4 c. fresh tomatoes, chopped and peeled
¼ c. onion, finely chopped
1–4 jalapeno peppers, seeded and finely chopped

1 T. oil, olive or vegetable
1 T. vinegar
1 t. ground cumin
1 t. salt
1 garlic clove, minced

In a bowl combine all ingredients and mix well. Serve with chips.

Makes 1 quart

Arlene Miller (Waitress)

MEXICAN LAYER DIP

1 can refried beans
16 oz. sour cream
1 pkg. taco seasoning mix
mild salsa or taco sauce

2 c. cheese, grated
lettuce, chopped
tomatoes, chopped
green onions, chopped

First place refried beans in 9"x13" dish. Combine sour cream with taco seasoning mix. Spread on top of beans. Layer the rest of ingredients in the order given. Serve with nacho chips.

Angela Miller (Daughter-in-Law of Bob & Sue)

MILD MEXICAN SALSA

10 tomatoes, peeled and chopped
3 c. onions, chopped
2 green peppers, chopped
3–4 jalapeño peppers, chopped- seeds and all

12-oz. can tomato paste
½ c. white vinegar
1 T. salt
1 T. garlic powder

Put all the ingredients in a large pan. Bring the mixture to a boil and simmer for two hours. Cool and serve with your favorite chips. Note: If you like a hotter sauce, just add more jalapeño peppers.

Luan Westfall (Purchasing Manager)

SALSA

10–16 lbs. tomatoes
10 cloves garlic
6 sweet green peppers
4 chili peppers
8 jalapeño peppers
2 large onions

2 stalks celery
¾ c. sugar, optional
¼ c. salt
1½ T. oregano
½ c. clear gelatin
¾ c. white vinegar

Chop or process vegetables in food processor, put into large kettle. Bring to boil and boil for 10 minutes. After boiling add sugar, salt, oregano, and gelatin mixed with the vinegar. Cook for several more minutes. Put into pint jars and process for 20 minutes in a boiling water canner. Note: More peppers can be added for a spicier salsa.

Makes 15–20 pints   Cassie Berney (Village Shops)

TACO BEAN DIP

8 oz. salsa
8 oz. sour cream
16 oz. refried beans
1 c. sharp cheddar cheese

1 c. lettuce, finely shredded
¼ c. green onions, chopped
2 T. black olives, sliced

Mix together or layer and serve with tortilla chips.

Kathy Miller (Daughter-in-Law of Bob & Sue)

TACO DIP

1 lb. hamburger
1 onion, chopped
1 pkg. taco seasoning
2 cans refried beans
1 c. sour cream

½ c. mayonnaise
1 small can black olives
2 tomatoes or salsa
8-oz. pkg. shredded cheese

Fry hamburger and onions until browned. Then add taco seasoning and refried beans. Put in 8–9″ dish. Mix sour cream and mayonnaise and put on top of hamburger. Then put black olives and tomatoes or salsa on top of sour cream mixture. Put cheese on top. Serve with tortilla chips. Add lettuce for a taco salad.

Susie Kauffman (Waitress)

VEGGIE DIP

32 oz. Hellmann's® mayonnaise
16 oz. sour cream
2 T. parsley flakes

2 t. dill weed
1 t. Accent® seasoning

Mix fresh jar of mayonnaise and sour cream, then add other ingredients. Serve with all kinds of vegetables. Do not use refrigerated Hellmann's®; it comes out lumpy. Keeps up to a month in an airtight container in refrigerator.

Delora Harker (Bakery Production)

PIZZA DIP

8 oz. cream cheese, softened
½ c. sour cream
¼ t. dried oregano
¼ t. garlic powder

¾ c. pizza sauce
½ c. pepperoni, chopped
1 c. mozzarella cheese, shredded
tortilla chips

Mix first four ingredients until well blended. Spread in a lightly greased 9″ pie pan. Spoon pizza sauce evenly over cream cheese mixture and sprinkle with pepperoni. Bake at 350° for 10 minutes. Sprinkle with mozzarella cheese and bake 10 minutes more or until cheese is melted. Serve with tortilla chips.

Serves 4

Polly Miller (Bakery)

APPLE SANTA

medium shiny red apple
large marshmallows
raisins
red cherry fruit rolls

corn syrup
toothpicks
cotton

For each Santa attach marshmallows for arms, legs, and head to an apple with toothpicks. Add raisins for eyes and a nose. Make the peaked cap from the fruit roll. Using corn syrup attach a cotton beard and trim if necessary. Prop the apple in the back with toothpick.

Mary K. Schmucker (Cook)

CHEDDAR CHEESE SPREAD

8-oz. container sharp Cheddar
    cheese spread
1 stick light margarine

8-oz. pkg. light cream cheese
¼ t. garlic powder
2 T. parsley flakes

Let the cheese spread, margarine, and cream cheese come to room temperature. Place all the ingredients into a bowl and blend well with a mixer. Place the mixture in a container and refrigerate until ready to use. Serve with your favorite crackers.

Luan Westfall (Purchasing Manager)

CHEESE BALL

3 lbs. cream cheese, softened
4 pkgs. Eckrich Slender®
    sliced beef

1 t. seasoned salt
1 t. Accent® seasoning

Mix cream cheese, accent, and seasoned salt together into a ball. Cut beef slices in ½" squares. Spread pieces of meat on cutting board then roll cheese so that meat covers ball on all sides. Serve with Ritz® style crackers.

Delora Harker (Bakery Production)

 Worry is a misuse of imagination.

CHEESE BALL

2 8-oz. pkgs. cream cheese
1 pkg. chipped chopped beef
1 jar Old English® cheddar cheese
½ t. Accent® seasoning
6 green onions, stems also, chopped fine
1 T. Worcestershire sauce
¼ t. garlic powder

Form in 1 or 2 balls and before serving roll in nuts and parsley.

Pam Frey (Bakery)

CHEESE BALL

8-oz. pkg. cream cheese, softened
8-oz. pkg. American cheese, softened
¼ t. garlic salt
2 T. Worcestershire sauce
¼ t. liquid smoke
1 oz. finely chopped smoked ham
⅓ c. chopped pecans

Cut cream cheese into small cubes and stir. Slowly add cubed American cheese and mix, then add the last 4 ingredients. Form into a ball. Cover with plastic wrap and refrigerate.

LORD, who may abide in Your tabernacle?
Who may dwell in Your holy hill?
He who walks uprightly,
　And works righteousness,
　And speaks the truth. . . .
　　　　　　　　Ps. 15:1–2

DOUBLE DELICIOUS SPREAD

1 c. mayonnaise
parsley flakes, as desired
1 envelope Hidden Valley® ranch dressing mix
2 c. sour cream

Combine all ingredients. Mix well. Good on crackers or vegetables.

Pam Frey (Bakery)

PINEAPPLE CHEESE BALL

2 8-oz. pkgs. cream cheese,
   softened
1 small onion, diced
8 oz. crushed pineapple,
   well drained
1 small green pepper, diced

1 T. seasoned salt
½ pkg. sliced ham, chopped
   (optional)
parsley
chopped nuts

Combine cream cheese, onion, pineapple, pepper, seasoned salt, and ham. Roll into a ball. Roll into parsley and crushed nuts. Refrigerate until hard. Variation: May be made without ham, but add 1 c. pecans to cheese ball, and roll in 1 c. pecans.

Arlene Miller (Waitress)
Luella Yoder (Kitchen/Buffet)

DENVER SANDWICH RING

3 c. Bisquick® baking mix
⅔ c. cooking oil
½ c. milk
2 eggs

⅔ c. chopped onion
⅔ c. chopped green peppers
3 c. cubed ham

Mix everything together and drop onto ungreased pizza pan around outer edge, forming a ring. Bake at 425° for 15 minutes or until golden brown. Serve with cheese sauce.

Martha Hochstedler (Cook)

KELLOGG'S CORN FLAKES® FRUIT PIZZA

4 c. Kellogg's Corn Flakes®
   (makes 1 cup crushed)
2 T. sugar
2 T. margarine, softened

2 T. Karo® Light Syrup
2 8-oz. pkgs. light cream cheese
7-oz. jar marshmallow cream
3 c. sliced fresh or canned fruit

Preheat oven to 350°. In medium-size bowl combine crushed Corn Flakes®, sugar, softened margarine, and syrup. Press mixture evenly and firmly in bottom of 12" pizza pan. Bake 5 minutes or till lightly browned. Cool. Combine cream cheese and marshmallow cream and spread over crust. Chill for 1 hour or until firm. Arrange fruit over cream cheese mixture.

Serves 12

Katie Miller (Bakery)

MOM'S SAUERKRAUT BALLS

1 lb. pork sausage
1 medium onion, chopped
1 stick butter
1 c. flour
2½ c. chicken broth
3 lbs. sauerkraut, drained and rinsed

Coating:
2 c. flour
2 eggs
1 c. milk
2 c. cracker crumbs

Brown sausage in large skillet, add chopped onion. Sauté until onion is translucent. Add butter. When butter is melted add 1 cup of flour to thicken. Add the broth and then sauerkraut. Mix well and chill several hours or overnight. Form mixture into balls (a little smaller than a golf ball) dip in flour, then in egg wash made of 2 eggs and 1 cup of milk, and then finally roll in cracker crumbs. Roll balls in your hands to help them hold together. Chill and then deep fry until golden brown. Serve hot.

Serves 12   Glenda Koshmider (Restaurant Gifts)

MUSHROOM LOGS

1 lb. mushrooms
½ c. butter
6 T. flour
1½ t. salt
½ t. Accent® seasoning

2 c. light cream
2 t. lemon juice
1 t. onion salt
2 loaves white bread

Sauté mushrooms, chopped finely, in butter. Add flour, salt, and accent. Stir in cream and cook until thick, stirring constantly. Add lemon juice and onion salt. Cut off crusts from each slice of bread. Roll slices flat with rolling pin. Spread each slice with mushroom mixtures and then roll up like a jelly roll. Freeze slightly and cut into thirds. Freeze until ready to serve. Bake at 375° for 15 to 20 minutes. Can make this a week ahead and freeze.

Makes 2–3 dozen   Sharon Schlabach (Waitress)

 The extra mile is never crowded.

PINEAPPLE LI'L SMOKIES®

1 c. packed brown sugar
3 T. all purpose flour
2 t. ground mustard
1 c. pineapple juice

½ c. vinegar
1½ t. soy sauce
2 lb. Li'l Smokies® mini smoked
   sausage links

In a large saucepan, combine sugar, flour and mustard. Gradually stir in pineapple juice, vinegar and soy sauce. Bring to a boil and cook for 2 minutes, stirring constantly. Add sausages; stir to coat. Cook for 5 minutes or until heated through. Serve warm.

Makes 8 dozen   Anna Mary Yoder (Waitress)

PINWHEELS

8 tortilla shells
8 oz. chives and onion cream
   cheese

½ c. shredded cheese
8 slices of sliced roast beef
   and/or sliced ham

Spread 2 T. cream cheese on each tortilla shell. Sprinkle with cheese and lay a slice of beef or ham on each tortilla. Roll up and refrigerate for 3–4 hours or overnight. Slice in 1–1½" slices and serve with salsa.

Serves 8   Martha Coblentz (Bakery)

SOUTHWEST CHEESECAKE

16 oz. cream cheese, softened
2 c. shredded cheddar cheese
2 c. dairy sour cream, divided
1½ packets taco seasoning
3 eggs, room temperature

4-oz. can chopped green chilies,
   drained
⅔ c. salsa
tortilla chips

Combine cheeses and beat until fluffy. Stir in one cup sour cream and taco seasonings. Beat in eggs, one at a time. Fold in chilies. Pour into 9" springform pan and bake at 350° for 35–40 minutes or until center is just firm. Remove from oven. Cool for 10 minutes. Spoon remaining sour cream over top of cake and return to oven for 5 minutes. Cool completely on wire rack. Refrigerate, covered, overnight. Remove from pan. Place on serving plate. Top with salsa. Serve with tortilla chips.

Linda Miller (Cashier/Hostess)

 The meek shall inherit the earth. . . .
Ps. 37:11

VEGGIE BARS

2 tubes crescent rolls
¾ c. Hellmann's® mayonnaise
1 pkg. ranch dressing mix
2 8-oz. pkgs. cream cheese, room temperature
½ c. fresh broccoli, chopped
½ c. green pepper, chopped
½ c. scallions, chopped
½ c. carrots, chopped
½ c. tomato, chopped
½ c. black olives, chopped
¾ c. shredded cheddar or colby cheese

Spray 11"x14" baking sheet. Roll out tubes of crescent rolls onto baking sheet and press out to edges. Bake at 350° for 8–10 minutes. Mix together mayonnaise, ranch dressing, and cream cheese. May process in food blender to make creamy. When crust is cooled, spread the dressing on top. Should be ¼" thick. Sprinkle vegetables on top in order listed. Sprinkle cheese on top of vegetables. Press down with wax paper. Keep refrigerated until served. Cut into squares.

Makes 12–24 bars   Barbara Skarbek (Cashier/Hostess)

TACO RING

1½ lb. hamburger
1 pkg. taco seasoning
2 pkgs. crescent rolls
1 pkg. shredded cheese
1 head lettuce, chopped
10 oz. sour cream
2–3 roma tomatoes, chopped
1 lg. bell green pepper

Brown hamburger and add taco seasoning, drain. Place unbaked crescent rolls on pizza pan, putting wide ends in the middle with the pointed ends facing out (like a flower.) Put a small scoop of seasoned hamburger on each wide end. Add shredded cheese if desired. Fold the pointed ends toward the middle over the hamburger. Bake at 325° for 20–25 minutes. Cut the top off of the pepper and remove seeds. Put salsa inside pepper and place in middle of taco ring. Then place lettuce and tomatoes around pepper. Put small amount of sour cream on crescent roll and serve. Serve with ranch dressing.

Serves 5–10   Rachel Yoder (Waitress)

YUMMY VEGGIE PIZZA

Crust:
1 c. lukewarm water
2 T. or 2 pkgs. yeast
2 t. sugar
1 t. garlic powder
2 t. onions, chopped finely
½ t. salt
1 T. parsley flakes
3 c. flour

Dressing:
1 c. light or fat-free salad dressing, mayonnaise
2 T. mustard
2 T. honey
¼ c. Splenda® sweetener

Toppings:
2 c. lettuce, shredded
carrots, shredded
¼ c. cauliflower
broccoli, shredded
¼ c. tomato, optional
2 hard-boiled eggs, sliced
½ c. cheese, shredded
1 c. cold turkey meat cuts, chopped

Put warm water into 3 qt. bowl. Add yeast, sugar, garlic, salt, onions, and parsley flakes. Mix together and add 2½ c. flour to mix. Add last ½ c. flour, mix. Don't get dough too dry. Dough should be slightly sticky. Let set to rise until double in size. Press out onto 16" round pan or large cookie sheet. Let rise until doubled in pan. Bake at 375° for 10–12 minutes or until slightly brown on top. Cool. For the honey mustard dressing, mix together dressing ingredients until well mixed and then place on top of cooled pizza crust. Place toppings on top of dressing in the order given. You may add or take away from this list and put on the veggies you love the most. Makes a meal in itself or is good served with soup.

Serves 6–8   Ryan Zimmerman (Cashier/Host Manager)

 SWEET AND SOUR LI'L SMOKIES®

2 lb. Li'l Smokies® mini smoked sausage links
⅔ c. Heinz Chili Sauce®
⅔ c. orange marmalade*

In large skillet, heat Li'l Smokies® 5–6 minutes or until heated through. Stir in chili sauce and marmalade. Cook, stirring occasionally until sauce thickens and Li'l Smokies® are glazed. Variation: Other jams or jellies may be substituted such as peach, grape, plum or apricot.

Linda Miller (Waitress)

CAPPUCCINO MIX

2 c. coffee creamer
2 c. dry milk
4 c. instant chocolate milk mix
¾ c. instant coffee
1½ c. white sugar
1½ c. powdered sugar

½ t. cinnamon
¼ t. nutmeg
½ t. salt

Mix all ingredients together and store in an airtight container. Use 2 to 3 tablespoons mix per cup of hot water when ready to serve.

Norma Lehman (Bakery)
Sharon Frye (Waitress)

CAPPUCCINO MIX

2 c. dry milk
1 c. powdered sugar
⅔ c. Nesquik®

1 c. French vanilla creamer
½ c. instant coffee

Mix all ingredients together. Store in an airtight container. Use 2–3 tablespoons of mix to 1 cup of hot water when ready to serve.

Martha Miller (Hostess/Cashier)

HOMEMADE CAPPUCCINO MIX

3 8-oz. cans French vanilla creamer
¾ c. regular creamer
2 c. instant coffee

1½ c. powdered sugar
½ c. hot chocolate mix w/ marshmallows
¼–½ t. nutmeg

Mix ingredients well. Put desired amount in a cup and add hot water.

Jody Yoder (Waitress)

Dry fresh bread when you need croutons or crumbs. One quart of cubes in a rectangular dish will dry in 6–7 minutes. Stir a few times.

COFFEE PUNCH

1 c. water
3 c. sugar
¼ c. instant coffee
1 gallon milk

½ gal. vanilla ice cream,
   softened
½ gal. chocolate ice cream,
   softened

Bring water to boil, add sugar and coffee until dissolved. Cool. Then combine coffee mixture and milk. Just before serving, gently stir in softened ice cream. Serve immediately.

Serves 65 (½–cup Servings)   Norine Yoder (Restaurant Gifts)

HOT CHOCOLATE MIX

8 qts. dry milk
6 oz. coffee creamer

1-lb. box Nesquik®
1 lb. powdered sugar

Mix all ingredients together. Put ¼ c. mix into 1 c. hot water.

Joyce Schmucker (Kitchen)
Norma Lehman (Bakery)

DELICIOUS PUNCH

12 oz. grape concentrate
6 oz. orange juice concentrate
¼ c. lemon juice

1½ c. water
¼ c. sugar (scant)
2-liter bottle ginger ale

Mix all ingredients together. You may add ice to serve.

Ellen Mishler (Administration)

FROTHY ORANGE DRINK

6-oz. can frozen orange juice
   concentrate
1 c. water
1 c. milk

½ c. sugar
1 t. vanilla extract
8–10 ice cubes

Combine all ingredients in a blender. Cover and process until drink is thick and slushy. Serve immediately.

Makes 4 cups   Martha Miller (Hostess/Cashier)

ORANGE JULIUS® STYLE DRINK

6 oz. orange juice concentrate
4 T. sugar
1 c. milk

16–18 ice cubes
1 t. vanilla or maple flavoring
1 c. milk

Put first 5 ingredients in blender and blend well. Add remaining cup of milk and serve immediately. Delicious served with popcorn.

Sue Miller (Owner)

PEDDLERS PUNCH

3 c. water
2 c. sugar
46 oz. pineapple juice
3 c. orange juice

¼ c. lemon juice
2–3 ripe bananas
1 t. red food coloring
2 qts. club soda

Put water and sugar in saucepan and bring to a boil. Let cool to room temperature. Add pineapple, orange, and lemon juices. Put the bananas in blender with small amount of juice, blend, and add to the punch. Stir in red food dye to make a nice red color. Freeze syrup (everything except club soda) overnight. Thaw just until slushy; add club soda and serve.

Verna Lickfeldt (Restaurant Administration)

It is better to suffer wrong than to do it, better to be sometimes cheated than never to trust.

PUNCH

1 pkg. cherry Kool-Aid®
1 pkg. strawberry Kool-Aid®
2 c. sugar
3 qts. water

6-oz. can orange juice concentrate
6-oz. can lemon juice concentrate
2 qts. ginger ale

Mix all ingredients together and serve.

Makes 1½ gallons

Sue Miller (Owner)

SOUTHERN ICED TEA

20 small Lipton® tea bags
3–4 c. sugar

1 lemon

Place tea bags in pan of water and bring to a boil. Cut off heat and allow tea to brew for at least 10 minutes. Meanwhile, cut ends off lemon and cut in quarters. Put in blender with some water and chop for several seconds and then strain. Cover bottom of 2-gallon container with ice. Pour brewed tea over ice. Add more water to make 2 gallons. Add sugar to reach desired taste. Stir well. Serve cold over ice.

Makes 2 gallons   Wendy Miller (Bakery Sales)

STRAWBERRY FRUIT PUNCH

32-oz. can pineapple juice
12-oz. can frozen lemonade, undiluted
12-oz. can frozen orange juice, undiluted

2 cans water
1 pt. frozen sliced strawberries
2 qt. chilled ginger ale

Mix together first 5 ingredients. Add ginger ale just before serving.

Serves 20   Joyce Miller (Sunshine Farm Manager)

STRAWBERRY SMOOTHIE

½ c. sliced strawberries, frozen or fresh
⅓ of a banana

¼ c. vanilla yogurt
¼ c. orange juice
1 ice cube

Combine in blender all ingredients. Whirl until smooth.

Makes a 10-oz. serving. Can be frozen to make 4 strawberry pops.

Joyce Miller (Sunshine Farm Manager)

Don't slam the door. You may want to go back.

The night is far spent, the day is at hand. Therefore let us cast off the works of darkness, and let us put on the armor of light. Let us walk properly, as in the day, not in revelry and drunkenness, not in lewdness and lust, not in strife and envy. But put on the Lord Jesus Christ, and make no provision for the flesh, to fulfill its lusts.

Receive the one who is weak in the faith, but not to disputes over doubtful things. For one believes he may eat all things, but he who is weak eats only vegetables. Let not him who eats despise him who does not eat, and let not him who does not eat judge him who eats; for God has received him.

Rom. 13:12–14:3

STRAWBERRY/BANANA SHAKES

1½ ripe banana
1 pint strawberries
½ orange
6 ice cubes

1 t. vanilla
1 T. Nesquik®
1 qt. vanilla ice cream

Blend all ingredients together.

Serves 4–5   Mary Stalter (Waitstaff)

WEDDING PUNCH

3 large cans frozen orange juice
2 large cans frozen lemonade
2 cans (1 qt.) pineapple juice

4 qts. 7-Up®
½ c. sugar, optional

Combine all juices, adding water as directed on frozen juice cans. Add 7-Up®, sugar if desired, and ice.

Serves 100   Lorene Mast (Kitchen)

Canning & Miscellaneous

GENERAL OVEN CHART

Very Slow Oven = 250°–300°
Slow Oven = 300°–325°
Moderate Oven = 325°–375°
Hot Oven = 400°–450°
Very Hot Oven = 450°–500°

BREADS
Baking Powder Biscuits
450° for 12–15 minutes

Muffins
400°–425° for 20–25 minutes

Quick Breads
350° for 40–60 minutes

Yeast Breads
375°-400° for 45–60 minutes

Yeast Rolls
400° for 15–20 minutes

CAKES
Butter Loaf Cakes
350° for 45–60 minutes

Butter Layer Cakes
350°–375° for 25–35 minutes

Cupcakes
375° for 20–25 minutes

Chiffon Cakes
325° for 60 minutes

Sponge Cakes
325° for 60 minutes

Angel Food Cakes
325° for 60 minutes

COOKIES
Bar Cookies
350° for 25–30 minutes

Drop Cookies
350°–375° for 8–12 minutes

Rolled and Refrigerated Cookies
350°–400° for 8–12 minutes

PIE SHELLS
450° for 12–15 minutes

FILLED PIES
450° for 10 minutes, lower to 350°
for 40 minutes

ROASTS
Beef Roast
Rare = 325° for 18–20 min./lb.
Medium = 325° for 22–25 min./lb.
Well Done = 325° for 30 min./lb.

Chicken
325°–350° for 30 min./lb.

Duck
325°–350° for 25 min./lb.

Fish Fillets
500° for 15–20 min./lb.

Goose
325°–350° for 30 min./lb.

Ham
350° for 20–30 min./lb.

Lamb
300°–350° for 35 min./lb.

7-DAY SWEET PICKLES

7 lbs. cucumbers, sliced

Syrup:
1 qt. vinegar
8 c. sugar
1 T. salt
2 T. pickling spice in sack

Day 1: Cover cucumbers with fresh boiling water and let stand for 24 hours. Drain and repeat on days 2, 3, and 4. Day 5: Prepare syrup and bring to a boil and pour over cucumbers. Make sure cucumbers are covered. Day 6: Drain and reheat syrup to boiling and pour over cucumbers. Day 7: Drain and reheat syrup to boiling. Add cucumbers and bring to the boiling point. Pack hot in jars.

Makes 4–6 quarts   Angela Miller (Daughter-in-Law of Bob & Sue)

KETCHUP

2 gallons tomato juice
8 T. salt
2 onions, diced
2 or 3 c. vinegar

20 drops oil of cinnamon
20 drops oil of cloves
8 c. sugar
12 T. Perma-flo® modified starch

Combine first six ingredients, then boil down ⅓ of juice. Sift sugar and Perma-flo® together and add slowly to juice. Keep stirring and then let it boil real good and put in jars to seal. Very good!

Loranna Hochstetler (Kitchen)

FROZEN PICKLES

25 cucumbers
10 onions
¼ c. salt

ice cubes
3 c. vinegar
4 lbs. sugar

Slice cucumbers and onions so they are paper thin. Put them in a pan and add salt. Cover with ice cubes, let stand 24 hours. Then cook together vinegar and sugar till sugar is dissolved, cool. Drain onions and cucumbers, then cover with vinegar mixture and freeze.

Martha Hochstetler (Bakery)

STRAWBERRY-KIWI FREEZER JAM

2¾ c. strawberries, crushed
1¼ c. kiwi fruit, peeled and chopped

3¼ c. sugar
1 pack Certo® light pectin crystals

Measure prepared fruits into a large bowl. Measure sugar into a separate bowl and set aside. Combine Certo® with ¼ cup of the measured sugar. Gradually add to fruit, stirring well. Let stand 30 minutes, stirring occasionally. Stir in remaining sugar and continue to stir for 3 minutes until most of the sugar is dissolved. Pour into clean jars or plastic containers. Cover with tight lids and let stand at room temperature until set; may take up to 24 hours. Store in freezer or for 3 weeks in the refrigerator.

Makes 6 cups   Cassie Berney (Village Shops)

 **MUSH**

1¼ c. corn meal
2 T. flour
4 c. water

⅔ t. salt
¼ c. milk

Spray pan with non-stick spray. Mix corn meal and flour together and then set aside. Bring water and salt to a pre-boil. Add milk gradually. Add corn-meal mixture, stirring thoroughly. Reduce heat and simmer for 20 minutes.

MAYONNAISE

2 c. white sugar
2 T. flour
2 large eggs, beaten
1 t. salt

2 T. dry mustard
1 c. vinegar
1 c. hot water

Combine sugar, flour, eggs, salt, and dry mustard and mix well. Then add vinegar and water. Cook to a boil, stirring constantly until thick. Remove from heat and let cool. Place in container and refrigerate. Mix with equal part of Miracle Whip® when using for potato salad.

Lorene Mast (Kitchen)

STEAK MARINADE

1½ t. salt
1 t. pepper
1 t. chili powder
1 t. celery seed
¼ c. Worcestershire sauce

¼ c. brown sugar
¼ c. vinegar
¼ c. ketchup
2 c. water
1 t. meat tenderizer, unseasoned

Put all ingredients in a saucepan and bring to a boil. Cool slightly and pour over steaks. Marinate for 7–8 hours.

Jody Yoder (Waitress)

TARTAR SAUCE

1 c. mayonnaise
¼ c. milk

¼ c. sugar
2 T. sweet pickle relish

Combine all ingredients. Serve with fish.

Anita Yoder (Daughter of Bob & Sue)

CINNAMON SYRUP

½ c. Karo® Light Syrup
1 c. sugar
¼ c. water

1 t. cinnamon
½ c. evaporated milk

Bring first 4 ingredients (except evaporated milk) to a boil for 2 minutes. Cool for 5 minutes and then add evaporated milk. Recipe can be doubled. Great on waffles, pancakes, and corn bread. Store in refrigerator.

Amanda Strebin (Bakery Sales)

CINNAMON ORNAMENTS

1 c. cinnamon
1 T. cloves, ground
1 T. nutmeg

¾ c. applesauce
2 T. white glue

In a large bowl, combine spices, and then stir in applesauce and glue. Work 2–3 minutes to form a ball. If balls are too dry, add more applesauce. If too wet, add more cinnamon. Use cookie cutters to form any shape of ornament, then let ornaments dry.

Anita Yoder (Daughter of Bob & Sue)

PAP (BRY)

2 c. milk
3 rounded T. cornstarch
3 T. sugar

¼ t. salt
¼ c. milk

Bring milk to a boil. Mix cornstarch, sugar, salt, and additional milk together. Add to boiling milk and cook one minute stirring constantly. Serve sprinkled with brown sugar. This is very good for baby's first food.

Sue Miller (Owner)

IMITATION PLAY DOH®

2 c. flour
3 T. vegetable oil
4 t. cream of tartar

2 c. water
1 c. salt
food coloring

Mix all ingredients together in a pan. Cook over medium heat until mixture starts boiling or forms a ball (2–3 min.). Remove from heat and cool enough to be handled. Knead dough like bread until smooth and supple.

Danielle Yoder (Grandaughter of Bob & Sue)

COUGH REMEDY

1 lemon, sliced thin
½ pint flax seed

1 qt. water
2 oz. honey

Simmer lemon, flax seed and water for 4 hours. Do not boil. Strain while hot. Add honey. If it is less than 1 pint, add water to make 1 pint. Take 4 times a day and after each coughing spell. This remedy will be effective in 4–5 days. For children, give less. Keep refrigerated.

Lorene Mast (Kitchen)

EASTER EGG COLORING

1 T. white vinegar
½ c. boiling water

food coloring

Put vinegar in a cup and then add boiling water. Add whatever coloring you want to that cup. Dip in your cooked egg till it's the right color.

Lorene Mast (Kitchen)

Index

100 GOOD COOKIES 174
15-MINUTE CHICKEN AND RICE
    DINNER 97
2-LAYER FINGER JELLO® 276
7-DAY SWEET PICKLES 301

A

AFTER SCHOOL TREATS 273
AMERICAN CHOP SUEY 110
AMISH BEAN SOUP 70
AMISH COOKIES 174
AMISH SCRAMBLE 38
ANGEL CRUNCH 228
ANGEL FOOD CAKE DESSERT 237
APPETIZERS
    2-Layer Finger Jello® 276
    Apple Santa 287
    Cheddar Cheese Spread 287
    Cheese Ball 287, 288
    Denver Sandwich Ring 289
    Double Delicious Spread 288
    Kellogg's Corn Flakes® Fruit Pizza
      289
    Linda's Meatballs 89
    Mom's Sauerkraut Balls 290
    Mushroom Logs 290
    Pineapple Cheese Ball 289
    Pineapple Smokies 291
    Pinwheels 291
    Southwest Cheesecake 291
    Sweet and Sour Smokies 292
    Taco Ring 292
    Veggie Bars 293
    Yummy Veggie Pizza 293
APPLE CAKE 151
APPLE CARAMEL DIP 281
APPLE CRISP 237
APPLE CRUMB PIE 207
APPLE DANISH 29
APPLE DIP 281
APPLE MUFFINS 31
APPLE SANTA 287

APPLE SQUARES 238
APPLESAUCE CAKE 159
APRICOT FLUFF SALAD 56
AUNT ANNIE'S STYLE SOFT PRETZELS
    273
AUNT RUTH'S STRAWBERRY SALAD 46

B

BACON WRAPPED CHICKEN 97
BAKED BARBECUED CHICKEN 100
BAKED BEANS 139
BAKED FRENCH TOAST 30, 35
BAKED MASHED POTATOES 130
BAKED OATMEAL 41
BAKED PINEAPPLE CASSEROLE 113
BAKED SPAGHETTI 118
BAKES RICE PUDDING 241
BANANA BREAD 20
BANANA CAKE 152, 153
BANANA CHOCOLATE CHIP COOKIES
    Banana Chocolate Chip Cookies 174
BANANA OATMEAL BREAD 21
BANANA SQUARES 242
BARBECUED CHICKEN 99
BARS
    Can't Leave Alone Bars 189
    Cherry Fruit Bars 189
    Chess Brownies 189
    Chewy Date Nut Bars 190
    Chocolate Cheese Layered Bars 190
    Chocolate Chip Bars 191
    Chocolate Chip Marshmallow Bars
      191
    Chocolate Chip Squares 192
    Chocolate Scotcheroos 192
    Cowboy Bars 192
    Easy Chocolate Chip Bars 193
    Frosted Banana Bars 193
    Frosted Chocolate Chip Bars 194
    Frosted Raisin Cremes 194
    Fudge Nut Bars 195
    Fudgy Toffee Bars 195

German Chocolate Brownies with
  Cream Cheese 195, 196
Granola Bars 196
Marshmallow Brownie Delight 197
Mound Bars 197
Peanut Butter Chocolate Chip
  Granola Bars 198
Pumpkin Pie Squares 198
Rhubarb Custard Bars 199
Rice Krispies® Cereal Bars 199
Rice Krispies® Treats 200
Strawberry Bars 200
Sugar Cream Pie Squares 200
Yummy Bars 201
BASIL CHICKEN AND DUMPLING
  CASSEROLE 92
BEEF CRESCENT CASSEROLE 111
BEEF ENCHILADAS 125
BEEF FAJITAS 124
BEEF MACARONI AND CHEESE 101
BEEF WITH CAULIFLOWER AND SNOW
  PEAS 110
BEST BREAD PUDDING 30
BEST-EVER PEANUT BUTTER PIE 207
BETH'S MEATZZIA PIE 101
BEVERAGES
  Cappuccino Mix 294, 295
  Coffee Punch 295
  Delicious Punch 295
  Frothy Orange Drink 295
  Homemade Cappuccino Mix 294
  Hot Chocolate Mix 295
  Orange Julius® Style Drink 296
  Peddlers Punch 296
  Punch 296
  Southern Iced Tea 297
  Strawberry Fruit Punch 297
  Strawberry Smoothie 297
  Strawberry/Banana Shakes 298
  Wedding Punch 298
BLACK BOTTOM CUPCAKES 201
BLACK BOTTOM PIE 207, 208
Black Forest Cake 153
BLACK FOREST DUMP CAKE 153
BLACKBERRY COBBLER 242
BLACKBERRY DELIGHT 243
BLACKBERRY MUFFINS 31

BLACKBERRY PINWHEEL COBBLER 243
BLENDER BANANA BREAD 21
BLT DIP 283
BLUEBERRY BUCKLE 243, 244
BLUEBERRY COFFEE CAKE 154
BLUEBERRY SQUARES 238
BREAD 26, 32, 36, 41
  Amish Scramble 38
  Apple Danish 29
  Apple Muffins 31
  Baked French Toast 30, 35
  Baked Oatmeal 41
  Banana Bread 20
  Banana Oatmeal Bread 21
  Best Bread Pudding 30
  Blackberry Muffins 31
  Blender Banana Bread 21
  Bread Pudding 30
  Breakfast Casserole 38
  Breakfast Haystacks 39
  Breakfast Pizza 39
  Bubble Bread 22
  Butter Bright Pastries 33
  Cheese Souffle 39
  Chili Cheese Corn Muffins 32
  Cinnamon Rolls 34
  Corn Bread 22
  Cornmeal Yeast Bread 23
  Crescent Breakfast Pizza 40
  Danish Roll Glaze 35
  Dinner Rolls 24
  Easy Croissants 24
  Easy Oatmeal Bread 23
  Egg and Sausage Breakfast Casserole
    40
  Hot Porridge 41
  Maple Pecan Coffee Ring 35
  Marilyn's Easy White Bread 24
  Melt-in-Your-Mouth Biscuits 26
  Mom's Bread Pudding 31
  Mom's Homemade Bread 26
  Mom's Pancakes 37
  Nutty French Toast 36
  Oatmeal Brown Sugar Pancakes 37
  Oven French Toast with Nut Topping 3
  Overnight Buns 25
  Overnight Dinner Rolls 25

306

Pumpkin Bread 26
Raisin Bran® Muffins 32
Scrambled Egg Muffins 33
Skier French Toast 37
Soft Pretzels 27
Strawberry Bread 27
Turtle Bread 28
Whole Wheat Bread 28
Winter Garden Scrambled Eggs 41
Zucchini Muffins 32
BREAD PUDDING 30
BREAKFAST CASSEROLE 38
BREAKFAST HAYSTACKS 39
BREAKFAST PIZZA 39
BROCCOLI AND CAULIFLOWER
    CASSEROLE 141
BROCCOLI AND CREAMED CORN
    CASSEROLE 140
BROCCOLI CASSEROLE 140
BROCCOLI DELIGHT SALAD 64
BROCCOLI SALAD 63
BROCCOLI SLAW 61
BROCCOLI SOUP 71
BROCCOLI-CORN CASSEROLE 141
BROCCOLI-HAM HOT DISH 141
BROWN SUGAR COOKIES 175
BROWN SUGAR NUT CAKE 159
BRY (PAP) 304
BUBBLE BREAD 22
BUCKEYES CANDY 228
BURRITO CAASSEROLE 122
BUTTER BRIGHT PASTRIES 33
BUTTER CRISP ICE CREAM TOPPING 270
BUTTERCREME ICING 167
BUTTERMILK COOKIES 176
BUTTERSCOTCH PECAN DESSERT 244
BUTTERSCOTCH PIE 208
BUTTERSCOTCH PUDDING 245

C

CABBAGE CASSEROLE 142
CABBAGE SALAD 65
CACTUS SOUP 71
CAKES
    Apple Cake 151
    Applesauce Cake 159

Banana Cake 152, 153
Black Forest Cake 153
Black Forest Dump Cake 153
Blueberry Coffee Cake 154
Brown Sugar Nut Cake 159
Carrot Cake 154
Chocolate Cherry Cake 159
Chocolate Chip Nut Cake 159
Chocolate Chip Pudding Cake 158
Chocolate Mint Cake 159
Chocolate Salad Dressing Cake 158
Chocolate Snack Cake with Variations
    158
Chocolate Spice Cake 159
Chocolate Zucchini Cake 160
Coffee Cake 155
Cream Filled Coffee Cake 155
Crumb Cake 160
Delicious Chocolate Cake 160
Double Chocolate Chip Cake 159
Dump Cake 161
Earthquake Cake 161
Easy Coffee Cake 156
Fresh Apple Cake 152
Fruit Swirl Coffee Cake 156
Graham Streusel Coffee Cake 157
Heavenly Hash Cake 161
Mahogany Chiffon Cake 170
Maple Nut Cake 159
Mary Emma's Coffee Cake 157
Mississippi Mud Cake 162
Oatmeal-Molasses Cake 159
Old-Fashioned Walnut Cake 159
One-Step Angel Food Cake 162
Our Lord's Scripture Cake 162
Payday Cake 163
Pumpkin Cake 159
Sour Cream Spice Cake 163
Strawberry Pecan Cake 164
Texas Sheet Cake 164
Tropical Carrot Cake 154
Turtle Cake 165
White Sheet Cake 165
White Texas Sheet Cake 166
Zucchini Cake 166
CALIFORNIA BLEND VEGETABLE
    CASSEROLE 146

307

CANDIES
Angel Crunch 228
Buckeyes Candy 228
Caramels 228
Carters Candy 229
Cashew Brittle 229
Chip Kisses 229
Chocolate Carmel Candy 230
Chocolate Covered Chips 275
Christmas Bark Candy 230
Cream Cheese Candy Mints 231
Date Pecan Balls 231
Gram's Homemade Caramels 231
Mints 232
Ohio Buckeye Candy 232
Peanut Butter Fudge 232
Peanut Clusters 233
Puppy Chow® Style Candy 178
Special K® Cereal Candy 233
CANNING
7-Day Sweet Pickles 301
Frozen Pickles 301
Ketchup 301
Strawberry-Kiwi Freezer Jam 302
CAN'T LEAVE ALONE BARS 189
CAPPUCCINO MIX 294, 295
CARAMEL CHIFFON PIE 209
CARAMEL CORN WITH CASHEWS 273
CARAMEL FROSTING 167
CARAMEL SWEET POTATOES 134
CARAMELS 228
CARMEL APPLE SALAD 50
CAROL'S BEST PECAN PIE 212
CARROT CAKE 154
CARROT CASSEROLE 144
CARROT COOKIES 176
CARTERS CANDY 229
CASHEW BRITTLE 229
CASHEW CRUNCH 274
CELERY CASSEROLE 145
CHEDDAR CHEESE SPREAD 287
CHEDDAR MIX 274
CHEESE BALL 287, 288
CHEESE SOUFFLÉ 39
CHEESE TACOS 127
CHEESY BEEF SPIRALS 104
CHEESY POTATO SOUP 72

CHEERIO® CLUSTERS 274
CHEESY POTATOES 128
CHERRY APPLE SALAD 51
CHERRY CHIFFON DESSERT 245
CHERRY FRUIT BARS 189
CHERRY PIES 209
CHESS BROWNIES 189
CHEWY DATE NUT BARS 190
CHICKEN & VEGETABLES 100
CHICKEN CASSEROLE 91, 93
CHICKEN ENCHILADA CASSEROLE 124
CHICKEN ENCHILADAS 125
CHICKEN FAJITA PIZZA 123
CHICKEN MARBELLA 98
CHICKEN NOODLE CASSEROLE 90
CHICKEN NOODLE SOUP 73
CHICKEN ON SUNDAY 95
CHICKEN PARMESAN 98
CHICKEN SPAGHETTI SUPREME 117
CHICKEN SUPREME 93
CHICKENETT FOR A BUNCH 91
CHILI CHEESE CORN MUFFINS 32
CHILIES RELLENNO 111
CHINESE CABBAGE SALAD 68
CHINESE PEPPER STEAK 87
CHIP DIP 283
CHIP KISSES 229
CHOCLATE CHEESE LAYERED BARS 190
CHOCOLATE CARMEL CANDY 230
CHOCOLATE CHERRY CAKE 159
CHOCOLATE CHIP BARS 191
CHOCOLATE CHIP CHEESECAKE 245
CHOCOLATE CHIP COOKIE DOUGH
    CHEESECAKE 246
CHOCOLATE CHIP COOKIES 177
CHOCOLATE CHIP MARSHAMALLOW
    BARS 191
CHOCOLATE CHIP NUT CAKE 159
CHOCOLATE CHIP PUDDING CAKE 15
CHOCOLATE CHIP SQUARES 192
CHOCOLATE-COVERED CHIPS 275
CHOCOLATE CREAM CHEESE PIE 210
CHOCOLATE ÉCLAIR 249
CHOCOLATE LUSH 250
CHOCOLATE MINT CAKE 159
CHOCOLATE PEANUT BUTTER
    COOKIES 177, 178

CHOCOLATE PUDDING 251
CHOCOLATE SALAD DRESSING CAKE 158
CHOCOLATE SANDWICH COOKIES 178
CHOCOLATE SCOTCHEROOS 192
CHOCOLATE SNACK CAKE WITH VARIATIONS 158
CHOCOLATE SPICE CAKE 159
CHOCOLATE ZUCCHINI CAKE 160
CHRISTMAS BARK CANDY 230
CINNAMON CREAM CHEESE SQUARES 251
CINNAMON ORNAMENTS 303
CINNAMON POPCORN 275
CINNAMON ROLLS 34
CINNAMON SYRUP 303
CLOTHES PIN COOKIES 179
COCONUT CRUNCH 252
COCONUT CUSTARD PIE 210
COCONUT PIE 210
COFFEE CAKE 155
COFFEE PUNCH 295
COLD SOUP 72
COLESLAW 61
COMPANY ROAST BEEF 83
COMPANY SPECIAL CHICKEN SALAD 59
CONCORD GRAPE PIE 211
COOKIES
  100 Good Cookies 174
  Amish Cookies 174
  Banana Chocolate Chip Cookies 174
  Brown Sugar Cookies 175
  Buttermilk Cookies 176
  Carrot Cookies 176
  Chocolate Chip Cookies 177
  Chocolate Peanut Butter Cup Cookies 177, 178
  Chocolate Sandwich Cookies 178
  Clothes Pin Cookies 179
  Cream Wafers 180
  Easter Story Cookies 173
  Favorite Peanut Butter Oatmeal Cookies 180
  Fire Truck Cookies 181
  Fudgy Bonbons 181
  Giant Spice Cookies 182

Grandma's Soft Brown Sugar Cookies 182
Gumdrop Cookies 183
Holiday Sugar Cookies 183
Just Right Chocolate Chip Cookies 177
Kieflies (Hungarian Christmas Cookies) 184
Mom's Overnight Cookies 184
Mom's Pumpkin Cookies 203
Mom's Ranger Cookies 185
Monster Cookies 185
No Bake Cookies 185
Oatmeal Lace Cookies, No Flour 186
Oatmeal Raisin Cookies 186
Orange Cookies 187
Pan Cookies 187
Sandwich Cookies 187
Sour Cream Cookies 188
Sugar Cookies 182, 183
Vanilla Nut Icebox Cookies 188
CORN BAKE 144
CORN BREAD 22
CORN CHOWDER 72
CORN FLAKES® CRUMB CRUST 211
CORNMEAL YEAST BREAD 23
COTTAGE CHEESE SALAD 45
COWBOY BARS 192
CRANBERRY APPLE CRISP 241
CREAM CHEESE CANDY MINTS 231
CREAM CHEESE PECAN PIE 211
CREAM FILLED COFFEE CAKE 155
CREAM OF ASPARAGUS SOUP 73
CREAM OF TOMATO SOUP 76
CREAM PEAR PIE 212
CREAM WAFERS 180
CREAMED CABBAGE WITH CHEESE 143
CREAMY APPLE SQUARES 239
CREAMY CARROTS 145
CREAMY CHOCOLATE CHIP NUT ROLL 250
CREAMY FROSTING 167
CREAMY ORANGE FLUFF 252
CREAMY PINEAPPLE PIE 213
CREAMY RICE PUDDING 253
CREAMY WHITE FROSTING 168
CRESCENT BREAKFAST PIZZA 40

309

CRESCENT CHICKEN 93
CROCKPOT PIZZA 119
CRUMB CAKE 160
CUPCAKES
    Black Bottom Cupcakes 201
    Orange Cream Cupcakes 202
    Snickerdoodle Cupcakes 202

D

DAD'S CASSEROLE 105
DAIRY DELICIOUS DIP 283
DANISH POTATO SALAD 60
DANISH ROLL GLAZE 35
DATE PECAN BALLS 231
DATE PUDDING 253
DEATH BY CHOCOLATE 254
DELICIOUS CHOCOLATE CAKE 160
DELICIOUS PUNCH 295
DENVER SANDWICH RING 289
DESSERTS. *See also* Bars, Cakes, Candies,
    Cupcakes, Ice Cream, Pies.
    Angel Food Cake Dessert 237
    Apple Crisp 237, 238
    Apple or Blueberry Squares 238
    Baked Rice Pudding 241
    Banana Squares 242
    Blackberry Cobbler 242
    Blackberry Delight 243
    Blackberry Pinwheel Cobbler 243
    Blueberry Buckle 243, 244
    Butterscotch Pecan Dessert 244
    Butterscotch Pudding 245
    Cherry Chiffon Dessert 245
    Chocolate Chip Cheesecake 245
    Chocolate Chip Cookie Dough
        Cheesecake 246
    Chocolate Éclair 249
    Chocolate Lush 250
    Chocolate Pudding 251
    Cinnamon Cream Cheese Squares
        251
    Coconut Crunch 252
    Cranberry Apple Crisp <u>241</u>
    Creamy Apple Squares 239
    Creamy Chocolate Chip Nut Roll 250
    Creamy Orange Fluff 252

    Creamy Rice Pudding 253
    Date Pudding 253
    Death by Chocolate 254
    Double Berry Dessert 254
    Easy Éclair Dessert 249
    Fat-Free Sugar-Free Apple Crisp 239
    Frozen Fruit Dessert 254
    Frozen Strawberry Dessert 255
    Grape Dessert 255
    Hot Fudge Pudding 256
    Ice Cream Sandwich Dessert 256
    Ice Cream Sundae Dessert 267
    Jiffy® Rhubarb Dessert 257
    Layered Banana Pudding 257
    Lazy Man's Cobbler 258
    Lemon Fluff 258
    Lime Mint Dessert 258
    Mrs. Bowden's Dessert 259
    New York Cheesecake 246
    No-Bake Cherry Cheesecake 247
    Oreo® Cookie Dessert 259
    Oreo® Fudge Cookie Dessert 260
    Oreo® Pudding Dessert 260
    Peaches 'N' Cream Cheesecake 247
    Peanut Butter Mousse Dessert 260
    Pecan Pie Squares 261
    Pineapple Rings 261
    Pumpkin Crunch 261
    Pumpkin Pie Dessert 262
    Quick Apple Crisp 240
    Red Raspberry Dessert 262
    Sour Cream Apple Squares 240
    Strawberry Angel Food Cake 263
    Strawberry-Pineapple Delight 263
    Strawberry Pizza 263
    Strawberry Shortcake 264
    Strawberry Trifle 264
    Striped Delight 264
    Tapioca Pudding 265
    Toffee Mocha Cream Torte 265
    Turtle Pecan Cheesecake 248
    Twinkie® Style Dessert 266
DINNER ROLLS 24
DIPS
    Apple Caramel Dip 281
    Apple Dip 281
    BLT Dip 283

Chip Dip 283
Dairy Delicious Dip 283
Easy Nacho Dip 284
Fresh Salsa 284
Fruit Dip 282
Jodi's Dip 282
Mexican Layer Dip 284
Mild Mexican Salsa 285
Pizza Dip 286
Salsa 285
Sugar-Free Fruit Dip 282
Taco Bean Dip 285
Taco Dip 286
Veggie Dip 286
Yummy Fruit Dip 282
DOUBLE BERRY DESSERT 254
DOUBLE CHOCOLATE CHIP CAKE 159
DOUBLE DELICIOUS SPREAD 288
DRESSINGS, BREAD 107
DRESSINGS, SALAD 68
French Dressing 70
Hot Bacon Dressing 69
Oil and Vinegar Dressing 69
Ranch Dressing 69
Salad Dressing 70
Tally Ho Salad Dressing 68
Zesty French Dressing 68
DUMP CAKE 161
DUTCH BOY LETTUCE 67

E

EARTHQUAKE CAKE 161
EASTER EGG COLORING 304
EASTER STORY COOKIES 173
EASY CHOCOLATE CHIP BARS 193
EASY COFFEE CAKE 156
EASY CROISSANTS 24
EASY ECLAIR DESSERT 249
EASY GOURMET POTATOES 129
EASY NACHO DIP 284
EASY OATMEAL BREAD 23
EASY PIECRUST 227
EASY SLOPPY JOES 135
EGG AND SAUSAGE BREAKFAST
    CASSEROLE 40
ELEPHANT EARS 275

EMERALD ISLE MOLD 52
ENCHILDA CASSEROLE 126
ESSENHAUS® RECIPES
    Amish Scramble 38
    Apple Crisp 237
    Broccoli Soup 71
    Cheese Ball 288
    Chicken Noodle Casserole 90
    Chicken Noodle Soup 73
    Coleslaw 61
    Essenhaus® Barbecue Ribs 89
    Essenhaus® Barbecue Sauce 90
    Ham & Green Bean Casserole 105
    Mush 302
    New England Clam Chowder 77
    Noodles 106
    Nutty Crackers 277
    Parsley Potatoes 133
    Potato Soup 78
    Sausage Gravy 147
    Sugar-Free Apple Pie Filling 225
    Sugar-Free Blueberry Pie Filling 226
    Sugar-Free Cherry Pie Filling 226
    Sugar-Free Peach Pie Filling 227
    Sugar-Free Vanilla Pie Filling 227
    Taco Salad Meat 58
    Tapioca Pudding 265
    Yellow Gravy 146
ESSENHAUS® BARBECUE RIBS 89
ESSENHAUS® BARBECUE SAUCE 90

F

FAMILY FAVORITE CHICKEN CASSEROLE
    92
FAT-FREE SUGAR FREE APPLE CRISP
    239
FAVORITE PEANUT BUTTER OATMEAL
    COOKIES 180
FETTUCCINE ALFREDO 112
FINGER JELLO® 276
FIRE TRUCK COOKIES 181
FISH STICK SUPPER 138
FLUFFY FROSTING 168
FOIL-BAKED FISH FILLETS 137
FRAN'S QUICK AND EASY CHICKEN
    BREASTS 100

FREEZING
  Frozen Pickles 301
  Strawberry-Kiwi Freezer Jam 302
FRENCH DRESSING 70
FRENCH PEACH PIE 213
FRESH APPLE CAKE 152
FRESH SALSA 284
FRIED ICE CREAM 268
FRIED PECANS 276
FROSTED BANANA BARS 193
FROSTED CHOCOLATE CHIP BARS 194
FROSTED RAISIN CREMES 194
FROSTINGS
  Buttercreme Icing 167
  Caramel Frosting 167
  Creamy Frosting 167
  Creamy White Frosting 168
  Fluffy Frosting 168
  Glossy Chocolate Icing 168
  "Philly" Frosting 169
  Soft Lemon Frosting 169
  Sour Cream Frosting 169
FROTHY ORANGE DRINK 295
FROZEN FRUIT DESSERT 254
FROZEN FRUIT SALAD 46
FROZEN GRAPE SALAD 51
FROZEN PICKLES 301
FROZEN STRAWBERRY DESSERT 255
FRUIT DIP 282
FRUIT SALAD 50
FRUIT SWIRL COFFEE CAKE 156
FUDGE NUT BARS 195
FUDGE SAUCE FOR ICE CREAM 270
FUDGE TOFFEE BARS 195
FUDGESICLE® STYLE DESSERT 266
FUDGY BONBONS 181

G

GARLIC FRIES 132
GERMAN CHOCOLATE BROWNIES
    WITH CREAM CHEESE 195, 196
GIANT SPICE COOKIES 182
GLAZED MEATLOAT 84
GLOSSY CHOCOLATE ICING 168
GRAHAM STREUSEL COFFEE CAKE 157
GRAM'S HOMEMADE CARAMELS 231

GRANDMA'S CASSEROLE 103
GRANDMA'S ICE CREAM PIE 214
GRANDMA'S SOFT BROWN SUGAR
    COOKIES 182
GRANDMA'S SOUP 73
GRANDMA'S SOUR EGG SOUP 74
GRANOLA BARS 196
GRAPE DESSERT 255
GUMDROP COOKIES 183

H

HAM & GREEN BEAN CASSEROLE 105
HAM SWISS CHEESE BAKE 86
HAMBURGER BARBECUE 90
HEARTY ITALIAN SANDWICHES 115
HEAVENLY HASH CAKE 161
HERSHEY ® PIE 214
HOLIDAY CHOCOLATE PRETZEL RING
    277
HOLIDAY SUGAR COOKIES 183
HOMEMADE CAPPUCCINO MIX 294
HOMEMADE PUMPKIN ICE CREAM 26
HOMESTEAD CHICKEN AND DRESSIN
    106
HOMESTEAD SALAD 62
HOT BACON DRESSING 69
HOT CHOCOLATE MIX 295
HOT FUDGE PUDDING 256
HOT PORRIDGE 41
HOT SPICY DOGS 89
HUNGARIAN CHRISTMAS COOKIES
    (KIEFLIES) 184
HUNGARIAN GOULASH 108
HUNGARIAN MEATBALLS 88
HUSH PUPPIES 114

I

ICE CREAM 269
  Butter Crisp Ice Cream Topping 270
  Fried Ice Cream 268
  Fudge Sauce for Ice Cream 270
  Fudgesicle® Style Dessert 266
  Homemade Pumpkin Ice Cream 269
  Ice Cream 269
  Ice Cream Crunch 266

Ice Cream Sundae Dessert 267
Mint Ice Cream Dessert 267
Peach Slush 267
Strawberry Topping for Ice Cream 270
Vanilla Ice Cream 269
Watermelon Look Sherbet Mold 268
ICE CREAM CRUNCH 266
ICE CREAM SANDWICH DESSERT 256
ICE CREAM SUNDAE DESSERT 267
ITALIAN CHICKEN BREASTS 98
ITALIAN HERITAGE CASSEROLE 112

J

JELLO® SALAD 54
JODI'S DIP 282
JUST RIGHT CHOCOLATE CHIP
    COOKIES 177

K

KELLOGG'S CORN FLAKES® FRUIT PIZZA
    289
KENTUCKY POTATOES 131
KIDNEY BEAN SALAD 45
KIEFLIES (HUNGARIAN CHRISTMAS
    COOKIES) 184
KRISPY ICE CREAM PIE 215

L

LAMB STEAKS WITH PEACHES 87
LAYERED BANANA PUDDING 257
LAZY MAN'S COBBLER 258
LEMON CAKE PIE 215
LEMON FLUFF 258
LEMON PIE 216, 217
LETTUCE SALAD 63
LETTUCE SALAD FAVORITE 65
LI'L CHEDDAR MEAT LOAVES 85
LIME MINT DESSERT 258
LINDA'S MEATBALLS 89
LINDA'S TACO SOUP 75

M

M.K.K.'s FISH BATTER 137
MAHOGANY CHIFFON CAKE 170

MAIN DISHES
    15-Minute Chicken and Rice Dinner
        97
    American Chop Suey 110
    Baked Spaghetti 118
    Basil Chicken and Dumpling
        Casserole 92
    Beef Crescent Casserole 111
    Beef Enchiladas 125
    Beef Macaroni and Cheese 101
    Beef with Cauliflower and Snow-Peas
        110
    Broccoli-Ham Hot Dish 141
    Burrito Casserole 122
    Cabbage Rolls 143
    Cheese Tacos 127
    Cheesy Beef Spirals 104
    Chicken Casserole 91
    Chicken Enchilada Casserole 124
    Chicken Noodle Casserole 90
    Chicken Spaghetti Supreme 117
    Crockpot Pizza 119
    Dad's Casserole 105
    Easy Sloppy Joes 135
    Enchilada Casserole 126
    Fettuccine Alfredo 112
    Fish Stick Supper 138
    Grandma's Casserole 103
    Ham & Green Bean Casserole 105
    Ham Swiss Cheese Bake 86
    Hearty Italian Sandwiches 115
    Hungarian Goulash 108
    Italian Heritage Casserole 112
    Mary B. Special 111
    Mary's Casserole 108
    Mashed Potato Casserole 130
    Mexican Pizza 126
    Night Before Casserole 104
    Overnight Casserole 103
    Party Ham Casserole 86
    Pizza Biscuit Bake 120
    Pizza Dough 122
    Pizza Hot Dish 121
    Pizza Rounds 122
    Pizza Sandwiches 121
    Pizza Sticks 120

Poor Man's Steak 84
Poppy Seed Chicken Casserole 94
Potato Pancakes 132
Quiche Chicken and Almonds 101
Quiche Lorraine 112
Saffron Seafood and Rice Paella 114
Sausage Casserole 109
Scalloped Potatoes and Ham 129
Skillet Supper 106
Sloppy Joe Bake 136
Sloppy Joes 136
Spaghetti Pie 117
Spaghetti Pizza 116
Stromboli Sandwiches 115
Summer Skillet 113
Super Chicken Casserole 91
Supper Popover 116
Sweet Sloppy Joes 136
Taco Casserole 126
Tuna Cheese Toasties 138
Turkey-Stuffed Peppers 85
Underground Ham Casserole 109
Virginia's Easy Lasagna 119
Wet Burrito Casserole 123
Zesty Taco Joes 135
MAKE-ITS-OWN-CRUST COCONUT PIE 219
MAPLE NUT CAKE 159
MAPLE PECAN COFFEE RING 35
MARILYN'S EASY WHITE BREAD 24
MARSHMALLOW BROWNIE DELIGHT 197
MARY B. SPECIAL 111
MARY EMMA'S COFFEE CAKE 157
MARY'S CASSEROLE 108
MARY'S CHILI 74
MASHED POTATO CASSEROLE 130
MAYONNAISE 302
MEATS
  Beef Fajitas 124
  Beth's Meatzzia Pie 101
  Chinese Pepper Steak 87
  Company Roast Beef 83
  Denver Sandwich Ring 289
  Easy Sloppy Joes 135
  Essenhaus® Barbecue Ribs 89
  Essenhaus® Barbecue Sauce 90

Foil-Baked Fish Fillets 137
Glazed Meatloaf 84
Hamburger Barbecue 90
Hot Spicy Dogs 89
Hungarian Meatballs 88
Lamb Steaks with Peaches 87
Li'l Cheddar Meat Loaves 85
Linda's Meatballs 89
M.K.K.'s Fish Batter 137
Meat Loaf 84
Mom's Sauerkraut Balls 290
Porcupine Meat Balls 88
Salisbury Steak 83
Steak Marinade Recipe 303
Swiss Steak 83
Touchdown Beans 139
Tuna Macaroni Casserole 102
MEAT LOAF 84
MELON SALAD WITH ORANGE LIME DRESSING 47
MELT-IN-YOUR-MOUTH BISCUITS 26
MEXICAN LAYER DIP 284
MEXICAN PIZZA 126
Microwave Hints 272
MILD MEXICAN SALSA 285
MIMI'S DOWN HOME CREAM PIE 218
MINT ICE CREAM DESSERT 267
MINTS 232
MISCELLANEOUS
  Cinnamon Ornaments 303
  Cinnamon Syrup 303
  Easter Egg Coloring 304
  Imitation Play Doh® 304
  Mayonnaise 302
  Mush 302
  Pap (Bry) 304
  Steak Marinade Recipe 303
  Tartar Sauce 303
MISSISSIPPI MUD CAKE 162
MIX-IN-PAN CRUST 225
MIXED VEGETABLE SALAD 65
MOM'S BREAD PUDDING 31
MOM'S HOMEMADE BREAD 26
MOM'S OVERNIGHT COOKIES 184
MOM'S PANCAKES 37
MOM'S PUMPKIN COOKIES 203
MOM'S RANGER COOKIES 185

MOM'S SAUERKRAUT BALLS 290
MONSTER COOKIES 185
MOUND BARS 197
MRS. BOWDEN'S DESSERT 259
MULLIGAN SOUP 77
MUSH 302
MUSHROOM LOGS 290
MUSTARD PRETZELS 279

N

NEW ENGLAND BAKED BEANS—
    CROCK-POT® 140
NEW ENGLAND CLAM CHOWDER 77
NEW YORK CHEESECAKE 246
NIGHT BEFORE CASSEROLE 104
NO-BAKE COOKIES 185
NO-BAKE CHERRY CHEESECAKE 247
NOODLES 106
NUTTY CRACKERS 277
NUTTY FRENCH TOAST 36

O

OATMEAL BROWN SUGAR PANCAKES
    37
OATMEAL LACE COOKIES, NO FLOUR
    186
OATMEAL RAISIN COOKIES 186
OATMEAL-MOLASSES CAKE 159
OHIO BUCKEYE CANDY 232
OLD-FASHIONED CREAM PIE 218
OLD-FASHIONED LEMON PIE 218
OLD-FASHIONED WALNUT CAKE 159
ONE-STEP ANGEL FOOD CAKE 162
ORANGE CREAM CUPCAKES 202
ORANGE JELLO® SUPREME 57
ORANGE JULIUS® STYLE DRINK 296
OREO® FUDGE COOKIE DESSERT 260
OREO® COOKIE DESSERT 259
OREO® PUDDING DESSERT 260
ORIENTAL CABBAGE SALAD 64
ORIENTAL CHICKEN WITH WALNUTS 96
OUR LORD'S SCRIPTURE CAKE 162
Oven Chart 300
OVEN FRENCH TOAST WITH NUT
    TOPPING 36

OVEN FRIED POTATOES 133
OVERNIGHT BUNS 25
OVERNIGHT CASSEROLE 103
OVERNIGHT DINNER ROLLS 25

P

PAN COOKIES 187
PAP (BRY) 304
PARSLEY POTATOES 133
PARTY HAM CASSEROLE 86
PARTY MIX 278
PAYDAY CAKE 163
PEA AND PEANUT SALAD 62
PEACH CRUMB PIE 214
PEACH SLUSH 267
PEACHES 'N' CREAM CHEESECAKE 247
PEANUT BUTTER CHOCOLATE CHIP
    GRANOLA BARS 198
PEANUT BUTTER FUDGE 232
PEANUT BUTTER MOUSSE DESSERT 260
PEANUT CLUSTERS 233
PEAR PIE 212
PECAN PIE SQUARES 261
PEDDLERS PUNCH 296
"PHILLY" FROSTING 169
PIE CRUST 226
PIES
    Apple Crumb Pie 207
    Best-Ever Peanut Butter Pie 207
    Black Bottom Pie 207, 208
    Butterscotch Pie 208
    Caramel Chiffon Pie 209
    Carol's Best Pecan Pie 212
    Cherry Pie 209
    Chocolate Cream Cheese Pie 210
    Coconut Custard Pie 210
    Coconut Pie 210
    Concord Grape Pie 211
    Corn Flakes® Crumb Crust 211
    Cream Cheese Pecan Pie 211
    Cream Pear Pie 212
    Creamy Pineapple Pie 213
    Easy Pie Crust 227
    French Peach Pie 213
    Grandma's Ice Cream Pie 214
    Hershey® Bar Pie 214

Key Lime Pie 215
Krispy Ice Cream Pie 215
Lemon Cake Pie 215
Lemon Pie 216, 217
Make-Its-Own-Crust Coconut Pie 219
Mimi's Down Home Cream Pie 218
Mix-in-Pan Crust 225
Old-Fashioned Cream Pie 218
Old-Fashioned Lemon Pie 218
Peach Crumb Pie 214
Pear Pie 212
Pie Crust 226
Pineapple Pie 219
Pumpkin Chiffon Pie 219
Pumpkin Custard Pie 220
Pumpkin Pie 220
Rhubarb Crumb Pie 220, 221
Rhubarb Pie 221
Shaker Lemon Pie 217
Strawberry Glazed Pie 222
Strawberry Pie 222
Strawberry-Rhubarb Jello® Pie 223
Sugar-Free Apple Pie Filling 225
Sugar-Free Blueberry Pie Filling 226
Sugar-Free Cherry Pie Filling 226
Sugar-Free Peach Pie Filling 227
Sugar-Free Vanilla Pie Filling 227
Sweet Potato Pie 223
Two Crust Blackberry Pie 224
Vinegar Pie 224
PINEAPPLE CHEESE BALL 289
PINEAPPLE PIE 219
PINEAPPLE RINGS 261
PINEAPPLE LI'L SMOKIES 291
PINWHEELS 291
PIZZA BISCUIT BAKE 120
PIZZA DIP 286
PIZZA DOUGH 122
PIZZA HOT DISH 121
PIZZA ROUNDS 122
PIZZA SANDWICHES 121
PIZZA SOUP 79
PIZZA STICKS 120
PLAY DOUGH 304
POOR MAN'S STEAK 84
POPCORN BALLS 278
POPPY SEED CHICKEN 94

POPPY SEED CHICKEN CASSEROLE 94
POPPY SEED CHICKEN FOR A BUNCH
    95
PORCUPINE MEAT BALLS 88
POTATO PANCAKES 132
POTATO SOUP 78, 79
POULTRY
    15-Minute Chicken and Rice Dinner
        97
    Bacon-Wrapped Chicken 97
    Baked Barbecued Chicken 100
    Barbecued Chicken 99
    Basil Chicken and Dumpling
        Casserole 92
    Chicken & Vegetables 100
    Chicken Casserole 91, 93
    Chicken Enchilada Casserole 124
    Chicken Enchiladas 125
    Chicken Fajita Pizza 123
    Chicken Marbella 98
    Chicken on Sunday 95
    Chicken Parmesan 98
    Chicken Spaghetti Supreme 117
    Chicken Supreme 93
    Chickenett for a Bunch 91
    Crescent Chicken 93
    Family Favorite Chicken Casserole
    Fran's Quick and Easy Chicken Brea
        100
    Homestead Chicken and Dressing
        106
    Italian Chicken Breasts 98
    Oriental Chicken with Walnuts 96
    Poppy Seed Chicken 94
    Poppy Seed Chicken Casserole 94
    Poppy Seed Chicken for a Bunch 9!
    Seasoned Salt Chicken 99
    Super Chicken Casserole 91
    Swiss Chicken 96
    Turkey-Stuffed Peppers 85
    Zesty Italian Chicken Breasts 97
PRETZEL CRUST SALAD 60
PUDDING FRUIT SALAD 48
PUMPKIN BREAD 26
PUMPKIN CAKE 159
PUMPKIN CHIFFON PIE 219
PUMPKIN CRUNCH 261

PUMPKIN CUSTARD PIE 220
PUMPKIN PIE 220
PUMPKIN PIE DESSERT 262
PUMPKIN PIE SQUARES 198
PUNCH 296
PUPPY CHOW® STYLE CANDY 278

Q

QUICHE CHICKEN AND ALMONDS 101
QUICHE LORRAINE 112
QUICK AND EASY RECIPES
  Bacon Wrapped Chicken 97
  Beef Crescent Casserole 111
  Best Ever Peanut Butter Pie 207
  Black Forest Dump Cake 153
  Blender Banana Bread 21
  Broccoli and Creamed Corn Casserole 141
  Bubble Bread 22
  California Blend Vegetable Casserole 146
  Cheesy Potatoes 128
  Chicken & Vegetables 100
  Chicken Parmesan 98
  Chocolate Chip Bars 191
  Chocolate Chip Pudding Cake 158
  Dump Cake 161
  Earthquake Cake 161
  Easy Coffee Cake 156
  Easy Éclair Dessert 249
  Easy Gourmet Potatoes 129
  Easy Nacho Dip 284
  Fran's Quick and Easy Chicken Breasts 100
  Frozen Fruit Salad 46
  Fruit Dip 281
  Fudgesicle® Style Dessert 266
  Garlic Fries 132
  Holiday Chocolate Pretzel Rings 277
  Ice Cream Crunch 266
  Ice Cream Sandwich Dessert 256
  Jiffy® Rhubarb Dessert 257
  Krispy Ice Cream Pie 215
  Linda's Taco Soup 75
  Mix-in-Pan Crust 225
  Oreo® Cookie Dessert 259

  Peanut Clusters 233
  Pizza Sandwiches 121
  Potato Soup 78
  Quick Apple Crisp 240
  Quick Apple Salad 48
  Seasoned Pretzels 279
  Spaghetti Pie 117
  Strawberry Pineapple Delight 263
  Strawberry Shortcake 264
  Sweet and Sour Smokies 292
  Sweet Sloppy Joes 136
  Taco Bean Dip 285
  Taco Soup 74
  Watermelon-Look Sherbet Mold 268
  Zesty Italian Chicken Breasts 97
  Zesty Taco Joes 135
QUICK APPLE CRISP 240
QUICK APPLE SALAD 48

R

RACHEL'S RANCH PARTY MIX 279
RAISIN BRAN® MUFFINS 32
RANCH DRESSING 69
RED RASPBERRY DESSERT 262
RHUBARB CRUMB PIE 220, 221
RHUBARB CUSTARD BARS 199
RHUBARB PIE 221
RICE KRISPIES® CEREAL BARS 199
RICE KRISPIES® TREATS 200
RIVEL SOUP 78
ROSEMARY RED POTATOES 130

S

SAFFRON SEAFOOD AND RICE PAELLA 114
SALAD DRESSINGS. See Dressings, Salad.
SALADS
  Coleslaw 61
  Ramen® Salad 59
  Taco Salad Meat 58
  Taffy Apple Salad 51
SALISBURY STEAK 83
SALSA 285
SANDWICH COOKIES 187
SAUSAGE CASSEROLE 109

SAUSAGE GRAVY 147
SCALLOPED CORN 145
SCALLOPED PINEAPPLE 113
SCALLOPED POTATOES 128
SCALLOPED POTATOES AND HAM 129
SCRAMBLED EGG MUFFINS 33
SEAFOOD SALAD 58
SEASONED PRETZELS 279
SEASONED SALT CHICKEN 99
SHAKER LEMON PIE 217
SIDE DISHES
  Baked Beans 139
  Baked Mashed Potatoes 130
  Baked Pineapple Casserole 113
  Broccoli and Cauliflower Casserole 141
  Broccoli and Creamed Corn Casserole 140
  Broccoli Casserole 140
  Broccoli-Corn Casserole 141
  Cabbage Casserole 142
  California Blend Vegetable Casserole 146
  Caramel Sweet Potatoes 134
  Carrot Casserole 144
  Celery Casserole 145
  Cheesy Potatoes 128
  Chiles Rellenno 111
  Corn Bake 144
  Creamed Cabbage with Cheese 143
  Creamy Carrots 145
  Dressing, Bread 107
  Easy Gourmet Potatoes 129
  Essenhaus® Barbecue Sauce 90
  Garlic Fries 132
  Hush Puppies 114
  Kentucky Potatoes 131
  New England Baked Beans—
    Crock-Pot® 140
  Noodles 106
  Oven-Fried Potatoes 133
  Parsley Potatoes 133
  Rosemary Red Potatoes 130
  Sausage Gravy 147
  Scalloped Corn 145
  Scalloped Pineapple 113
  Scalloped Potatoes 128

Spaghetti Sauce 118
Spinach Balls 146
Sweet and Sour Cabbage 143
Sweet Potato Casserole 133
Sweet Potato Soufflé 135
Sweet Potatoes on Pineapple Rings 134
Sweet Potatoes with Marshmallows 134
Swiss Potato Casserole 131
Tater Tot® Casserole 109
Tomato Gravy 147
Touchdown Beans 139
Triple-Corn Spoon Bread 145
Variety Baked Beans 139
Yellow Gravy 146
SKIER FRENCH TOAST 37
SKILLET SUPPER 106
SLOPPY JOE BAKE 136
SLOPPY JOES 136
SNACKS
  2-Layer Finger Jello® 276
  After School Treats 273
  Aunt Annie's Style Soft Pretzels 273
  Caramel Corn with Cashews 273
  Cashew Crunch 274
  Cheddar Mix 274
  Cheerio® Clusters 274
  Chocolate-Covered Chips 275
  Cinnamon Popcorn 275
  Elephant Ears 275
  Finger Jello® 276
  Fried Pecans 276
  Holiday Chocolate Pretzel Rings 277
  Mustard Pretzels 279
  Nutty Crackers 277
  Party Mix 278
  Popcorn Balls 278
  Puppy Chow® Style Candy 278
  Rachel's Ranch Party Mix 279
  Seasoned Pretzels 279
  Spiced Pecans 277
  Strawberry Smoothie 297
  Trail Mix 280
  White Chocolate Party Mix 280
  White Trash 280, 281
SNICKERDOODLE CUPCAKES 202

SOFT LEMON FROSTING 169
SOFT PRETZELS 27
SOUPS
   Amish Bean Soup 70
   Broccoli Soup 71
   Cactus Soup 71
   Cheesy Potato Soup 72
   Chicken Noodle Soup 73
   Cold Soup 72
   Corn Chowder 72
   Cream of Asparagus 73
   Cream of Tomato Soup 76
   Grandma's Soup 73
   Grandma's Sour Egg Soup 74
   Linda's Taco Soup 75
   Mary's Chili 74
   Mulligan Soup 77
   New England Clam Chowder 77
   Pizza Soup 79
   Potato Soup 78, 79
   Rivel Soup 78
   Taco Soup 74
   Tomato Hamburger Soup 76
   Tomato Soup 75, 76
   Vegetable Beef Soup 80
   Zucchini Soup 80
SOUR CREAM APPLE SQUARES 240
SOUR CREAM COOKIES 188
SOUR CREAM FROSTING 169
SOUR CREAM SPICE CAKE 163
SOUTHERN ICED TEA 297
SOUTHWEST CHEESECAKE 291
SPAGHETTI PIE 117
SPAGHETTI PIZZA 116
SPAGHETTI SAUCE 118
SPECIAL K® CEREAL CANDY 233
SPICED PECANS 277
SPINACH BALLS 146
SPINACH SALAD 67
STEAK MARINADE RECIPE 303
STRAWBERRY ANGEL FOOD CAKE 263
STRAWBERRY BARS 200
STRAWBERRY BREAD 27
STRAWBERRY FRUIT PUNCH 297
STRAWBERRY GLAZED PIE 222
STRAWBERRY PECAN CAKE 164
STRAWBERRY PIES 222

STRAWBERRY-PINEAPPLE DELIGHT 263
STRAWBERRY PIZZA 263
STRAWBERRY-RHUBARB JELLO® PIE 223
STRAWBERRY SHORTCAKE 264
STRAWBERRY SMOOTHIE 297
STRAWBERRY TOPPING FOR ICE CREAM
   270
STRAWBERRY TRIFLE 264
STRAWBERRY-KIWI FREEZER JAM 302
STRAWBERRY/BANANA SHAKES 298
STRIPED DELIGHT 264
STROMBOLI SANDWICHES 115
Substitutions 20
SUGAR COOKIES 182, 183
SUGAR CREAM PIE SQUARES 200
SUGAR-FREE APPLE PIE FILLING 225
SUGAR-FREE BLUEBERRY PIE FILLING
   226
SUGAR-FREE CHERRY PIE FILLING 226
SUGAR-FREE FRUIT DIP 282
SUGAR-FREE PEACH PIE FILLING 227
SUGAR-FREE VANILLA PIE FILLING 227
SUMMER SKILLET 113
SUPER CHICKEN CASSEROLE 91
SUPPER POPOVER 116
SWEET AND SOUR CABBAGE 143
SWEET AND SOUR LI'L SMOKIES 293
SWEET POTATO CASSEROLE 133
SWEET POTATO PIE 223
SWEET POTATO SOUFFLÉ 135
SWEET POTATOES ON PINEAPPLE
   RINGS 134
SWEET POTATOES WITH
   MARSHALLOWS 134
SWEET SLOPPY JOES 136
SWISS CHICKEN 96
SWISS POTATO CASSEROLE 131
SWISS STEAK 83

T

TACO BEAN DIP 285
TACO CASSEROLE 126
TACO DIP 286
TACO RING 292
TACO SALAD 57
TACO SALAD MEAT 58

TACO SOUP 74
TAFFY APPLE SALAD 51
TALLY HO SALAD DRESSING 68
TAPIOCA PUDDING 265
TARTAR SAUCE 303
TATER TOT® CASSEROLE 109
TEXAS SHEET CAKE 164
TOFFEE MOCHA CREAM TORTE 265
TOMATO GRAVY 147
TOMATO HAMBURGER SOUP 76
TOMATO SOUP 75, 76
TOUCHDOWN BEANS 139
TRAIL MIX 280
TRIPLE-CORN SPOON BREAD 145
TROPICAL CARROT CAKE 154
TUNA CHEESE TOASTIES 138
TUNA MACARONI CASSEROLE 102
TURKEY-STUFFED PEPPERS 85
TURTLE BREAD 28
TURTLE CAKE 165
TURTLE PECAN CHEESECAKE 248
TWINKIE® STYLE DESSERT 266
TWO-CRUST BLACKBERRY PIE 224

U

UNDERGROUND HAM CASSEROLE 109

V

VANILLA ICE CREAM 269
VANILLA NUT ICEBOX COOKIES 188
VARIETY BAKED BEANS 139
VEGETABLE BEEF SOUP 80

VEGGIE BARS 293
VEGGIE DIP 286
VINEGAR PIE 224
VIRGINIA'S EASY LASAGNA 119

W

WATERMELON-LOOK SHERBET MOLD 268
WEDDING PUNCH 298
WET BURRITO CASSEROLE 123
WHITE CHOCOLATE PARTY MIX 280
WHITE SHEET CAKE 165
WHITE TEXAS SHEET CAKE 166
WHITE TRASH 280, 281
WHOLE WHEAT BREAD 28
WINTER GARDEN SCRAMBLED EGGS

Y

YELLOW GRAVY 146
YUMMY BARS 201
YUMMY FRUIT DIP 282
YUMMY VEGGIE PIZZA 293

Z

ZESTY FRENCH DRESSING 68
ZESTY ITALIAN CHICKEN BREASTS 97
ZESTY TACO JOES 135
ZUCCHINI CAKE 166
ZUCCHINI MUFFINS 32
ZUCCHINI SOUP 80